# Professional Services Marketing Handbook

# Professional Services Marketing Handbook

How to build relationships, grow your firm and become a client champion

Edited by Nigel Clark
Foreword by Charles Nixon

LONDON   PHILADELPHIA   NEW DELHI

**Publisher's note**

Every possible effort has been made to ensure that the information contained in this book is accurate at the time of going to press, and the publishers and authors cannot accept responsibility for any errors or omissions, however caused. No responsibility for loss or damage occasioned to any person acting, or refraining from action, as a result of the material in this publication can be accepted by the editors, the publisher or any of the authors.

First published in Great Britain and the United States in 2015 by Kogan Page Limited

Apart from any fair dealing for the purposes of research or private study, or criticism or review, as permitted under the Copyright, Designs and Patents Act 1988, this publication may only be reproduced, stored or transmitted, in any form or by any means, with the prior permission in writing of the publishers, or in the case of reprographic reproduction in accordance with the terms and licences issued by the CLA. Enquiries concerning reproduction outside these terms should be sent to the publishers at the undermentioned addresses:

| | | |
|---|---|---|
| 2nd Floor, 45 Gee Street | 1518 Walnut Street, Suite 1100 | 4737/23 Ansari Road |
| London EC1V 3RS | Philadelphia PA 19102 | Daryaganj |
| United Kingdom | USA | New Delhi 110002 |
| www.koganpage.com | | India |

© Nigel Clark and Charles Nixon, 2015

The right of Nigel Clark and Charles Nixon to be identified as the authors of this work have been asserted by them in accordance with the Copyright, Designs and Patents Act 1988.

ISBN      978 0 7494 7346 4
E-ISBN    978 0 7494 7347 1

**British Library Cataloguing-in-Publication Data**

A CIP record for this book is available from the British Library.

**Library of Congress Cataloging-in-Publication Data**

Clark, Nigel.
  Professional services marketing handbook : how to build relationships, grow your firm and become a client champion / Nigel Clark, Charles Nixon. – 1st Edition.
     pages cm
  ISBN 978-0-7494-7346-4 (paperback) – ISBN 978-0-7494-7347-1 (ebk)  1. Professions–Marketing.  2. Consulting firms.  3. Marketing.  I. Nixon, Charles.  II. Title.
  HD8038.A1C53 2015
  658.8–dc23
                                                                                              2015000917

Typeset by Graphicraft Limited, Hong Kong
Print production managed by Jellyfish
Printed and bound by CPI Group (UK) Limited, Croydon CR0 4YY

*For Belinda and Hilary*

# CONTENTS

*List of figures* x
*List of tables* xi
*List of contributors* xii
*Foreword* xiii
*Acknowledgements* xiv
*About the editor* xv

**Introduction: leadership themes in professional services marketing** 1

**THEME ONE** Growth 17

**Introduction to the Growth theme** 19

**01 Growth and globalization** 22
**Richard Grove**, *Director of Marketing, Business Development & Communications, Allen & Overy LLP*

**02 Implementing a growth strategy: lessons from Asia Pacific** 37
**Daniel Smith**, *Senior Business Development and Marketing Manager, Asia Pacific, Baker & McKenzie*, and **Claire Essex**, *Director of Business Development and Marketing, Asia Pacific, Baker & McKenzie*

**03 Developing international networks** 48
**Clive Stevens**, *Executive Chairman, Kreston Reeves*

**Lessons on Growth** 57

**THEME TWO** Understanding 59

**Introduction to the Understanding theme** 61

**04 Listening, understanding and responding to clients** 64
**Louise Field**, *Head of Client Service & Insight, Bird & Bird LLP*, and **Tim Nightingale**, *Founder, Nisus Consulting*

## Contents

**05   Closing the commerciality gap**   78
*Ben Kent*, Managing Director, Meridian West

**06   What legal clients want**   89
*Lisa Hart Shepherd*, CEO, Acritas

**Lessons on Understanding**   103

### THEME THREE   Connecting   105

**Introduction to the Connecting theme**   107

**07   From communities to cohorts**   110
*Nick Masters*, Head of Online, PwC

**08   Thought leadership: transforming insights into opportunities**   119
*Alastair Beddow*, Associate Director, Meridian West

**09   Conversation is king: connecting thought leadership and sales**   133
*Dale Bryce*, President, Asia-Pacific Professional Services Marketing Association

**Lessons on Connecting**   142

### THEME FOUR   Relationships   143

**Introduction to the Relationships theme**   145

**10   The importance of client relationship management**   148
*Gillian Sutherland*, Director, Global Key Account Management Buildings+Places, AECOM

**11   Developing internal and external relationships**   162
*Susan D'aish*, Business Relationship Director, MacRoberts LLP

**12   The primacy of relationships: how and why clients choose**   173
*Dan O'Day*, Vice President, Thomson Reuters Elite

**Lessons on Relationships**   181

## THEME FIVE  Managing  183

### Introduction to the Managing theme  185

**13  It's all about value: managing marketing and business development**  188
*Matthew Fuller*, Director of Marketing and Business Development EMEA, White & Case LLP

**14  Managing transformational change**  199
*Amy Kingdon*, Marketing & Communications Director, UK & Europe, and *Eleanor Campion*, Communications Executive, UK & Europe, Atkins

**15  Understanding and exceeding partner expectations**  209
*Jessica Scholz*, Business Development Manager, Freshfields Bruckhaus Deringer, Germany

**16  The role of marketing KPIs in professional services firms**  219
*Giles Pugh*, Principal, SutherlandsPugh

### Lessons on Managing  232

## Conclusion  235

**17  The future for professional services marketing: becoming a client champion**  237

*References*  251
*Further reading*  253
*Index*  254

# LIST OF FIGURES

**FIGURE 0.1**  Changing client needs   1
**FIGURE 0.2**  The professional's role is changing   2
**FIGURE 0.3**  The marketer's role is changing   5
**FIGURE 0.4**  Client, firm and marketer changing together   5
**FIGURE 1.1**  Single vs multi-country matter profitability   24
**FIGURE 1.2**  Brand positioning   25
**FIGURE 1.3**  Network growth   28
**FIGURE 3.1**  How international networks develop over time to meet client needs   51
**FIGURE 4.1**  The marketing paradox   67
**FIGURE 4.2**  Qual vs quant: how to choose   70
**FIGURE 4.3**  Responsibility for listening to clients   72
**FIGURE 5.1**  Future challenges   79
**FIGURE 5.2**  The seven habits of a commercial adviser   80
**FIGURE 5.3**  Why professionals struggle to be commercial   84
**FIGURE 8.1**  Five simple criteria for assessing excellence in thought leadership   121
**FIGURE 10.1**  Stages of development in a client-to-adviser relationship   149
**FIGURE 10.2**  How client relationships work   150
**FIGURE 10.3**  A design for a client relationship management programme   157
**FIGURE 13.1**  Balancing proactivity and reactivity in business development   194
**FIGURE 16.1**  Stages in the development of KPIs   222
**FIGURE 16.2**  The impact of KPIs and influencing change   231
**FIGURE 17.1**  The five themes for the marketing and business development leader   238
**FIGURE 17.2**  'Inside out' vs 'outside in' views of the world   244
**FIGURE 17.3**  The client life cycle   246

# LIST OF TABLES

| | | |
|---|---|---|
| **TABLE 0.1** | Top 10 characteristics of a professional services firm | 9 |
| **TABLE 4.1** | The differences between qual and quant | 69 |
| **TABLE 6.1** | Important steps for improving brand health and client relationships | 102 |
| **TABLE 8.1** | Meridian West 'Megatrends Map' for thought leadership topics | 126 |
| **TABLE 10.1** | Selection criteria for identifying relationship clients | 154 |
| **TABLE 11.1** | Differences between transactional and relationship marketing | 163 |
| **TABLE 16.1** | Categories of marketing metrics for professional services firms | 225 |
| **TABLE 16.2** | Web metrics and their effectiveness | 228 |
| **TABLE 17.1** | The traditional response vs the client champion response | 242 |
| **TABLE 17.2** | The client life cycle response | 247 |

# CONTRIBUTORS

- **Alastair Beddow,** Associate Director, Meridian West
- **Dale Bryce,** President, Asia-Pacific Professional Services Marketing Association
- **Eleanor Campion,** Communications Executive, UK & Europe, Atkins
- **Susan D'aish,** Business Relationship Director, MacRoberts LLP
- **Claire Essex,** Director of Business Development and Marketing, Asia Pacific, Baker & McKenzie
- **Louise Field,** Head of Client Service & Insight, Bird & Bird LLP
- **Matthew Fuller,** Director of Marketing and Business Development EMEA, White & Case LLP
- **Richard Grove,** Director of Marketing, Business Development & Communications, Allen & Overy LLP
- **Lisa Hart Shepherd,** CEO, Acritas
- **Ben Kent,** Managing Director, Meridian West
- **Amy Kingdon,** Marketing & Communications Director, UK & Europe, Atkins
- **Nick Masters,** Head of Online, PwC
- **Tim Nightingale,** Founder, Nisus Consulting
- **Dan O'Day,** Vice President, Thomson Reuters Elite
- **Giles Pugh,** Principal, SutherlandsPugh
- **Jessica Scholz,** Business Development Manager, Freshfields Bruckhaus Deringer, Germany
- **Daniel Smith,** Senior Business Development and Marketing Manager, Asia Pacific, Baker & McKenzie
- **Clive Stevens,** Executive Chairman, Kreston Reeves
- **Gillian Sutherland,** Director, Global Key Account Management Buildings + Places, AECOM

# FOREWORD

I have been involved with the professional services sector since my time as Marketing Director at Société Générale during its takeover of Touché Remnant. While different rules of competitive engagement then applied, what struck me at the time was the courtesy and concern for client care that firms in the sector displayed and practised. This is a trait that was ahead of its time when compared with other industries.

Since then, the professional services sector's emphasis on customer relationships and the management and nurturing of prospects and enquirers through what we now call the sales funnel has become distinctive. These areas have not only served the sector well during the recession, but also proved an innovating aspect of business practice as now applied worldwide in all sectors. Similarly, the evolution of marketing into business development (MBD) and the development of thought leadership as a business tool have been pioneering.

At Cambridge Marketing Colleges we offer a range of courses to several specialist sectors (Arts, Sports, B2B etc), so as Master I come across marketers in many sectors who are convinced that they are not up to scratch in their marketing. Yet, at the same time, they expound 'that marketing idea won't work here' or 'that concept does not apply to us'. Some of this has merit, up to a point, as all sectors are different. In contrast, in the professional services sector I see a very genuine concern to learn from elsewhere and a limited aspect of the 'it will not work here' culture. We teach a Diploma programme in marketing for professional services clients in the UK and Germany and have done so in the former case for eight years. In that time we have come across some genuinely innovative ideas and business practices.

Our dear friend Laurie Young struck a deep seam with his innovative book *Marketing the Professional Service Firm* and it is in this tradition that we have attempted with this new book to bring the discussion up to date and in line with the digital revolution. A shrinking world is not limited to the commercial landscape and, despite legal geographical boundaries, best practice from partner companies around the world is seeping into mainstream commercial practice.

The aim of this book is to add insight for MBD professionals on best practice experienced by leading firms around the world, so that they can help manage the development of their firms' marketing practices. It will also be of keen relevance to other sectors that should adopt some of these practices. In many ways the professional services world has a lot to teach commercial companies about customer service and client relationship marketing.

Overall, I believe that this book holds many of the techniques that will unlock value for MBD professionals and will now be recommended reading for all students and practitioners of professional services marketing.

*Charles Nixon*
*Chairman and Founder, Cambridge Marketing Colleges*

# ACKNOWLEDGEMENTS

The idea for this book came about following a conversation with Charles Nixon from Cambridge Marketing Colleges and Gail Jaffa from the Professional Services Marketing Group. They have both contributed a huge amount in helping turn the original idea into reality. Alongside Charles and Gail, Jasmin Naim, Megan Mondi and the team at Kogan Page have been constant sources of encouragement and advice.

The book would have remained just an idea without the commitment and cooperation of all the contributors. Their expertise, insights and enthusiasm come through in every chapter.

I have benefited from working and sharing experiences with many people in the professions during my career, a number of whom have contributed to this book. I would also like to thank Duncan Ogilvy, Mark Jeffries, Paul Jaffa, Peter Young, Barry Newby, Geoff Linke and Michelle Jones.

Finally, my wife, Hilary, has helped me make sure this book reads well, tells a coherent story and is not just a patchwork of ideas.

# ABOUT THE EDITOR

**Nigel Clark** has held senior marketing and business development roles in financial services, management consulting, legal, environmental, business services, engineering and project management firms. He currently works for Jacobs, one of the world's largest and most diverse providers of technical, professional and construction services. Nigel is a past director of the Professional Services Marketing Group (PSMG) and a current tutor for Cambridge Marketing Colleges, specializing in teaching courses to professional services marketers.

# Introduction
## leadership themes in professional services marketing

The market for professional services and consulting firms is changing. A number of factors are influencing that change, but without doubt the principal reason is client requirements.

Across sectors – law, accounting, property, engineering, management consulting and others – clients are asking for more from their professional services advisers. This is not a new trend, as there has been a steady evolution from clients wanting to buy a product or service to needing advice – the idea of the 'Trusted Advisor' was first put forward by David Maister (Maister, Green and Galford, 2000). However, today clients are going further and many want their advisers to anticipate and deliver full-service, commercial solutions to meet their changing needs (Figure 0.1).

**FIGURE 0.1**   Changing client needs

With new client demands comes the requirement for professional services firms to change their business model (Figure 0.2). Firms have to recognize that they are no longer in business just to provide technically excellent products and services. They need to go the extra mile to anticipate, understand and deliver commercial solutions to their clients. This has to be done in a manner and style that not only resolves their clients' challenges, but also delivers a great experience in the process. Clients want relationships with their advisers that cover all points – technical excellence, service provision, and client experience – not just a narrow set defined by the firm's technical disciplines. They are looking for a partner that cares about business outcomes as much as they do.

**FIGURE 0.2** The professional's role is changing

To meet these needs the modern professional services firm needs to recruit, retain and develop a team of people that thinks first and foremost about the client and is ready to address all of their challenges.

Thankfully it's been clear for many years that whatever expertise an individual or team has in their chosen discipline, a successful career or practice cannot be achieved unless that technical ability is paired with strong client relationship skills. The ability to attract, develop and retain clients has always been a prerequisite for success in a professional services firm.

More recently and across the professions, firms have started to realize that there is a limit to how far that combination of technical skill and relationship management can take you. That limit is rooted in a failure to understand that developing client relationships cannot be a singular or team activity alone.

Like all critical business activities, client relationship development has to be led from the top, but it cannot be the sole preserve of individual partners, directors and senior managers. It has to be a shared, whole-firm obsession which then embraces and influences company-wide concerns such as strategy, structure, systems and skills.

The widening gap between individual and firm-wide capability in these areas has been exacerbated by clients now demanding better solutions and an improved experience. No firm can achieve those outcomes for clients without such considerations permeating the DNA and values of the business.

Until recently, there had been a gap in the capability and capacity of professional services firms to deliver on that obsession. This begs the question as to what type of individual or team discipline is best placed to help plug that gap.

## The need for marketing

The UK Chartered Institute of Marketing still defines marketing as 'The management process responsible for identifying, anticipating and satisfying customer requirements profitably' (Chartered Institute of Marketing, 2014). I always say that marketing is about seeing the world through the eyes of your client – first understanding and then acting on what they need and want – and everything else should then flow from there.

Whatever your preferred definition, it is exactly this client-focused capability and mindset that professional services firms should be looking for in their people. All marketing and business development professionals should recognize skills such as identifying market trends, understanding client requirements and recognizing competitive advantage as their natural territory. These skills lie at the heart of our professional capability and credibility.

These skills need to be honed and delivered in an environment where the principal point of contact between the client and the firm is the team of technical practitioners delivering the advice or service required. The marketing and business development teams often do not have the benefit of a direct channel of engagement or communication with the client. They need the ability to build their client understanding through their technical colleagues. Their relationship and engagement with their colleagues firm-wide – their internal clients – are critical and prerequisites for success.

Unfortunately, marketers in professional services firms have for too long been pigeonholed as only external communications experts, designing and implementing plans to push out the latest PR or promotional campaign. Similarly, business developers have been wrapped up in coordinating and finessing urgent client pitches, delivering to ever-tighter timescales. However, in both cases, the individuals or teams involved are usually kept remote from the client and used in support of the partners or managers leading the client engagement.

These individuals and teams are recognized as providing critical capabilities to the business and adding skills and professionalism to their firms, but they are rarely seen as setting the agenda or offering strategic capabilities for their firms. Marketing and business development professionals have been seen as valuable foot soldiers, but not officer material – helping to win battles, but not define how or where those battles should be fought.

## Marketing, business development, sales...

The roles and titles of those leading and contributing to the development of client relationships vary within professional services firms. At first, people joined firms in marketing roles as the majority of their responsibilities covered promotional and communications activities. Increasingly, business development roles have developed as firms have professionalized the client development and sales process. Some people hold sales roles, but it remains a term or title little used in professional services firms.

In addition, people holding marketing, business development or sales roles can either be specialists from those areas that have joined to bolster the firm's capabilities or technical practitioners – lawyers, accountants, consultants – who have stepped across either temporarily or permanently into such positions.

The title held or career path pursued by such individuals does not really matter. Most firms are now finding that a blend of skills and experiences is needed to progress the development of client relationships. The title and role are not important – the commitment to the client is.

In this book we will use marketing and business development interchangeably and will not get hung up on the distinctions. We will make few references to sales because, although it remains a critical step in the process, the overall objective is the progression of the client relationship, not the individual sale. A sale is a necessary but not sufficient condition for a successful client relationship.

## The barriers to marketing leadership

There are a number of barriers that prevent people in marketing and business development roles progressing into leadership positions within professional services firms. The best-known and most pernicious is the division drawn between 'fee-earners' and 'non-fee-earners', which suggests that only a technical professional can lead the growth and development of the firm – everyone else being in a 'support' function.

The terms fee-earner and non-fee-earner, although well intentioned by themselves, suggest a culture where a) the principal role of a lawyer/accountant/consultant etc is to get money out of the client, and b) if someone isn't a technician, then their role is defined by what they don't do, that is, earn fees, not by what they contribute.

It is never very clear what clients think of the terms fee-earner and non-fee-earner. It doesn't indicate immediately that a firm's focus is on everyone working in the best interest of the client's requirements.

Historically, professional rules prevented anyone from a 'support' function achieving partner, or even quasi-partner, status, and so sitting on the senior management team of the firm. Those rules have now largely been removed, but it remains common for the head of marketing or business development to report into a 'Marketing Partner', rather than have a direct line to the Managing Partner/Director or Chief Executive Officer.

I have been party to many a conversation where professional services marketers have bemoaned their status in firms when similar positions in consumer businesses command much greater power and influence. They complain about the 'support' status of marketing and business development in the professions and the cultural traditions that preserve leadership positions for the partners of the firm. They see a 'glass ceiling' that cannot be penetrated without partner status.

What those in professional services firms have failed to recognize is that in a consumer-led business, with maybe millions rather than hundreds of customers, the marketers understand their business's customers better than anyone else and champion their cause. That knowledge earns influence at the top table reserved for partners or directors in professional services firms, who are also typically the 'owners' of the firm's key client relationships.

The real reason that many marketing and business development leaders do not make it is that they know little of additional value about the firm's clients and what they are really looking for. It's a bitter pill to swallow, but they neither earn nor deserve a place at the top table. The 'glass ceiling' is not one of heritage and prejudice, but one of knowledge and insight.

## The new breed of marketers

What marketers and business developers need to show their firms is that they can deliver the insight and intelligence that their consumer marketing colleagues frequently offer. Some firms will need people in these roles to specialize in, and take a lead on, both developing client relationships and guiding their colleagues in the necessary skills to deliver that whole-firm client relationship obsession. The more advanced firms will offer the opportunity to become a complete client champion – the voice of the client – helping to shape and deliver the client solution and experience (Figure 0.3).

**FIGURE 0.3** The marketer's role is changing

Thankfully, we are now seeing that new breed of marketing and business development professional step forward: leaders who do not accept that they are a 'support function' working in a subsidiary role to the firm's partners or directors. They are individuals and teams working alongside the current and future leadership of the business to design, shape and drive successful client strategies.

This book is for this new breed of professionals – not only marketing, business development and sales specialists, but also the firm's technical practitioners – who want to play a full role in their firm's obsession with client relationship development. This means stepping up as a leader in the business and having a material and measurable impact on everything the client demands from your firm. If you see yourself as merely a member of a support function who just delivers tasks, then stop reading here; read on if you want to be involved in setting the agenda and both lead and increase the impact and influence you have on your firm.

This book will help you understand how the development of your role and career can, in fact must, match the changing requirements of your clients and the corresponding opportunities for your firm (Figure 0.4).

**FIGURE 0.4** Client, firm and marketer changing together

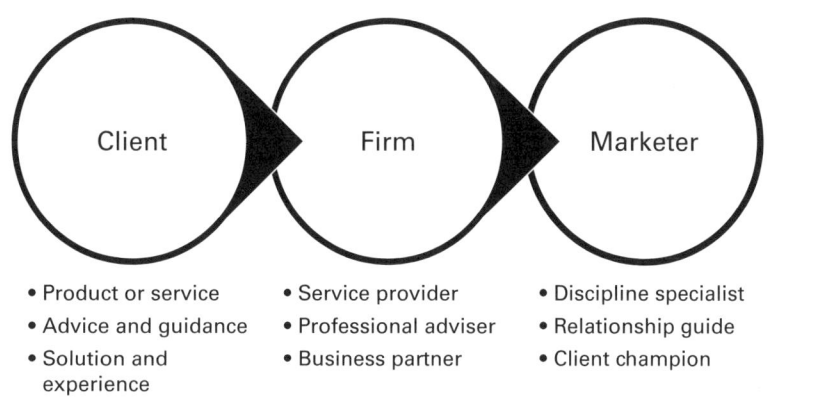

# Today's top marketing leadership themes

To give you the ammunition to step up in your firm and become a client champion, we focus in this book on the themes we think are most relevant today to the modern professional services marketer. We also concentrate on how you apply knowledge of those themes and learn from experience and practical examples. Your value to your firm will come from knowing not just what to do, but how to do it.

Theory is critical – you have to be able to back up your advice and decisions with a solid foundation of knowledge and fact-based evidence – but you will not gain sufficient influence if you cannot both evidence and justify your plans for putting ideas into practice. This, therefore, is not a book that covers the A to Z of professional services marketing and client development theory. There are many good texts already covering that ground. In fact, if you are starting out on your journey of developing knowledge and skills in this area, I would encourage you to start with a text or course not specific to the professions. The core theories and models of marketing and client or customer development hold universal truths that transcend industry sector boundaries. Much is written about why the professions are different, but there is more that can be learnt from mainstream product or service marketing theory.

This book is therefore less about the 'why' and 'what' of marketing theory and more about the 'how' of marketing practice. It takes the themes we believe are relevant to all professional services leaders today and explores how some of the world's most successful firms are tackling them.

These themes are:

1 Growth – identifying and choosing markets and clients;
2 Understanding – listening and responding to client needs;
3 Connecting – connecting with clients and stakeholders;
4 Relationships – developing and managing client relationships;
5 Managing – influencing the marketing organization.

We have chosen these themes for the following reasons.

## *Growth*

We start with growth because identifying and selecting markets and clients is a common and persistent obsession for all businesses. 'Who do you want to work for?' and 'How far and fast can you go?' are two questions that always consume a business leader's thinking.

We could have called this theme 'strategy', but in today's market your business strategy is undoubtedly driven by a growth objective. Firms are today refocusing on growth, and so marketers are challenged to help identify the right markets and clients to focus on.

They also need to consider whether the firm's business model needs to change to realize that growth, what globalization means for the growth imperative, and whether the firm can retain its DNA and values as it grows.

## Understanding

Throughout this book we will propose that a marketer needs to be the client champion in their firm, helping the business to listen and respond to client needs. So few firms do this well that it has to be a priority for improvement.

Firms need to understand better what clients want and tailor their approach accordingly, and marketers must champion that client-focused approach in their firms. If listening and understanding clients are innate skills that all professionals need to develop, marketers must use them to change their firms for the better. They must also use what the latest research says about client requirements and their expectations of their professional advisers.

## Connecting

This is more than just 'old school' marketing communications. Businesses need to move away from marketing campaigns that just pump out messages on products or services that interest them. Connecting is about building a conversation with clients and other key stakeholders. Here, marketers must combine all aspects of their role as discipline specialist, relationship guide and client champion.

'Content marketing' is a hot topic across different industries and media, which professional services firms must understand and grasp. Even if content is king and firms have something valuable to say, being heard is increasingly difficult in a world of cluttered communications. Marketers must understand how to cut through the noise, build connections and generate business.

## Relationships

Firms now obsess about relationships, but developing and managing your most important client relationships successfully requires processes, capabilities and a shift in mindset that goes far beyond a trite phrase or plug-in software solution.

Great firms are built on great client relationships, but the development and management of those relationships cannot be left to chance, and marketers can set the pace in key account management. They must understand how to identify and focus on the relationships that really matter – and what you do with the others. The firm might be clear on what they want from a relationship, but by definition it is a two-way process – so marketers should build understanding of what the client wants from their relationship too.

## Managing

This is where it all comes together, both as a leader in the marketing and business development team but also the wider firm. A marketer cannot achieve all of the above on their own, so their impact will most likely be measured by the influence they have on the team around them and the wider audience of the firm.

If great firms are built on great client relationships, the marketing organization must add to the value of those relationships, thrive and be credible in the wider firm and be clearly accountable for its actions and results. Marketing leaders need to develop and lead their team but, more importantly, the marketing capacity of the whole firm. Then they must measure and demonstrate the value of marketing through tangible results.

We explore each of these five themes through the eyes of a team of expert contributors whose experiences, of both success and failure, cover the full range of professions, size of firms and geographic locations. Whether you work for a global law firm, a regional accountancy practice or a small management consultancy, there are lessons and advice here that you can use tomorrow in your business. Moreover, if you work outside the professions, for instance in another service delivery business, you can compare and contrast your experiences with those of our experts.

Each theme has a short introductory chapter explaining its relevance, followed by three or four chapters authored by a theme expert. We then summarize lessons for each theme.

After these themes we return in a concluding chapter to exploring how the role of a client champion will evolve and what the future looks like for marketing and business development professionals.

## Characteristics of a professional services firm

We stand by the assertion that there are more similarities than differences in best-practice marketing and business activities across sectors. The claim that everything about professional services marketing is different is overplayed. Nevertheless, there are some characteristics of the professional services sector that are important to understand.

The following are what we consider to be the 10 most important characteristics of a professional services firm that define the sector in comparison to others (Table 0.1). If you ignore these characteristics you will limit your ability to influence and impact the success of your firm. They should all be familiar to experienced marketers, but there is no harm in regularly reviewing whether you are paying enough attention to each in your marketing, business development and management programmes.

Some of these characteristics arise because we operate in a people-dominated service rather than a physical product market, others because firms are principally interested in business customers (clients, to use the preferred professional services term) rather than consumers, and a few are just peculiarities of the professions and related disciplines. All of them are important for marketers to understand and consider when designing and implementing policies, plans and programmes.

**TABLE 0.1** Top 10 characteristics of a professional services firm

| Characteristic | Definition | Consideration for marketers |
|---|---|---|
| 1. Perishability | As a former colleague once put it, 'Consulting is like being in the airline business. Every day a plane takes off with seats for all your consultants and you want to make sure a client is paying for every one of them to fly. You can't sell a seat today for yesterday's flight.' Many businesses deal with perishability – think of soft fruit in a supermarket – but professional services and consulting businesses have a particular challenge. There are some results- or success-based charging models, but most firms sell time, and time expires every minute, hour and day. | Your role may be to plan for the future and implement campaigns that will deliver market, client and project opportunities, but you must not ignore the fact that your operational colleagues always have one eye on what they and their teams are doing today, tomorrow and next week. You have to see the short- and long-term pictures together. There will be no tomorrow if you cannot sell today. Utilization/billability/chargeable time is an obsession in firms, so you should think about that too and understand the finance fundamentals underpinning the business. |
| 2. Professional pyramid | The pyramid comes in all shapes and sizes, with multiple layers, but it exists in every firm. At the top you have the partners, directors and senior management. They may own the business; they certainly set the agenda and manage most of the clients and all of the people. Below them are those aspiring to make the top tier; they might not run the client relationships, but they are probably delivering day to day your most important projects. Towards the bottom is the majority of the team: the engine room of the business, churning out the projects, racking up the chargeable time and making most of the profit for the firm. | You probably work with, worry about and listen to that top tier most of your time. If you're lucky, in the right firm culture and doing a great job, they may even consider you one of them. If you are not, you are unlikely to realize the influence and impact we talk about through the book. You are right to aim the majority of your time here, because that is where client interaction, relationships and sales are concentrated, but don't ignore the other tiers. The middle tier contains the leaders of the future and they will value your advice on developing their client skills. Help them now and they should repay you when they make it to the top. You may also find it easier to gain traction here, especially with new ideas and programmes, than you might with the top tier. The lower tier will have a thirst for knowledge, again in developing client-friendly skills. Also, they are a massive part of the brand experience for your client. If you can instil the right behaviours here, early in their careers, they will do your job for you. |

**TABLE 0.1** *continued*

| Characteristic | Definition | Consideration for marketers |
|---|---|---|
| **3. Intellect and challenge** | Your 'product' is highly intelligent, very professional and passionate about what they do. Once convinced by a course of action, it will be a highly effective and compelling force, but it will not necessarily accept the course proposed and will require convincing. It will also have doubts and uncertainties on certain activities; in particular, marketing and business development, because the natural role of a professional is to 'advise' or 'tell', not 'enquire' and 'understand'. | You are privileged to work in such an intellectually stimulating environment. If you value debate, collaboration and a constant desire to improve, you will thrive. You will also find an audience that values your professionalism, because it is the bedrock of a firm and you bring something new to the mix. However, don't expect to get your way just because you say so and you 'understand marketing'. Expect to be challenged, always have data to justify your case and, while being determined and resolute, be prepared to change and reach a collegiate outcome. You will also need loads of emotional intelligence to read a room and work out how to get a sometimes-disparate group to the right outcome. |
| **4. Consistency** | People are different in the way that a product, eg a widget, is not. That's what makes working with people interesting, stimulating and fun. Your clients want all the intellect, innovation and ideas that come from human interactions, but they also want the job delivered as planned and, probably, would like the experience to be similar, if not identical, to their last project. If you deliver projects to different standards and styles, dependent on the vagaries of the individual or team involved, you don't have a firm or a brand: you just have a ragbag collection of individuals who happen to trade under the same banner. | Consistency and brand are essential bedfellows, so if you care deeply about the latter you need to obsess about the former, too. Behaviours, training, processes, systems, method statements etc may not seem the natural territory for a marketer, but they all help to underpin consistency in a firm. Get involved! |

**TABLE 0.1** *continued*

| Characteristic | Definition | Consideration for marketers |
|---|---|---|
| 5. Intangibility | Not only are two widgets the same, but you can also pick them up. They have substance. You can see and touch what you're buying before you part with your cash. You can probably even ask for a sample to try first. You can meet a lawyer, accountant or engineer etc but you can't see what they are going to advise or design before you sign the contract. A client can start small and give the firm a minor commission before risking a large, critical one, but in most instances you can't take home that sample before committing to any purchase. | You have to do all you can to minimize the client's fear of intangibility. You have to help demonstrate expertise and experience – 'we may not have done this for you, but we've completed successful projects for other similar clients'. You have also to show empathy and identify ways that you and the client can share in developing a solution and build trust. If you can help the client shape the outcome, they will have more faith in you to deliver it when they finally sign the contract. And don't ignore the symbols of tangibility: smart offices, well-dressed professionals, impeccable behaviours… all play a part in reassuring the client and building confidence that there is more to your sales pitch than just words. |
| 6. Project risk | In many instances the cost of professional advice is not a client's largest project outlay: consider the advisers' fees as a percentage of an acquisition cost or your solicitor's costs when you buy a house. But the risk to the client of making the wrong choice of adviser and receiving bad advice far outweighs the fee paid. There is an old adage in UK law: 'A General Counsel has never been fired for hiring a "magic circle" law firm.' What is the risk to the client of hiring you? | You and the firm will think about various aspects when taking on the project – what is the revenue/profit, how will we resource it, what is the delivery risk, what are the contract terms, how much insurance cover must we offer etc. That is all important information, but you need to see your appointment in the context of the client's overall project. What is the cost of that? Where are their risks? Irrespective of the fee, how important are you to the whole equation? Focus on that, not your metrics alone. |

**TABLE 0.1** *continued*

| Characteristic | Definition | Consideration for marketers |
|---|---|---|
| **7. Client concentration** | To use a quote from George Orwell's *Animal Farm*: 'All animals are equal. But some animals are more equal than others.' All your clients are important, but some are probably more important than others, ideally in both revenue and profit terms. Many firms glibly use the 80:20 rule and say that 80% of the revenue or profit comes from 20% of the clients. However, in our experience, in most firms it is at least that order of magnitude and sometimes even more concentrated. | You should understand your client concentration ratio and know exactly who fits in that 'more equal' bracket. Those clients should be your focus for any client relationship programme and underpin your thinking on strategy, market choices, service development, skills and recruitment etc. You should understand these clients better than anyone else. You should also work out how to manage the other 80–90% of clients. |
| **8. Switching costs** | Choosing a professional adviser is not necessarily for life but, like a pet, it should be for longer than Christmas. The client may just want someone to 'do a job', but it's more likely that they are looking for a firm to work with over a period of time, even if it is a series of discrete transactions. In part, that is because, as social animals, we like to develop relationships, but also switching costs for professional advisers are high. To change advisers, a client needs to find someone else they trust and then invest in bringing them up the curve of knowledge about their business and particular circumstances. | If you are the incumbent adviser, you should recognize the cost of switching and do everything you can – assuming that the relationship is mutually beneficial and profitable – to cement it. Invest in the relationship, identify compatibility in contacts, work on the points that will make the relationship 'sticky' and hard to undo. If you are looking to remove an incumbent, you need to reduce the switching costs: build empathy, understanding and trust ahead of the appointment, try to climb the client's knowledge curve by stressing compatibility through other sector experience and make personal connections. |
| **9. Purchase complexity** | Formal and informal purchasing procedures now dominate decision processes in professional adviser appointment: rules and regulations, framework agreement, procurement panels and portals, purchasing departments etc all complicate a process that might once have been just one person's decision and completed in a single meeting. | Understand the procurement processes in your client's business and do not think that direct appointment is inevitable or within your contact's grasp. Build your network of client contacts beyond your principal contact. Construct a relationship map and overlay the client process so that you can understand who influences, recommends and decides an appointment. That will show if you know the right people well enough and where else you need to focus your relationship effort. |

**TABLE 0.1**  *continued*

| Characteristic | Definition | Consideration for marketers |
|---|---|---|
| 10. Brand | Your brand is about what you stand for and how you are different from everyone else. But it is not decided by you, it's defined by how your clients and other key stakeholders see you. They decide your brand – not you – and whether it is consistent or differs depending on the audience. In professional services firms, brands are notoriously difficult to define and shift, in many cases because of some of the points above, eg consistency and intangibility. Perception is reality and changing perceptions takes time. It is much easier to destroy a brand overnight than it is to build one up. | You should work hard and communicate consistently what your brand stands for and how you are different, but you should also invest in understanding how successful you are in getting your message across, how others see you and work out how to close any gaps. Recognize that any changes you want to make will take time – branding is a long-term process. And, of course, brand is not about colours and logos, although they have a part to play because we are all susceptible to visual stimuli.<br><br>Remember, everything you do in response to points 1–9 could impact your client's perception of your brand. |

# Differences between professional services firms

I believe these characteristics hold true for most, if not all, professional services firms, but of course there will still be some differences driven by the business and culture of individual firms.

One obvious difference will be the technical discipline or sub-sector in which the firm operates. All professionals share characteristics such as intellect, technical qualifications, the adviser role, client service and a high level of commitment to standards (see Characteristic number 3), but lawyers, accountants and engineers, for example, are not interchangeable in their nature, training or common behaviours.

This book is not about the style and preferences of individual professions. If you are joining a professional services firm for the first time or switching between professions, I would advise you to spend some time getting to know how your particular colleagues think and operate. You could do much worse than spend time over a coffee or lunch with a few of them to understand why they chose their profession and what for them are its defining characteristics, practices and preferred operating styles.

With regard to marketing and business development, there is a stereotype that says management consultancies and accounting firms are more advanced in their thinking and practice than law firms and other professions. That may have been the case 10 to 15 years ago, but I think it is now a dangerous assumption to make. It is also risky to assume that the 'Big 4' accountants or the 'Magic Circle' law firms are ahead of their smaller or more regional competition. I have encountered firms that are leaders and laggards of all sizes and in all professions. It is probably a cliché, but the first sign of a business or sector in decline is often when it adopts the complacent belief that it has achieved an unassailable lead and has nothing to learn from others.

One difference that is always quoted as setting professional services firms apart from other industries is the peculiar nature of partnership. There are not many sectors where the owners and managers of a business are one and the same, make up a significant number of the staff and have usually been with the firm for most of their careers. I have worked in and with firms that are partnerships, privately owned by third parties and publicly traded, and in my experience the ownership structure drives more differences in a firm's culture and style than the individual nature of the profession.

Overall, partnership drives many positive characteristics: a strong and consistent culture, leadership continuity, passionate and involved owners, commitment to career development, more control over the firm's destiny and direction, and fewer external shocks, to name but a few. There is an inherent conservatism in partnership, which I touch on in the introduction to our 'Growth' theme, but, from my experience, the premise that partnership also drives an inevitable 'us and them' culture is unfounded.

There are partnerships where those who have ascended to that rarefied position see themselves, and are treated, as an untouchable 'super race', but that is not desirable and, indeed, actively discouraged in most modern partnerships. Partnership should not imply a right to management or the authority to overrule on operational decisions. Partners need to be accountable and take their responsibilities as owners seriously, but quite rightly they expect management and leadership to come from all levels and quarters of the business, not least the marketing and business development team.

Given the predominance of the partnership model in the professions and the firms contributing to this book, throughout the five themes we talk a lot about partners and the need for marketing and business development leaders to establish strong and mutually trusting relationships with their firm's owners. It is a defining and necessary feature of anyone wanting to achieve a leadership role.

If you are unable to earn peer status with your firm's partners, or with whoever leads your business if you have a different ownership structure, then you are unlikely to achieve the influence or demonstrate the impact that we talk about in this book.

## Characteristics, differences and excuses

I would encourage you to get under the skin of the characteristics of your particular firm, be they driven by its profession, ownership structure, history, geography or size. You should also understand its differences – you may call it distinctive culture – that set the firm apart from others in its sector or the wider professional services industry.

However, you should not focus too much on either characteristics or culture, and certainly not use them as a reason for accepting the status quo. The difference in characteristics between the professions and other industries and within the professions themselves can be overstated and used too often as a reason to avoid or abandon a progressive agenda. A line of thinking or response that starts with 'that will never work here because…' is usually a poor opening gambit and little more than an excuse for inaction.

Of course, you need to be flexible and adaptable – no pyrrhic victories please – and find out how ideas and solutions will fit your firm, but the needs and preferences of your clients and your own professional judgement, experiences and skill should be your primary drivers for decision and action. That is especially the case in marketing and business development, where successful leadership demands new thinking, fresh ideas and positive action.

I would encourage you to take the ideas in this book, whichever firm or sector they come from, and test truthfully how they can add to the success of your firm and your career.

# THEME ONE
## Growth

# Introduction to the Growth theme

*"The consequences for human welfare involved in questions like these are simply staggering: once one starts to think about them, it is hard to think about anything else."*
**(ROBERT LUCAS, NOBEL PRIZE-WINNING ECONOMIST)**

The questions Robert Lucas had in mind here concerned the growth of a national economy, and in particular that of developing nations. The managing partner or CEO of a professional services firm may focus more on growth questions concerning their own business rather than an overall economy, but we are sure they would identify with Lucas's sentiment that 'it is hard to think about anything else'.

Any leadership team will recognize the relentless pressure to grow the top and bottom lines of a business. Innumerable business strategies, improvement programmes and change initiatives are justified, launched and frequently flounder on the promise of delivering renewed and sustained growth, without a question asked as to why that is important.

In a business with external owners, the pressure for growth is expected and rarely questioned, with shareholders demanding an improving return on their investment through either capital appreciation or distributed earnings. Whatever management's priorities or personal opinions, that external pressure will be relentless. In contrast, the shareholders of most professional services firms sit within the business, principally as partners or directors. They then hold dual and sometimes contradictory roles of shareholder and business manager, setting and striving respectively to hit the same growth targets.

We have witnessed many partnership and senior management conversations where, as shareholders, individuals have urged their leadership team to strive for improved performance, motivated by the impact that it will have on their future earnings. Then, at a later date when sitting in a business operations role, the same individuals will expound equally vociferously that their team or personal targets are impossible to hit.

A firm may also have a community of senior shareholders, maybe approaching retirement, who are nervous that any investment in growth will endanger their earning potential on a shorter time horizon. Knowing that they will not benefit from longer-term growth, they often urge the management of the business to be more cautious, adopt a 'steady as she goes' mentality and realize profit now rather than build for the future.

If the views and objectives of the business owners and operators are to align, whether or not they are the same person, they need to agree on the need for, as much as the pace of, growth. Why grow, at what pace and with which risk profile are questions that every professional services firm should not be afraid to ask and, more importantly, define a clear, mutually shared response. In our experience, there is often extensive discussion and planning about how much growth is needed without corresponding consideration of pace and, in particular, the acceptable risk profile.

Without getting wrapped up in the importance or not for a firm to have a stated vision and statements of values and mission, if these documents do exist then they should provide some insight into the 'Why grow?' question for all your key stakeholders, not just your shareholders. In fact, a firm is unlikely to translate growth aspirations into a clear and shared strategy if the needs of other stakeholders are not addressed. Growth may be essential not only to improve returns for shareholders, but also to meet the ongoing needs of clients – both existing and new – and provide development and career progression for staff.

Hopefully, your clients are successful and expanding, so they need their advisers to grow to match their ambition. Equally, there is nothing like growth to open new doors and career pathways for the next generation of business leaders from within your existing staff. You should never hear the statement 'I can't progress until my boss leaves or retires!' in a fast-growing firm.

A corporate or business strategy is less likely to answer the 'why?' of growth, but should be crystal clear on the 'what?' and 'how?' If your strategy doesn't answer the question of what markets, clients and services and how you're going to achieve those aspirations, it's not a good strategy.

Finding the right answer to those questions has only proved harder in the past decade. A growth strategy used to be something that many professional services firms thought applied only to the 'big boys'. Only when firms were looking to enter new markets or cross borders did they feel the need to plan for growth. If you were a small to medium-sized firm, operating in a single market or geography, then surely growth just meant taking on a few more people each year, finding a few more clients, keeping the top and bottom line ticking over…?

Today though, whatever size firm you are, you have to recognize that you operate in a global marketplace. Your team may be in a single state or city, but where is your supply chain or outsourced service providers? And more to the point, even if your client looks like they are just around the corner, what are their aspirations and where are their customers, service providers and staff? For even the most straightforward business, you can find suppliers in Guangdong or Guatemala, service providers in Bangalore or Boston and customers wherever the Cloud will reach. Your firm may want to stay in Cincinnati or Sevenoaks, and technology may enable that scenario more than ever, but your aspirations and horizons cannot stop at the city or state boundary, so nor can your growth strategy.

In whatever way your firm is tackling the why, what and how of growth, as marketers and business development professionals you should want to be involved. The path to growth and accompanying business strategies may seem the preserve of shareholders, partners and senior management, but forward-thinking firms should welcome new and innovative thinking from all quarters. There is no better way to make your mark and flag up your future leadership potential than to contribute to strategy development and influence the why and what of growth, not just the how. Set the path – don't just follow it!

In this first section, we have three chapters that look at all aspects of the growth strategy question from three very different starting points and perspectives. We start with Richard Grove, Director of Marketing, Business Development & Communications at Allen & Overy, the global law firm. Allen & Overy has experienced impressive growth, breaking into new markets and geographies during the global recession at a time when most firms were focusing on consolidation and asking how they could get more from what they already had, not pushing out and forging new relationships. Richard looks at that path to growth and how you can achieve it without diluting the essence of the firm that your clients and staff fell for in the first place.

We follow this up with Daniel Smith and Claire Essex from another global law firm, Baker & McKenzie, but this time viewed from the perspective of their responsibility for marketing and business development in Asia. While marketers in the developed economies of Europe and the United States were asking themselves if a low/no-growth market was the new normal, Daniel and Claire were surrounded by booming markets. They address the question of how to choose the right path to growth and how to set priorities when everything looks like an opportunity.

We conclude this section with Clive Stevens, Executive Chairman at Kreston Reeves, a UK regional accountancy practice. Clive explores and explains the opportunity and challenges of professional networks, and specifically the development and continuing evolution of Kreston International, a global network of accountancy practices. He demonstrates that any size firm can push the boundaries on growth and expand their influence and reach beyond traditional markets.

# Growth and globalization

01

**RICHARD GROVE,** Director of Marketing, Business Development & Communications, Allen & Overy LLP

**Profile:** Richard has spent his entire career in marketing and business development, having started in consultancy, developing fast-moving consumer goods marketing strategies for the likes of Unilever Plc, PepsiCo and the Wellcome Foundation. He has 20 years' experience in large, international professional services firms and was appointed a director of Allen & Overy in 2007, with responsibility for the marketing, business development and communication functions across the firm's global network.

This chapter shares the growth and globalization experiences of Allen & Overy, one of the world's most respected law firms. It starts with a recent experience that demonstrates how multinational corporates operate in global markets and therefore expect their advisers to support them accordingly – is this an opportunity or a threat?

It is 10.30 on a Saturday morning at home in London. I'm browsing news and e-mails, coffee in hand. An e-mail pops up – one of our largest Asian clients needs advice on a mobile device app product launch by tomorrow (Sunday) night, in 46 jurisdictions. After a few minutes of mild panic, the global machine starts to jump into life on screen. Within a few hours there are 20 partners on a call. And by Sunday night at 6.00 pm we have delivered the advice for 46 jurisdictions.

## Background – capturing global growth opportunities

In recent years, despite the recession following the global financial crisis, the pace of globalization has continued to accelerate and its extent has deepened. A quick review of the Forbes Global 2000 (Forbes, 2014) shows that over the past decade the number of countries represented in that list of major companies and banks has risen from 42 to 62.

For advisory firms, globalization and cross-border expansion have first been driven by that growth in client diversity. We've seen our and our competitors' clients move into new markets as they seek to expand their customer base and pursue new engines of growth. An example of this is investment in international infrastructure markets. Those clients expect their legal advisers to be able to follow them into these new markets and provide them with the necessary support.

At the same time, many countries have opened up their domestic legal markets to external law firms – creating opportunities to win new domestic clients in these jurisdictions and support better inbound and outbound deals. Capital markets now operate globally and governments see globalization as a chance to use cross-border investment to stimulate their economies. This is also aided by the rise of digital technologies, which significantly favour a borderless world economy.

Sitting alongside these factors is the proliferation of both national and international regulation, especially for financial institutions. Not only is there now more complex regulation, but these regulatory frameworks have become more fragmented since the financial crisis. For clients, keeping abreast of all these constant changes has become much more demanding.

This offers law firms the opportunity to demonstrate their ability to interpret this increasingly fast-moving and complex regulatory landscape, along with the many different legal codes that will govern international commercial agreements, investments and financing arrangements across the globe.

So it's no surprise that client work is becoming more complex and cross-border in nature and reflects exactly the type of work that Allen & Overy is looking to win.

## A strategy for globalization and growth

Against this backdrop of globalization, we segmented our market by complexity, dividing it up by how many different jurisdictions a deal or transaction involved. We identified that the client work we did that involved five countries or more was 30 per cent more profitable than single-country domestic work (Figure 1.1). Furthermore, it was much better protected from being taken in-house by cash-strapped clients.

We also realized, importantly, that on a global playing field there is simply less competition. Fewer law firms are able to compete at that level. If you add to this the complexity of international deals and transactions, it represents a very attractive premium-priced market into which to sell very high-quality legal expertise.

So our strategy needed not only to identify new growth markets but also to position ourselves as the go-to firm for complex cross-border legal support. In a post-crisis climate of cost-cutting, we had to be sure to select markets with the best growth opportunities so as to deliver the best returns on investment to the partnership both in the short and long term.

This, coupled with maintaining our position in the relatively flat, mature markets such as France, Italy and the Netherlands, would provide a balanced business model in these (and future) times of uncertainty. High-growth emerging markets could offer an attractive 'hedge' against stagnation in mature markets in tough economic conditions. But, we also recognized that it is critical to manage global expansion carefully, so that consistently high-quality services continue to be provided to clients in all markets.

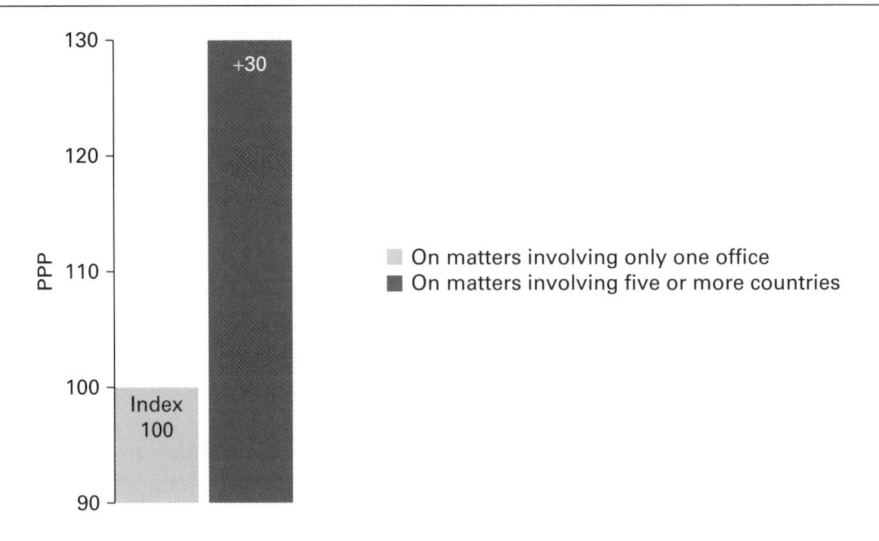

**FIGURE 1.1** Single vs multi-country matter profitability

```
130 -
                 +30
120 -

PPP 110 -           ▨ On matters involving only one office
                    ■ On matters involving five or more countries

100 -
      Index
      100
 90 -
```

Under the umbrella of this globalization and growth strategy we set out a number of marketing and communication initiatives. These included:

- strengthening the brand;
- defining and communicating clear strategic priorities;
- devising entry plans for new geographical markets for share of spend;
- actively managing client relationships;
- motivating cross-selling;
- building on our sector expertise;
- creating new products and service delivery models;
- using new technology.

## Setting the strategy

It's relatively easy for the senior management of a firm of 5,000 people to set a strategy, but little or no progress will be made unless all employees are aware of it and, more importantly, have bought into its intent. Published research tells us that the more aligned a workforce is with its strategy, the more successful it will be – and that is even more the case with an organization distributed over 30 countries. So as part of our strategy roll-out we conducted a survey of the partners' understanding of the firm's objectives to see how well they grasped what the business was currently trying to achieve – such as our existing globalization plans.

This survey revealed that only 45 per cent of non-management partners were familiar with the firm's strategic priorities. Some 85 per cent also didn't think their team or office was up to speed with it. In other words, the strategy hadn't properly filtered down to the ranks. This presented us with a real internal communications challenge.

To address that challenge we set up a strategic communications advisory group consisting of 12 partners, alongside members of the marketing and communications team. This group was tasked with figuring out how to make sure that everyone in the firm was on board with the strategy. I was struggling to find any magic formula to do this other than some tips I had gained from a conversation with Deloitte about their London Olympics 2012 sponsorship. They had set everyone in their firm the challenge to make their own personal contribution to the sponsorship programme.

To make it easier to communicate the strategy across the firm, the group distilled it down to three key phrases. They were: 'Global reach, local depth; lasting relationships, market leadership; high-performance culture'. And, both on paper and in our messaging, we put our brand positioning (see below under 'The role of the brand') at the centre of the strategic framework (Figure 1.2).

**FIGURE 1.2**  Brand positioning

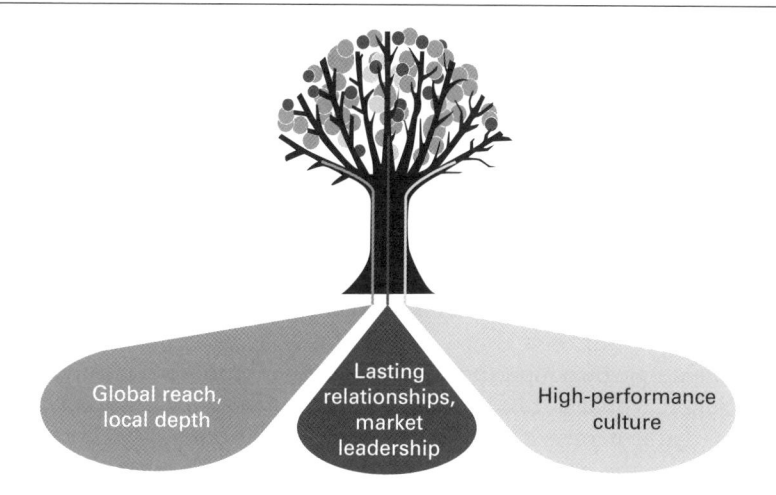

We used various media to explain the firm's strategy and what it might mean to everyone at an individual level. And even though we invested hours in creating high-impact communications and gathered all the partners from across the network for a face-to-face global meeting, it was the individual engagement that proved the key to success.

The internal communications campaign triggered a series of conversations about the strategy and even saw offices around the world helping each other implement it at a local level. With the brand and the marketing strategy well and truly embedded, it inevitably proved easier for the organization to direct its efforts more effectively to the globalization and growth agenda.

When we ran the same survey again a year later, we were pleasantly surprised to see that we had really 'moved the dial': 94 per cent of the partners were familiar with the strategic priorities and only 15 per cent thought their teams weren't up to speed with it. One would like to think that 4,500 people with map directions could lead those who might be a bit lost to the right destination!

## Debunking a myth about partnerships

Before tackling the firm's globalization and growth strategy in more detail, there is one point I want to address. There is a widespread myth that professional services firms lack sophistication in their approach to marketing by virtue of the constraints of a partnership structure.

This myth is based on a perception that partnerships are archaic structures reliant on a consensus-driven decision-making process, which moves at a glacial pace. This is supposedly in contrast to listed corporates, with their more dynamic and efficient 'command and control' management structures.

Having also served as Marketing Director of multinational, listed professional services companies, I can say that this perception couldn't be further from the truth – and the evidence bears this out. The major London-based law firms dominate their industry globally and are a great UK export success story. They have been far quicker to globalize than their US peers, investing in new markets and setting up the management infrastructure to exploit the opportunity.

US law firms have been slower to attack the global market, in large part simply because they enjoy such a huge domestic market, which dwarfs those of other countries. A large group seeking 'global' credentials is now following the few US firms that did 'go global'.

The partnership model has some very clear advantages in pursuing a globalization and growth strategy, especially in a world increasingly prone to volatility, uncertainty, complexity and ambiguity. It provides a strong degree of stability and even certainty from a strategic point of view.

A single global partnership can take a long-term approach to strategic planning and marketing. It would not be unusual to invest in entry to a new market with a business plan that generates a loss for two years. A CEO of a listed company might be very nervous at the prospect of doing this for fear of alienating a diverse set of shareholders and analysts.

This actually makes long-term planning and risk-taking much more challenging for listed companies. A partnership is capable of being truly entrepreneurial with a mere (in our case) 500 or so partners as stakeholders (ie owners), whereas a listed corporate or bank can be hamstrung by a huge and disparate collection of shareholders and analysts.

## Global reach, local depth

Generally speaking, tier 1 law firms have been globalizing through either mergers and acquisitions, organic growth or a combination of both approaches. For Allen & Overy the strategy since the global financial crisis has been largely built around organic growth, which has required strong marketing planning and support.

It's against this backdrop that we undertook a major global expansion drive not long after the financial crisis. This caused some surprise among market commentators because we were investing in new markets at a time when most law firms were putting expansion plans on ice and battening down the hatches.

Although counter-cyclical, this strategy offered us the opportunity to gain first-mover advantage in some markets at a time when there was less competition. The largely organic approach helped ensure we expanded as one global firm with a strong incentive to leverage rapid growth in market share from collaborative business development.

We understood that the broader the geographic coverage a law firm offers, the more likely it is to win business from large multinational corporations. A large global network enhances a firm's ability to offer the full range of services that many clients now seek from their professional advisers. Here's an extract from an e-mail from one of our marketing team that is not untypical of many I receive: 'We have received an RFP [Request For Proposal] from XXX for their global panel. It's two years since we won our place on their panel and we understand that they will further slim down the list of preferred firms (possibly by half) and channel more work into the hands of those firms that are successful.'

Many of the new markets we entered were and are very different in nature, ranging from some very mature, developed markets, such as Australia, to others that were truly emerging, such as Myanmar. We currently have 45 offices worldwide (Figure 1.3).

The common thread, though, that ran through all of these markets was the opportunity offered by globalization rather than the domestic market alone. We were witnessing growing cross-border trade and investment flows between various new and existing markets served by the firm and it was these flows that drew us in, not the opportunity to be in that market alone.

So, in 2010, when much of the world was still concerned about commercial survival in a tough global economy, we opened offices in Doha, Sydney, Perth and Jakarta. In 2011, while there was still a level of caution prevailing in the legal sector, new operations were started in Washington, DC and Casablanca. In 2012, when there was some discussion taking place about global economic recovery, offices were opened in Istanbul and Vietnam. Then in 2013, when the talk about the global economy was becoming more optimistic, the firm announced office launches in Myanmar and Barcelona.

## Market entry

Despite their diversity, all these countries represented different growth opportunities in the global market and each market entry was approached in a different way. For example, an analysis of the Moroccan market revealed a fast-growing gross domestic product (GDP), cross-border trade flows, a new trend for financial institutions and private equity firms to locate there as a North Africa hub, a major infrastructure investment programme, strong links with one of Allen & Overy's existing markets – France – and, most importantly, only one law firm dominating the high-end market. It was obvious that an international firm could secure first-mover advantage by agreeing to join forces with the key players. This resulted in the combination of Naciri & Associés with Allen & Overy.

**FIGURE 1.3** Network growth

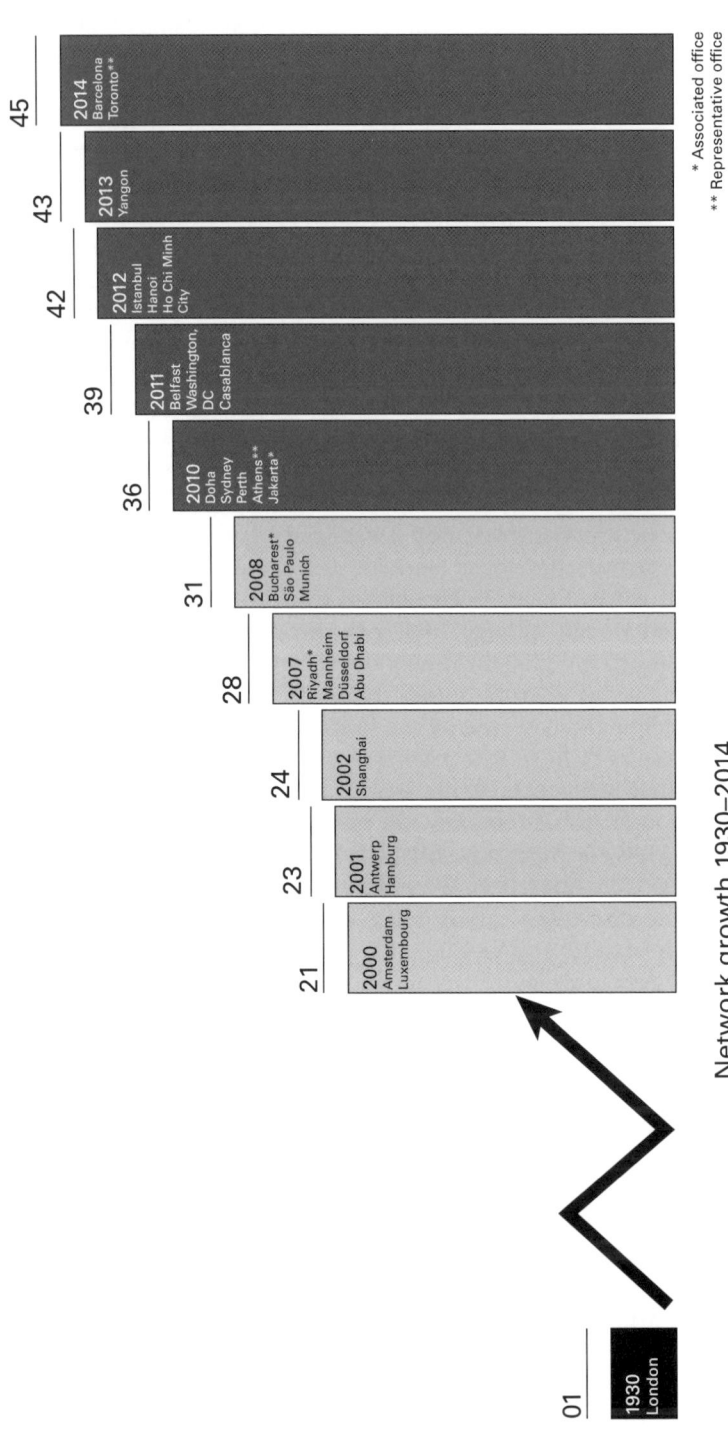

Network growth 1930–2014

| Year | Cities | Total |
|---|---|---|
| 1930 | London | 01 |
| 2000 | Amsterdam, Luxembourg | 21 |
| 2001 | Antwerp, Hamburg | 23 |
| 2002 | Shanghai | 24 |
| 2007 | Riyadh*, Mannheim, Düsseldorf, Abu Dhabi | 28 |
| 2008 | Bucharest**, São Paulo, Munich | 31 |
| 2010 | Doha, Sydney, Perth, Athens**, Jakarta* | 36 |
| 2011 | Belfast, Washington, DC, Casablanca | 39 |
| 2012 | Istanbul, Hanoi, Ho Chi Minh City | 42 |
| 2013 | Yangon | 43 |
| 2014 | Barcelona, Toronto** | 45 |

\* Associated office
\*\* Representative office

Australia, however, was a different beast – a mature market, where domestic firms focused on domestic work dominated the legal sector. The opportunity there was to open an operation that targeted inbound and outbound deals and transactions across a number of sectors, not least energy and natural resources.

The leading firms were too big to swallow in a full merger, so the only means of market entry was to use the strength of the brand and the opportunity for multinational work to hire what we considered to be 17 of the top lawyers in the country and open for business from a standing start. The market was changed forever as international firms followed. In an article entitled 'Australian law – do the first movers have it?' published on the Beaton Capital website, 7 January 2013, Warren Riddell said '…the market is polarizing into those that will have meaningful global reach and those that won't'.

With a lot of market analysis and a number of variations on market entry strategies, we opened 15 new offices over a five-year period, which helped grow revenues by 15 per cent and profits by 24 per cent. It is worth noting the impact on profitability of driving more revenue through a single global infrastructure and cost base.

Business plans for the new markets were accompanied by very detailed marketing plans for collaboration across offices to 'sell' the new market presence. The partners, as individual investors in the new offices and participants in a single profit pool, were strongly motivated to deliver those plans. The resulting cross-selling has contributed to the business plan targets for each new office being reached well ahead of schedule, and 70 per cent of Allen & Overy's work now involves two countries or more.

One of the many things we learnt from this was the value of having a strong brand (see below). We had worked on building the brand from 2009 and it helped open doors to the most attractive merger partners as well as getting us off to a quick start with clients. In every case we operated under the Allen & Overy name from Day 1.

## Best-friend alliances

Opening new offices represents a considerable investment and therefore it is impossible to have a presence in every country. In order to fulfil our positioning as the go-to firm for cross-border work, we also had to supplement our physical office network with an extended network of 'best friend' firms in markets where we had no presence.

In 2008, we set about establishing these best-friend alliances with a dedicated function to manage the non-exclusive relationships with those firms. This was the first combined physical office and best-friend alliance model on this scale in the legal market. In order to support the best friends of the firm we not only employed a relationship management team but we also invested in a dedicated knowledge-sharing and training programme, conferences, events, online forums, secondments, directories, and joint marketing and networking activities.

This has now grown to cover 118 countries over and above our own physical network of offices. Firms compete with each other to join the 'club', which provides Allen & Overy with access to clients in markets where we do not have a presence and reinforces the firm's global services offering with a 'local law' capability covering 99 per cent of the world's economy.

# The role of the brand

The brand was and is at the heart of the firm's strategy; it plays an important role in helping the firm expand into new markets and in capturing the highly complex premium-end work we are targeting.

To be clear, a brand is far more than just a logo or a trademark. We believe it has to communicate succinctly the firm's values, culture, objectives and positioning in the marketplace: in other words, to tell a story about what the firm represents and to create an emotional bond with clients and prospects. As such, it is both a promise and an expectation.

In turn, the brand, and what it represents, should penetrate the DNA of the firm and its culture. It should be integral to the firm's marketing, business development and communications strategies.

The positioning that Allen & Overy has chosen is to be 'the world's most advanced law firm', with a strong emphasis on 'advanced'. This is not about being the biggest or the best law firm – the former doesn't necessarily resonate with clients (so what?), and the latter is hard to define.

From a legal market perspective, 'advanced' is about us demonstrating that we are ahead of the curve: it's supporting clients facing very complex legal issues, which can span many jurisdictions. We think of it as more than just delivering high-quality advice and excellent service; it also means coming up with cutting-edge thinking to solve complex legal issues. The idea is for the branding to position the firm to work with top-tier global companies, providing the reassurance that we will meet their legal needs internationally and domestically.

'Advanced' also applies to other aspects of the business. These include working with the latest technologies, motivating the highest standards of staff performance (the internal brand) through attracting and retaining top lawyers (the employer brand), and being able to partner with the leading law firms in countries where Allen & Overy has no physical presence.

This positioning lends itself very well to thought-leadership-based marketing, which is one of the most effective forms of marketing for any professional services firm. A visit to allenovery.com will provide multiple examples of thought leadership, as will a visit to the websites of any of the big four accountancy firms, for example. When thought leadership content is woven into an integrated campaign, it can deliver a big impact to a firm's profile but also extend to act as a business development tool.

Branding is now increasingly important in the legal services market. As the market has become more competitive, there is a growing need to differentiate, to support premium pricing and to communicate the value proposition in increasingly commoditized markets. The brand also plays an essential role in a globalization programme as a badge of quality and as a 'credentials carrier' into new markets.

Brand did not feature in the language of law firms 10 years ago, yet it is now referred to as a key asset and differentiator. Without doubt, it is a vital element in a growth and globalization strategy.

# Aligning with the culture

In this story there is also a cultural aspect to consider – not just in terms of the branding per se, but also in the projection of the brand through the marketing strategy and then to the delivery of services to clients. A key challenge faced by many marketers is to make the brand part of an organization's culture. This is made somewhat easier if the brand is equally a reflection of that culture.

Professional services firms are very different from consumer product suppliers – a people business must have an authentic brand; if the brand is little more than an artificially manufactured veneer, the organization is unlikely to deliver on its promises to its clients. There is a risk of client expectations not being met, and that in turn could undermine the brand and the marketing strategy. At Allen & Overy we wanted to be sure that the brand and the business objectives were embedded into the firm's psyche and an integral part of its culture and vice versa.

The firm's culture also helps with recruiting and retaining the best people. A law firm can only be as good as the calibre of its people. A strong culture and identity should motivate and enthuse the workforce with a sense of pride. Being able to attract business from the world's largest banks and corporates makes for interesting and challenging legal work, which in turn attracts the best lawyers to work for and stay with the firm. There is a virtuous circle where having the best lawyers on your payroll means being able to deliver high-quality legal work, which helps attract and retain top clients. In effect, the firm's culture acts as a positive self-reinforcing dynamic.

# Building strong relationships

A physical presence in a market is only a platform from which to do the real work. With a strong brand in place and a culture that supports the growth and globalization strategy, it becomes easier to align the other aspects of marketing effectively.

Professional services firms are about people: relationship-building and cross-selling are the core components of a marketing plan to grow the top line from existing and new clients. Indeed, in an aggressively competitive market, these actions are a necessity simply to maintain market share.

Like any professional services firm, Allen & Overy employs a classic key account management programme supported by a client listening function and global client relationship management systems. Individual partners are given overall responsibility for individual clients, with a multinational, cross-practice client team (predominantly partners) supporting them to drive cross-selling activities. These activities are planned and orchestrated by a network of relationship managers who form part of the marketing function.

Strong relationships are crucial for understanding the challenges and needs of individual clients and prospects. However, this desire to build strong relationships is hardly a one-way street. Many in-house legal teams actually want to work with the external providers of legal services more on a partnership-type basis, especially where there is a consolidation of legal services suppliers to a small panel of core close advisers. They see it as in their own interest for their legal providers to develop an in-depth knowledge of their businesses. It makes them easier to work with and enhances their ability to bring value.

This client partnership approach is not necessarily second nature to the fee-earning members of professional services firms. Many a lawyer will regard his or her role as that of technical legal expert working to a brief on a deal or transaction. Lawyers tend instinctively to avoid extending their remit to encompass relationship management and the offering of strategic business advice. Interestingly, though a generalization, this is much less the case among US lawyers, who tend to adopt the role of strategic business adviser to their clients.

We realized that if we were to be effective in our client relationship management programme, we had to engage fee-earners to a much greater extent in the process, working closely with the marketing function and extending their relationships beyond general counsel to CFOs, CEOs and the board. Allen & Overy needed to move from being a transactional firm that was good at relationships to a relationship firm that was good at transactions.

To support that goal we introduced a programme called 'Strategic Conversations' across the firm, recognizing that relationships start with a dialogue, ideally at a business, not exclusively legal, level. The strength of lawyers' relationships with their clients is substantially linked to clients' level of dependence on those lawyers for good strategic business advice. The objective was to become 'trusted adviser', which is a step beyond legal adviser.

Preaching best practice to globally recognized technical experts in their field is not easy. This required skills in behavioural change. The issue was less about lawyers' desire to adopt that best practice but more about whether they believed they had 'permission' to adopt that role.

To address this and to give fee-earners the confidence to have a broader, deeper and better-quality interaction with clients, we conducted research among our clients as to their expectations of our fee-earners. The results showed that the clients wanted their lawyers to use their understanding of the business and market to help them manage their strategic challenges. Playing back the research to the partners opened the door to a different way of thinking and a different approach.

Questions that we now routinely ask include:

- How much do we engage with the client 'off deal'?
- Do we prepare well enough for client meetings?
- Do we question assumptions sufficiently?
- Do we know enough about the client's commercial imperatives?
- How can we best use our knowledge of the sector?
- Do we know what it is that clients will really value about our advice?

And many more.

This has become a valuable process for sharing experiences and ideas throughout the firm. It has helped us to realize the lessons we can learn from the routine collection of client feedback, which we share openly among colleagues and client relationship teams. The output from our client listening programme now flows into both the client relationship management process and fee-earners' performance reviews. It is very much considered as a tool for growth, rather than a threat.

The client relationship management function has delivered real growth for the firm. When considering investment in the marketing function, this deserves particular attention. If I ask partners how they would spend an additional 5 per cent on the marketing budget (and I do ask them), the majority will tell me 'client relationship management'.

In the past year alone we have recorded a 5 per cent growth in fee income and profitability among the clients that were included in the programme. There is a degree of 'if you visibly measure it you'll get results' in the learning from the teamwork between fee-earners and marketing staff. A perfect example was a priority target campaign in Asia Pacific that delivered a 29 per cent improvement in revenue and a 60 per cent increase in profitability.

## Motivating cross-selling and a sector approach to market

Strong relationships not only foster a greater mutual understanding, but also make it easier to cross-sell the firm's full range of services to clients across all the markets in which the clients operate. This is an obvious priority for a growth and globalization strategy; in fact the business case for every new market entry is predicated on a thorough cross-selling exercise to 'sell the whole firm'.

Effective cross-selling requires rigorous planning and follow-up. When we analysed our partners' cross-selling behaviour in their interaction with clients, we found a strong motivation to cross-sell across geographies within the same practice area. For example, our German corporate partners who had advised client A on an acquisition in Germany were only too happy to introduce that client to our new Turkish office partners to support their ambitions to expand into Turkey. There was an enhanced relationship of trust between partners who 'belonged' to the same practice area, sharing the same knowledge, skill set and experience.

When it came to measuring our success in cross-selling, we found that, on average, we were advising our top 50 clients in more than 20 different countries. When we looked at our top 10 clients, we discovered that each of them had worked with more than 90 of our partners across our office network. Overall, this adds up to 70 per cent of our work involving two offices or more. So we were certainly pleased with the leverage we were gaining from geographical cross-selling.

However, we saw less progress in cross-selling between practice groups. This, in my experience, is a much tougher challenge. One solution is to introduce a sector approach to market to reinforce the client teams. It also fits well with a globalization agenda. This has been adopted effectively by many professional services firms such as management consultancies, IT services firms and accountants, but law firms have found it harder to introduce as they cling on to geography- or practice-group-based organization structures.

Now we see fee-earners increasingly investing time in building an understanding of their clients' businesses and their sectors and sharing this across the client team that carries responsibility for growing the client account. This enables the client teams to identify pertinent business and market issues for the clients and to introduce other practices more easily. Ideally this is supported by sector-based thought-leadership campaigns designed to raise the profile of the firm within each chosen sector.

## New services, new products, new models

Finally, we looked at the way in which legal services were being delivered. We were seeing the emergence of a few new entrants to more mature markets, seeking to disaggregate elements of legal work that could be substantially standardized and delivered through streamlined processes at lower cost. To a large extent this trend was a response to pressure on prices from clients. But it also signalled the arrival in the legal sector of a change in the market that mirrored the re-engineering and outsourcing boom of the 1990s led by the IT service companies. Here was an opportunity to develop new revenue streams with new models of legal services delivery for clients preaching the mantra 'more for less'. The big issue for the marketing function was to be on the front foot and help to lead the development of new services and new models of service delivery before finding ourselves playing catch-up with impatient clients.

Some time ago, we commissioned independent research into how the delivery of legal services was, and still is, changing (Allen & Overy, 2014). If anyone doubted whether it was set to change, the surprisingly high response rate of 50 per cent to the research was an indication of market sentiment.

We identified that the change was driven by:

- Pressure on clients to achieve more for less: 86% of respondents identified that they are under pressure to deliver more value for less cost. This has led 51% of respondents to increase the amount of work done in-house, effectively shrinking the market available to law firms.
- Consolidation: 58% of respondents identified their organization as looking to consolidate its legal service providers with the intention of developing deeper relationships with fewer firms.

The second point was illustrated by a comment from the head of the legal function of a global bank: 'We would like to use a one-stop shop as we don't want to have to manage many different entities for our legal work; provided that quality is good we would be happy to use such a service.'

On the other hand, many organizations intend to increase their use of non-traditional providers of legal services. For example, over the next five years, the number of organizations using contract lawyers is anticipated to increase from two-thirds (63 per cent) to three-quarters (74 per cent). Penetration of specialist document review services suppliers will likely increase from a third (34 per cent) to just under half (48 per cent). This indicates disaggregation of some legal services away from the traditional law firm.

It is obvious that these trends represent a significant shift in spending patterns. Our globalization strategy obviously positioned us well for responding to the trend towards client consolidation of multiple suppliers into a few one-stop shops, but we also had to address the question of new service delivery models. This is an opportunity to capture market share and generate new revenue streams.

Our first new venture was Derivative Services, which now serves more than 185 institutions, providing online subscription products to help clients reduce legal, regulatory and operational risk. The products codify Allen & Overy's unique legal expertise and cover all aspects of derivatives trading and a range of compliance issues. A service that had been provided on a bespoke, hourly-rate basis was now available to clients as an on-demand, online service.

The next venture was the establishment of a Legal Services Centre in Belfast, offering specialist transaction-related services such as document reviews, drafting and research tasks. The timing of the launch was good – we saw the volume of work passing through the centre double year on year.

More recently we established Peerpoint, Allen & Overy's flexible resourcing business (see allenovery.com/peerpoint). Peerpoint provides a panel of experienced, high-calibre lawyers for temporary placements or for specific projects. This enables clients to reduce fixed costs in-house and to cover peaks in their resourcing requirements that might result from, for example, takeover activity or compliance needs.

## Summary

In conclusion, we identified eight key lessons on how to successfully plan and roll out a globalization and growth strategy:

1 **Develop a strong global brand**: this stands out in people's minds and against the competition as a promise and an expectation. It should act as a leadership platform, justify premium pricing, reflect the firm's values and have an emotional resonance with clients, partners, staff and recruits.

2 **Align your people with your strategy**: professional services firms can only be as good as their people. It is therefore critical that they all get behind the firm's growth strategy and work as one towards common objectives.

3 **Plan for new markets**: select new markets that offer a realistic opportunity to achieve market leadership. Construct an affordable business case that targets not just domestic growth but cross-border opportunities with existing markets and clients.

4 **Global and local**: offer global services to multinational clients and look for opportunities to globalize the infrastructure of the firm. Do not forget that a global relationship is comprised of personal relationships that will also require local, customized support.

5 **Build relationships**: law firms are basically in the relationship business. Develop strong relationships with clients by understanding their businesses and their markets. Become their trusted strategic adviser.

6 **Focus on cross-selling**: investment in globalization will be wasted without attention to cross-selling. This is easier to achieve across geographies than practice groups. With the right degree of planning and monitoring of progress it can make a big impact.

7. **Develop demonstrable sector expertise**: lawyers with deep industry knowledge are worth more to clients than those with just technical legal knowledge. It differentiates and adds value; it is a foundation of an effective strategic advisory role and confident cross-selling.
8. **Be a game changer**: be innovative in building new products and services that address shrinkage or acceleration of markets or, even better, that create new markets. Be prepared to be disruptive.

# Implementing a growth strategy
## lessons from Asia Pacific

**02**

**DANIEL SMITH,** Senior Business Development and Marketing Manager, Asia Pacific, Baker & McKenzie, and **CLAIRE ESSEX,** Director of Business Development and Marketing, Asia Pacific, Baker & McKenzie

**Profiles:** Daniel is a professional services business development and marketing specialist with 15 years' experience of international law firms and a 'Big 4' accountancy practice. He is currently based in Singapore, and is managing the portfolio of advisory practices for Baker & McKenzie in Asia Pacific. His current role ensures that he develops business and collaborates with partners from a number of varied cultures and backgrounds across the firm's network of 17 offices in the region, many of which are in emerging and frontier markets.

Claire has worked over the past 20 years in senior business development and marketing roles in the educational, financial and professional services sectors and focused on growing business in Africa, the Americas and Asia Pacific. Having grown up in Singapore, Claire returned to the region 10 years ago. In her current role she advises Baker & McKenzie's Asia Board and 350+ partners on developing relationships with clients and building reputation across the firm's industry and practice groups. She also designs business skills training for 1,000+ lawyers.

This chapter will look at the experience of developing and implementing a growth strategy in Asia Pacific, the most dynamic market for professional services firms in the past decade. At a time when firms in Western markets have faced limits on growth and the challenge of shrinking markets, Asia Pacific has pushed firms to keep pace and prioritize when every market looks like an opportunity. We will consider both opportunities and challenges in the region and what the lessons are for marketing and business development professionals, wherever they are located.

## Growth in Asia Pacific

The global financial crisis remains a vivid memory for all of us. Although markets in North America and Europe are showing signs of recovery, regular economic wobbles mean that uncertainty in developed markets will remain for years to come and low-growth economies are probably the new norm.

In contrast, the Asia Pacific market has become the world's economic engine, transforming the global business landscape. With economic power now inexorably shifting east, we need no longer rely solely on the West's traditional multinationals to be engines of growth. These businesses are now looking to the Asia Pacific market to re-energize their growth path, but are facing competition from emerging global Asian multinationals. A quick look at the Fortune Global 500 list of the largest international firms shows that nearly 20 per cent – 87 companies – are now from Asia (Fortune, 2014).

There is no denying that Asia represents the most dynamic economic region in the world. Since 2000, Asia has been the fastest-growing source of foreign direct investment and its businesses produce a quarter of the world's exports (International Monetary Fund, 2010). The IMF predicted growth of 2 per cent in 2013 for advanced economies, while the corresponding figure for Asia was nearly 7 per cent.

## Developing, emerging or frontier markets

Fifteen years ago, we were still talking about developing nations. We then started talking about Asia's emerging economies – China, Korea, Vietnam, Indonesia, Malaysia, Thailand. Then came frontier markets – Myanmar, and before too long we're sure Laos and Cambodia will make waves.

For many in Asia, the Asian financial crisis of 1997 still lives long in the memory. Many so-called economic 'tigers' had their claws clipped and it took some time to recover. Notwithstanding the occasional financial crisis, most believe that Asia will be the world's business engine for some time to come.

When we worked in London and Sydney, many professional services firms saw the development of Asia essentially as meaning the emergence of China, and possibly India. Calling China an emerging market today seems behind the times. Any economy that has propelled itself to be the second largest in the world, and is soon to become the world's largest, has clearly *emerged*. But even with this rapid development over the past decade, there is no doubt that China still offers huge potential for even more growth.

A memorable and humorous presentation one of us attended recently claimed that 'China' could be used as a legitimate answer to pretty much any business question. For example: How do we explain Africa's current rapid economic growth? Answer: China. Why has the Japanese economy stagnated for a generation? China. Why are property prices in London and Melbourne so high? China! All tongue-in-cheek of course, but you get the picture. There is no denying that China's emergence as an economic global super-power is having an impact on every aspect of business life.

Next time you travel to a hotel in Europe, take a moment to look at the breakfast buffet. We guarantee that there are more Chinese items on the menu now than there were a decade ago. Cornflakes and Coco Pops are making room for *congee* and *char siew baos*. In 2013, China overtook Germany as the number one source nation for international tourism. Expenditure by Chinese tourists abroad has increased eight-fold since 2000 (World Tourism Organization, 2013). Although many believed that the building blocks of global growth would come from the BRICS (Brazil–Russia–India–China–South Africa), it seems that only 'C' is currently realizing its full potential.

More recently, the Asian success story has expanded well beyond China. China's success has seen a wave of several other nations 'emerge' in its wake. In the past decade, South Korea has fast replicated what Japan achieved in the 1980s. Samsung, Hyundai and LG, for example, are now well-recognized international brands and highly regarded companies. Alibaba, Haier, ICBC and Tencent are starting to make waves. Many more will surely follow.

Although India has not replicated China's rapid success, it remains a key player in the global economy – and certainly in that of Asia. Its sheer size and population alone mean that it cannot be ignored in the global business ecosystem. India will soon have a fifth of the world's working-age population (Economist, 2013). India already has the second-largest labour force in the world behind China, so what it can offer multinationals in terms of intellectual capital and workforce is profound.

ASEAN (Association of South-East Asian Nations) as a region has started to attract huge attention in recent years. Considered separately, ASEAN's 10 nations are a disparate and diverse group. Indonesia, for example, is a member of the G20 and represents almost 40 per cent of the region's economic output. Myanmar is only just emerging from decades of isolation. GDP per capita in Singapore is higher than that of economies such as the United States, Germany and the United Kingdom, and way above neighbours such as Cambodia – where GDP per capita is 1/50th the level of Singapore. But with the ASEAN Economic Community (AEC) integration on the horizon, ASEAN's collective strength is hugely attractive to multinationals.

The growth of Asia Pacific economies has presented equivalent opportunities for professional services firms. Only a few decades ago, there were no more than a few law firms in Asia Pacific with international or regional capabilities. Fast forward to 2014 and there are now nearly 400 offices of international law firms. This incredible growth has been most noticeable since 2000, when the number of international legal offices has grown by almost 400 per cent. In one financial quarter in 2013 alone, international law firms made more than 60 announcements of new office openings.

# Challenges for business development and marketing professionals – lessons from Asia

With so many opportunities in Asia, you would think that those working in this dynamic region should have no problem advising their firms. While our friends in Europe and North America are struggling to get budgets or win more work from clients, surely business development and marketing in Asia is just plain sailing? There is no denying that Asia offers oceans of opportunity, but the waters are not always calm. In oceans, one can also easily lose sight of the destination.

We will shortly offer our views on how to realize the potential, but first we will address two significant challenges – staying focused and instigating change – and consider the implications for marketing and business development professionals wherever they work. We also share some ideas on alternative options for those resistant to change.

## *Staying focused*

You can argue that business development is easier with a smaller budget as it forces you to focus. Our time in London, Chicago and Sydney, in the years leading up to and just after the financial crisis, offered a completely different perspective on professional services business development from where we're operating now. Constraints and pressures demanded discipline and a requirement for focus, leadership and return on investment.

Then, business development investments were made on projects and initiatives that offered clear and tangible returns. Central proposal teams were only strengthened, for example, as clients moved into the habit of running large legal panels through formalized procurement processes. Efforts were also put into strengthening client programmes as, in uncertain markets, holding on to key clients was more important than ever. Larger marketing campaigns with less visible returns weren't encouraged. Speculative spend on generic brochures was reduced, and in some cases cancelled altogether. Anything that was 'nice to have' just didn't justify the resources and was cut.

These are all practices and habits that business development and marketing professionals should remember, even during the good times. Why so? Because many partners and professionals themselves are likely to forget! We speak in generic terms, of course, and certainly there are those who stay 'focused to the task', but I'm sure we've all been in meetings where discussions about the quality of wine at a function seems to take up twice as much time as the discussion around key objectives, targets or return on investment.

In markets where there seem to be opportunities at every corner, the scattergun approach proliferates. So how do you get your partners and fellow professionals to focus?

As a business development professional, you have to stay true to your firm's strategy. Be clear that you and your team are all aware of the firm's key strategic drivers, and plan and implement your business development and marketing efforts in alignment with those. The tactics of achieving your strategic goals should drive your activity.

This may all sound obvious, but it's not always easy to do. There will be lots of white noise. With partner demands, personal agendas and a lack of resources and time, business development professionals need to know how to tie all activities back to the strategy.

For example, if the firm has a clearly articulated focus on a key group of selected clients, make sure that every event or initiative considers this group prominently. If a set market sector has been identified as your firm's target area, you must advise your partners to really concentrate there.

Ultimately, business development professionals are employed to help the firm win new business. So work out what offers the best return on investment – whether it is from current or new clients. Moreover, make sure you stick to your firm's collective strategy; you will then find it easier to keep your partners and professionals focused on the right track.

## *Instigating change*

Marketing and business development professionals must see themselves as change agents. In our experience, we've found that many professionals are creatures of habit. They are highly technical, intelligent individuals, but they don't like to be told that what they are doing could perhaps be done better or at least differently. Furthermore, in many hierarchical cultures, and in Asia particularly, advising partners not to do something, or to do it differently, is not a straightforward matter. It is often also not that well received!

In Asia, it is not common to hear 'no' given as a response to anything. You can get several variations of 'yes'. Just trying to interpret a hesitation, a silence or even a direct 'yes' that means 'maybe' can be a skill in itself! The business culture, of course, is also nowhere near as direct as in Western countries, so it is important to allow for these nuances when advising a partner or group of lawyers.

In Europe or North America where being direct is usually expected, it is still difficult to convince professionals to do something different. The business development professional needs to offer the *reason* for change. Highly technical and intelligent individuals also need evidence. You have to ensure that your facts are correct, put forward your case and stick to your guns.

To illustrate the change challenge, we can look at our experience of shifting behaviours on some key business development and marketing tasks, such as proposals and pitches. We have seen far too many examples of proposal submissions that 'we are unlikely to win, but it would be rude not to'; or a pitch to potential clients whom your firm does not even know or have any established contact with; or a proposal without proper conflict or terms of engagement checks considered.

We will always argue you should be robust in your no-go decision. If you know it should really be a no-go proposal, but your partner is insistent, you should at least question the decision. You will not change a mindset overnight; it will take time, but with intelligent questioning and probing, your partners will start to get the message that a proposal isn't just about submitting a sub-par document 'just because we should'. Your questioning and general desire to be commercially inquisitive set you on the road to being an adviser rather than just an implementer.

One interesting example we encountered was when we were asked to put together a comprehensive proposal document for a client that we didn't want to win! We recall that the request from the partner was along the lines of 'we need to submit a document, but we really don't want to win it – so make sure it's a poor enough document that we don't get shortlisted'! In this case, the partner would have been prepared to submit a sub-par document, which could have implications for the firm, its brand reputation and the chance of future work with this client. We politely declined to put together the proposal and instead drafted a note for the partner to discuss the opportunity with the prospect, explaining our reasons.

In other situations, brochures and printed material can be produced so generically as to be of little use to anyone. Yet they are churned out by the thousands anyway, probably only to be discarded a few months later. Similarly, we choose to run seminar after seminar, without any great desire for follow-up or actions to enhance the sales pipeline.

## *Offering alternatives and driving change*

Despite advice to the contrary, many professionals will still see some of these basic marketing tools as the most appropriate to reach out to the market and their clients. If this is the case, a good business development professional will know their limits. There is no point banging your head against a brick wall. Instead, try to suggest changes incrementally. Don't change *what* your partner is trying to do, but suggest *how* things could be done differently. The adage of 'you won't know until you try it' works well here! And sometimes they just might like it. For example:

- If your partners love to produce brochure after brochure, or develop guidebooks, suggest reducing the number of hard copies and go online. As technology develops, this is an obvious evolution of the printed brochure or guidebook.
- If they are insistent on sending a generic brochure, as it's more comfortable to do that than not, make sure your partners follow it up. Point out that the brochure is just a general overview, but it could be followed up with something more specific and targeted.
- If the request is for lengthy newsletters with pages and pages of legal developments, suggest shorter, snappier blogs that can be read on a mobile device, where interestingly the usage in emerging economies is higher than in more mature markets. Ask your partner when they last read a lengthy newsletter from a service provider. If they say rarely, ask why they expect clients to be any different. If they insist, make sure the content is commercial.
- If they insist on producing hundreds of copies of printed materials for a seminar or conference, suggest that all presentations should be online well before your event so that clients can help themselves as they want. This saves on printing costs and often gets your presentations in early. As above, most people attend seminars with handheld devices these days, so information should be available online anyway.
- Suggest alternative ways of connecting with clients and instigating a conversation, for example webinars. These are really popular professional development tools for clients in emerging market tier 2, 3 and 4 cities.

As firms get more proficient with digital technology, such platforms can be used more effectively.

In all these instances, it is important to work with advocates. Every firm has partners or professionals who 'get it' from a business development and marketing perspective. If you work with them closely, they can be your voice too. Often you'll find that when advocates speak on your behalf, it's amazing how quickly things then move.

One of the bolder moves we have tried is to 'do first, ask for forgiveness later'. If you provide a good reason, show that you're acting in the firm's and the partners' best interest, you will find that things can get done differently and quickly. It can backfire, but less often than you might think. It is a tactic perhaps best used by more senior business development and marketing professionals, as it takes confidence and belief.

A less risky tactic is to pilot activities. If not everyone is convinced about making sweeping changes, choose a group of partners, a practice group or a country to trial something different. Then share the experiences. Use the pilot group to be your advocates. Once you have evidence of success, others will be more open to trying something different.

These points are true of business development professionals everywhere, not just in Asia, but the key point here is that to grow, you need to instigate and encourage change.

# Growth strategies in Asia

Having taken the challenges of growth and change into consideration and planned your approach accordingly, you can then focus on the opportunities. Based on our experiences of the past few years in the Asia Pacific market, below are our recommendations on how business development and marketing professionals, together with their firms, should develop and implement a growth strategy.

### *Long-term commitment*

Our expansion philosophy at Baker & McKenzie has been to go where our clients need us to be. This sounds obvious, but it takes a long-term vision and commitment to achieve. This simple philosophy of client service has led the firm to open in cities that others may not have considered, with 2013 being our 50th anniversary in Asia Pacific. This commitment to the region has not gone unnoticed.

It has also not gone unnoticed when other firms have entered a market, but hastily retrenched if the going gets tough. In Asia, building trust takes time – often a long time, so firms need to be prepared to invest for the long haul.

### *Have local strategies within a global context*

Asia is not homogeneous, yet how many of us have sat in meetings in Europe or the United States and heard comments such as 'what is our general strategy for Asia?' We have known Asia Pacific business development managers in the UK who have never even been to Asia, or only for personal visits. Living here and doing business in the region is a very different experience.

Even in a sub-region such as ASEAN, the countries and economies are so diverse. How can you have just one approach in a sub-region where one country has 50 times the GDP per capita of its neighbour? This diversity isn't just economic: it extends to culture, religion and language. Even though ASEAN has articulated its desire to be more integrated economically, for instance to develop an ASEAN Economic Community by 2015, business development and marketing professionals need to be aware of these cultural sensitivities and local preferences.

You must ensure that you talk to your national colleagues and various partners about what matters to them on the ground. How do they usually go to market? What is the expectation in the market? What is the expectation of their business development and marketing teams? That said, it is also important to remember that all markets and cultural norms change over time, so, on occasions, it is also sensible to question sensitively the norm.

## *Allow flexibility and autonomy*

For some countries, even the concept of business development and marketing is still fairly alien. For those who have moved from more developed professional services markets, you may not find the appetite for robust business development and marketing programmes. For example, in the UK and Australia, it is likely that firms are looking to phase out generic brochures and encourage partners to form strategic pursuit teams to win work from chosen clients. But this strategy will not work in markets where the concept of professional services marketing is so new. Often the partners are not ready for it – but, more importantly, neither are their clients.

Can you advise a partner that a brochure is a waste of time when the office has just opened and the market has no idea who you are? A good business development and marketing professional, like every firm exploring opportunities in Asia, needs to remain flexible and nimble. You must consider what is suitable for the market in which you are operating.

Many large international firms are also likely to suffer from the global vs local brand dichotomy. Even the largest international firms need to rely on a continual stream of local work. For every FTSE 100 or Fortune 500 company you work for, there are likely to be 10 local firms instructing your local offices. So you have to cope with a dual-brand perception. Are you a strong local firm or an international firm? In our experience, it is possible to be both, but in order to grow both markets, you will need to structure your business development and marketing functions appropriately.

## *Nurture key clients together*

Treat every client as if they were your only client. We've all heard this before, but it is of course easier said than done and, in truth, not entirely realistic. It is important, though, that any delivery team has this mindset.

Growing client breadth, and therefore the relationship, is tricky. It may sound crazy, but it is not unheard of for partners to refer clients to another firm in another country, even though their firm has an office in that country. Why would they do this? Partners want the best for their clients, but if they feel they would get a better quality of advice or service elsewhere, that is a serious management issue.

Any risk of a particular partner 'losing face' is hugely important in Asia. They would rather refer the work to another firm than risk such embarrassment. Connections are everything in Asia, so key client programmes for the collective, rather than individual, benefit are very difficult to implement. To instil a culture of 'a client of one is a client of all' is really tough to achieve in Asian markets.

However, firms must persist in the goal of robust key client programmes for the collective, not the individual. Again this sounds obvious, but not enough firms pay attention to the fact that 'hunting in packs' can offer greater rewards. The will and reputation of the individual still tend to prevail.

Even if priority client programmes are in place, the nuances of local office needs are often difficult to control. If these are not managed robustly, any benefit of network or scale can erode very quickly. Why should office X put their 'A team' on a small part of a larger project for a global priority client, if the returns for that office (or partner) are minimal, especially if it is at the expense of a local office priority Asian client – who may indeed turn out to be tomorrow's global client?

Addressing such issues requires strong leadership. Different firm structures will mean that there isn't one correct way to deal with this, but, generally speaking, the benefit of prioritizing clients who will benefit the wider firm should offer dividends in the long term, even if this could result in the loss of smaller local clients.

Senior management needs to ensure that benefits are shared and that those who follow best practice are rewarded and recognized accordingly.

## *Do the ordinary extraordinarily well*

Local autonomy should not mean compromising on standards or allowing local offices to do things that contradict the big-picture strategy. The best business development any professional can do is, of course, to do their job well. Do the ordinary extraordinarily well is the mantra of one of our colleagues. And it should be a mantra for all of us every day.

To achieve this, firms need to instil a mindset that quality is everybody's responsibility, not just the partners' or senior managers' or directors'. From the time a speculative call is answered to when the work is discharged, every step requires excellence. Leaving a phone to ring out several times or not connecting through to the right person, for example, may sound trivial, but it is the small things that count. It leaves an impression of the standards you uphold.

Every business development professional should lead the way. Be responsive, professional and commercial in the advice you give your partners; do the simple things well; build trust in doing so; and deliver work of a standard that you would be proud of every time.

## *Move your business development professionals up the value chain*

In countries where business development and marketing concepts are in their infancy, the business development function unfortunately is seen as little more than additional administrative support. In Asia, subservience and a 'them and us' attitude still exist strongly. For those from more egalitarian societies, the extent of this can take you a little by surprise.

Developing your business development professionals to challenge, be creative and take on more of an advisory role can be difficult. It also means that firms need to be brave enough to allow their business development professionals to do the job for which they are employed. That is to say, help partners generate work, win new clients, nurture current clients to expand the breadth and depth of client relationships, perform client reviews and so forth.

However, as we mentioned previously, it is not easy to direct and advise partners. Be aware of specific cultural nuances and be mindful of what works within the parameters of your partners' culture. Business development and marketing professionals need to be inquisitive, intuitive, commercial, robust, tenacious yet culturally sensitive.

## *Business development management needs an international outlook*

Management capabilities need to evolve. This isn't just true of the senior partnership, but of the professional support functions as well. As mentioned above, it is not unheard of for marketing and business development managers with global roles in Australian, UK or US international firms never to have lived or worked outside of Sydney, London or New York, respectively.

Leadership teams need a better understanding of global markets. Owing to the non-homogeneous reasons mentioned earlier, it pays for leadership teams to experience working cultures in different countries.

Central teams too need a mix of international experiences, while also focusing on strong local talent. This is particularly important in cultures where management styles and cultural expectations are very different.

At Baker & McKenzie, for example, our regional business development team includes a mix of Australian, American, British, South African, Indian, Japanese, Chinese, Singaporean and Filipino nationals – many of whom have lived in several different countries. Our national teams are also a mix of expatriates and locals. This blend of cultural backgrounds and international differences encourages debate, creativity and inclusivity rarely achieved in other professional environments.

In time, the reliance on expatriates in national or local offices will reduce, but firms will need to continue to manage the fine balance of national delivery with a regional or global identity.

Some professional services firms already have global training and mobility programmes in place to ensure that senior managers have a more international outlook and gain the experience required. This should continue to be encouraged.

## *Grow all processes together*

As firms enter new markets, the priority is often investment and gaining market share – margins are often a secondary priority. Ensuring sound operations from day one should also be prioritized. Firms need to consider the administration of work, business development and marketing, IT infrastructure, finance and so forth. All this should be done concurrently. This entire infrastructure needs to be set up to enable future growth. Without the right structure and support capabilities in place, growth is likely to be stalled or, at least, truncated.

## *Forming partnerships*

Recent years have seen an uptick in formal partnerships and mergers in the legal market. Taking this to its natural conclusion, one could see a future where the legal market goes the same way as the accountancy market, with a handful of big firms dominating.

The tough environment in which legal firms have operated since the global financial crisis has led to this increase in mergers, partnerships and consolidations with international friends. Different firms can call it different things – but essentially it's joining with another for purposes of growth.

Partnering is a popular growth strategy. We have seen many large British and international law firms merge with counterparts with bases in either Asia or Australia for wider global coverage. The merger of Australian firm Mallesons with Chinese firm King & Wood, for example, has changed the legal landscape. Here, one of Australia's most respected firms has indicated clearly to the market that the future is Asia.

# Summary

Business development and marketing professionals have a huge role to play in developing growth strategies, implementing change for the benefit of growth and helping partners set the path for success.

Senior business development professionals can help shape growth not only through personal action and the actions of their teams, but also by instilling a business development mindset through every facet of the firm – from the most senior of partners to the trainees. This mindset should start from the moment someone enters the firm and continue through their careers.

On the path to growth, marketing and business development professionals will face challenges, principally around staying focused on strategic imperatives and resistance to change.

As a business development professional, you must role-model the behaviours you want to see in others and continuously develop yourself. There are clear growth strategies you can pursue and you should identify and adapt what will work best for your firm.

# Developing international networks

03

**CLIVE STEVENS,** Executive Chairman, Kreston Reeves

**Profile:** Clive is Executive Chairman at Kreston Reeves, a top 30 UK accountancy practice, and International Board member at Kreston International, the worldwide accounting network. Clive also sits on the ICAEW Council and holds non-executive directorships with Locate in Kent and Turner Contemporary.

I will seek, in this chapter, to summarize the reasons for professional services firms to consider international markets for their services and the issues that arise in forming international relationships. I will refer to examples that I have encountered in the organizations with which I have had the privilege to be involved.

We will discuss how international groups grow and develop and the importance that personal trust and individual relationships have in determining the success or failure of such organizations. We will also look at the power of cohesive branding and the issues that arise when faced with considering changing from a local to an international brand.

## The internationalization of business

Business is more international than ever before. In the United Kingdom, the government has set ambitious targets to double the value of exports to £1 trillion by 2020.

This focus on international trade is as true for the professional services sector as any other industry. Indeed, professional services in all its guises is now arguably the largest sector of the UK economy and a significant exporter to the rest of the world. Similar trends are evident in other countries as well.

This is not just confined to the largest internationally organized firms. Even smaller professional services firms are seeing small and medium-sized (SME) clients needing advice and assistance with international trade. This has been driven by recent recessionary pressure forcing businesses to look for new markets overseas as well as advances in information technology making it much easier to make international contacts.

## Kreston Reeves and Kreston International's story

Kreston Reeves is a multi-site accounting practice based in London and the South East of England. The firm has 300 partners and staff. It offers a full range of business services – accounting and audit assurance, tax advice and compliance, insolvency and financial services advice – largely to SME businesses and entrepreneurs. The firm's partners have also developed their expertise and experience across a variety of industry sectors.

The firm recognized some time ago that it needed to develop an international capability to serve its largest clients and joined Kreston International in the 1980s. This was initially seen as a 'defensive' measure to enable the firm to retain clients with international aspirations rather than for them to look elsewhere for international expertise. At that time, Kreston was a loose association of like-minded accounting and audit practices throughout the world.

Kreston recognized that building effective relationships between the partners in member firms is paramount to its success. Its motto is 'People do business with people they know, like and trust'. Great store is placed on this at all Kreston conferences and gatherings around the world.

This was similar to, and compatible with, Kreston Reeves' local goals and values. To help align local and international goals and values, Kreston Reeves' partners agreed that, as the firm's Managing Partner at the time, I could stand as an International Board Director, and subsequently as Chairman, of Kreston International.

Today, Kreston International has moved to be a network of independent firms and has grown to be one of the top 15 such global networks, with nearly US$2 billion of global fees. In order to satisfy the increasing demand from clients for quality service provision, it now insists upon member firms complying with agreed quality standards and being subject to external quality review. It has established agreed business goals to develop expertise and business opportunities across the network. The member firms that comprise Kreston have moved from a 'defensive' stance to one of proactively seeking international opportunities.

## How international groups develop

Once a need for an international capability is recognized at a local level, the firm's management must decide how best to organize their business to satisfy that need. This will depend largely on the needs of the firm's clients.

There are three basic models being adopted today:

- international partnerships or businesses as practised by a few of the major international professional services firms;
- wholly owned subsidiary or branch operations in specific countries;
- associations or networks of like-minded independent firms.

A few of the major international professional firms that are dealing with larger global multinationals have generally found that the best solution for them is likely to be a single international firm. This enables them to enforce rigid disciplines and procedures across the world and deliver a seamless service to their clients. This is sensible in the context of delivery of services to public interest or quoted multinational businesses operating globally.

This type of model involves compulsory global branding and profiling, central control of the organization and high levels of cohesion and credibility essential to investors in multinational public interest businesses. At the highest levels in the marketplace, the benefits from this must clearly outweigh both the loss of independence at a local level, something that can be difficult for many smaller professional firms, and collective responsibility for vicarious liability issues.

Smaller niche firms may have clients that require services in a specific country or jurisdiction. Rather than adopt a global model, it is likely to be more cost-effective to establish a small branch or subsidiary in that country to serve their clients. For example, some professional services firms may serve clients based in France and may well establish a small office in Paris to do just that. This fulfils a specific need while at the same time maintaining independence from other larger firms.

However, many firms, like my own, may perceive a need for a more general international offering across the world and the services they offer. For them, joining an international association or network may well be the most effective way of gaining access to international expertise while at the same time maintaining local independence. This can be of particular benefit to those mid-sized firms serving the SME sector and therefore perhaps having a more irregular need for international services compared with the needs of those firms that service multinational clients.

The degree of independence required by local firms will determine whether a looser association is the preferred constitution or whether some loss of independence through a more formal network, particularly when it comes to collective branding and systems compliance, is worthwhile compared to the hopefully greater potential for winning client work.

The Kreston Reeves story is similar to those of many other professional services firms that do not compete with the larger international firms for large assignments from major multinational public companies. For Kreston Reeves, building contacts through the Kreston network has proved to be more cost-effective and efficient. It combines and balances the need of the partners in the firm for local autonomy with access to expertise in other countries as and when clients have a need for this.

Of course, clients' needs change over time and firms need to improve the level of service they offer as their clients grow and become more sophisticated in their own service needs. What therefore starts as a loose association of contacts will inevitably develop into a network that starts to share expertise and training. The network will also look to develop quality standards and reviews. Having incurred the cost of this, the network will then look for a return on this investment, which is likely to be based on increased referral work and proactively looking for international work opportunities.

The nature of any international relationship will depend upon the balance required by the firm's clients between global quality assurance and local autonomy and personal local relationships (Figure 3.1).

**FIGURE 3.1**  How international networks develop over time to meet client needs

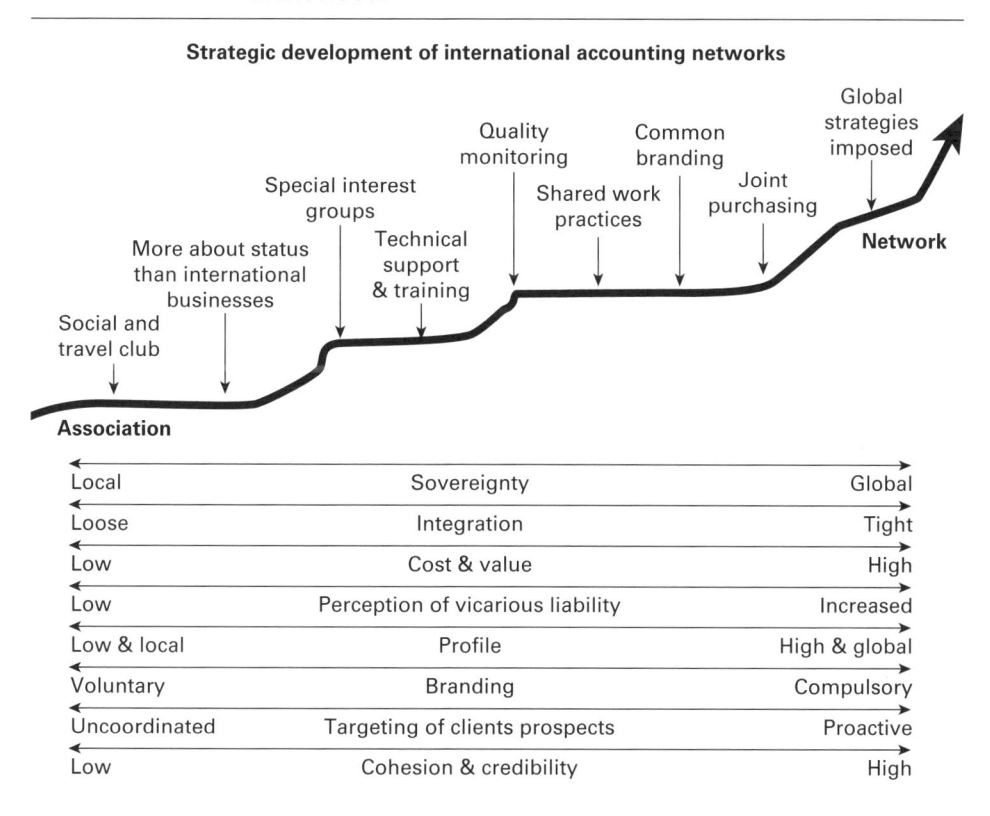

**Strategic development of international accounting networks**

Stages along the development curve (Association → Network):
- Social and travel club
- More about status than international businesses
- Special interest groups
- Technical support & training
- Quality monitoring
- Shared work practices
- Common branding
- Joint purchasing
- Global strategies imposed

| Local | Sovereignty | Global |
|---|---|---|
| Loose | Integration | Tight |
| Low | Cost & value | High |
| Low | Perception of vicarious liability | Increased |
| Low & local | Profile | High & global |
| Voluntary | Branding | Compulsory |
| Uncoordinated | Targeting of clients prospects | Proactive |
| Low | Cohesion & credibility | High |

# Building trust internationally

When firms pursue international work, they will find that it is essential to have a local presence on the ground to service that work. Without that presence being firmly in place, they are unlikely to capture the work opportunity. For this, two things are necessary: a strong local presence in the required countries; and personal collaboration between the partners of the network firms involved.

I have found that this is hard to achieve in a comprehensive and complete way throughout all international networks and associations. Its effectiveness rests on mutual trust, respect and confidence that one's clients will be looked after as well as you would do at home. While systematic processes are important and necessary, ultimately trust does not rest on collective branding, procedures or formal assurance reviews but on personal contact. As we say at Kreston International, 'People do business with people they know, like and trust'.

There is no shortcut to building this level of trust. It is the same level of trust that partners must develop in a domestic business – it just takes longer in an international context where contact may be infrequent and local business customs and behaviours may be different.

# How to build trust and personal contact

First, all groupings will organize a range of conferences and other opportunities so that members can meet face to face and build direct contact with each other. Countrywide, continental or world conferences are essential for individuals to meet and to build contacts – not just at Managing or Senior Partner level but at a variety of seniority levels within each member firm. Younger partners and managers can often develop relationships with their own peer group that have greater longevity as the careers of the individuals involved develop. Today, social media, such as LinkedIn, Facebook and so on can help build and maintain these contacts.

Another effective means of building personal contact is visits to other offices of member firms throughout the world. Whenever a partner or employee travels abroad, they should be encouraged to visit the local member firm to introduce themselves and meet their overseas colleagues. This has become part of the Kreston Reeves and Kreston culture.

Staff secondment to member firms, on a reciprocal basis, will also build individual contact – so important in trust-building. This will usually be a temporary assignment to help overcome peak demands in one firm or another. I have also found this to be an excellent way of retaining and developing the best people, as well as enabling long-term international relationships to develop.

All of these actions need individuals to make this happen effectively. It starts in a small way and builds. There is no shortcut.

Of course, nothing succeeds better than an individual identifying a need and actively working on a real fee-earning project to solve a client problem. This builds effective joint working with reward for the work undertaken. For this reason, asking partners in member firms to actively seek work opportunities within their existing client or contact base is essential to drive successful behaviours. But it starts with an individual willing to trust their network colleagues with such an assignment in the first place.

While hard to achieve, when this happens the results can be truly powerful, as the case study below shows.

## CASE STUDY    Kreston International

Kreston acts worldwide for a US-based freight-forwarding and logistics group that was founded in the late 1970s and, by the nature of its business, trades worldwide. With 400 people operating in 17 offices worldwide, it is essential that a range of services is delivered to this client across the globe in a consistent, proactive manner.

The client was originally advised by a multinational accountancy firm, but it switched when the client service partner left to join a Kreston firm. The client to partner relationship was so strong that when the client looked to expand into Europe it turned to a familiar face for guidance. The Kreston partner in the United States was able to pick up the telephone and talk with a colleague in the United Kingdom, whom he knew, had worked with before and implicitly trusted to look after his client.

Because of the trust and working relationship between the individual partners engaged on this assignment, distance and time differences have proved to be no barrier to looking after the client's needs. Having initially provided acquisition, structuring and strategy advice, the close working relationship between the US and UK firms has led the client to appoint Kreston as the sole supplier of business and tax services worldwide.

In addition to corporate finance, these services now include audit, international tax planning and outsourced and company secretarial services. Member firms work together across Europe, Japan, Australia and South America. In addition to meeting up annually, members are consistently communicating throughout the year to deliver services as a cohesive organization. The common desire and ability to deliver a world-class service by every member firm has led to Kreston member firms being the group's first port of call for its professional services worldwide.

This level of service could not be delivered without strong personal relationships between the Kreston colleagues involved. Without that, the delivery of a seamless professional service to the client would be impossible. This example demonstrates clearly why this is vital to the development of all international groupings.

Of course, relationships need to be nurtured, sustained and developed. They are built on regular contact and the exchange of reciprocal work opportunities and work referral. Very rarely will there be the opportunity to exchange referral opportunities simultaneously. Such opportunities tend to occur irregularly and there must be an understanding that if one party gives a work opportunity to another then that favour will be returned at some future point. This is why longevity of personal relationship is essential – there must be sufficient likelihood of future referral to stand any form of success.

## Reinforcing trust

In a general order of effectiveness, I would summarize the following activities, if consistently applied, as being essential in helping build trust at a personal level and consequently the ability to work together:

- personal networking at international conferences and training sessions;
- time spent in visiting local offices of member firms;
- international exchanges of staff;
- the referral of real work opportunities to other members;
- information-sharing – of both managerial and technical resources;
- the use of social media to reinforce personal contact.

In reality, this list is no different from the types of activity that one might undertake at a local level in any firm in the world. Personal networking between people will always foster deeper understanding of personalities, skill sets and interests. Indeed, many professional services firms will, even today, maintain that more new work opportunities come from direct referral from clients or other intermediaries than from any other marketing effort. This is true both domestically and internationally – the work and demonstrable expertise of a firm's partners and staff remains the best marketing tool a firm has.

## The power of branding

In the international accounting market, it is evident that the top 12 international networks have adopted global branding and have between them a significant majority of global network fee revenues. A similar story emerges in other professional services sectors. Global branding seems to work!

However, as associations and networks develop, branding is not the first matter to address: that is generally one of improving the consistency of work quality throughout the group – an essential precursor to promoting a consistent brand. Once that is addressed, the question then soon arises as to whether uniform branding can and will help in attracting further better-quality work opportunities.

Clearly the power of a collective brand operating across the world should make it easier to attract global clients requiring the services of the group. There is also little doubt that a link with an international brand should provide comfort and confidence for the client in terms of quality assurance.

Whether this remains true will largely depend upon the local client experience on the ground as regards the delivery of the services being bought. It will be essential for the group to police this, as the quality of the whole will be seen to be only as good as the weakest link – collective branding 'burns the boats' of those member firms in the group. They must enforce the very best quality and client service behaviours or risk being seen as unable to deliver consistently.

In my experience, this is a question of behaviours. In order to win multinational assignments the group will soon realize that a prerequisite will be multi-country project coordination and control. Consistency in delivery of service will also be essential, which comes down to collaboration between the local units involved in the project. This is why building trust at a personal level between the individuals concerned in delivering the project is essential.

Fundamental questions arise, such as who will be in charge and responsible for project coordination and delivery. How will billing arrangements be dealt with – at a local level or through one lead country? How do independent firms involved in service delivery take responsibility for professional liability in case things go wrong?

This all depends on how coordinated a service the client requires or is expecting, and these questions can only be solved by individuals with sufficient trust in each other to work together. In order to establish a truly global brand, they must be addressed at the outset, otherwise the group will fail to win significant multinational clients, as it will not be able to back up claims of being able to deliver a properly coordinated service.

Even with high levels of trust, it is very difficult to move existing member firms in a network to a uniform globally branded organization quickly. Each firm will have its own local culture, values and history that it will be loath to give up. Transitional arrangements that acknowledge the individual history and feel of each firm but still move them towards a common brand and cohesion will need to be agreed and implemented. This will take a lot of leadership skill and, again, a high level of personal trust in the leadership group within the network.

Fortunately, the power of branding for group member firms is not just international – it also gives comfort to clients about service quality in the local marketplace too. While international client work will be of interest and give firms professional challenges that they will not get in just their domestic markets, it is likely always to be a small percentage of the total workload of a professional firm.

For most firms, its domestic market should always produce more work opportunity than its overseas market. But international branding, with the promotion of the domestic brand across the world, can help win better-quality assignments locally, particularly where a firm's competitors are also branded internationally.

The power of international branding in a domestic market is the main reason why, in many networks, smaller member firms in less developed parts of the world will tend to be first adopters of network branding. It will show them in the best light against their local marketplace.

Firms in the developed world, where identities have been established for far longer, often believe (possibly arrogantly) that their local brand is well known and doesn't need to change. This does not always prove to be the case. Increasingly I believe that collective international branding will be seen to bring benefits to firms in the developed world – particularly when these long-established firms (albeit with good local brands) seek to move into new market areas or improve their ability to compete for larger or more profitable assignments.

To achieve growth through such branding strategies, it will be necessary to:

- Increase skills to enable firms to take on larger or more complex assignments.
- Ensure that the quality standards that are mandatory elsewhere in the world are applied equally in less-developed areas. Inevitably, collective branding must be backed up by strict quality control procedures to give the level of comfort and degree of trust that is required by all member firms and their clients.
- Build the trusted relationships between individual partners throughout the world on which work relationships are based.

# Regulation and external oversight

Many service firms operate in sectors with little in terms of an international regulatory framework, while other sectors, such as legal, auditing and the financial services, are very heavily regulated at home and abroad. They must demonstrate the highest levels of business and ethical behaviour to external regulators.

For those in a regulated service sector, the nature of the international grouping they join will determine the level of regulatory compliance that will be necessary.

In the auditing profession, loose associations are not currently regarded by audit regulators as a threat to audit independence and objectivity. However, closer networks that have common systems, common branding, adopt quality reviews and have generally closer ties will be seen by audit regulators as one organization and will have to consider whether this constitutes a threat to objectivity – particularly where there is joint pitching for work or financial interdependence.

When looking at international opportunities, industry regulatory requirements can constitute a significant cost in both time and money and these ought to be balanced against the prospects of work to be derived from international assignments. In some cases they can be significant enough to be factored into pricing decisions.

## Conclusion – the future

Following the financial crash, the world economy is starting to grow again. We are seeing a continuing shift to the emerging worlds of China, India, Africa and the East, where there will undoubtedly be strong growth as the number of people making up a wealthier middle class explodes and improved living standards emerge. In the developed world, while relative growth rates might be lower, economies will still do well in absolute terms.

While change can bring uncertainty and fear, there is no doubt that the world is becoming an increasingly smaller place and that over the next few decades opportunities for overseas trade will multiply exponentially. The big danger is to overlook the pace and scale of the changes taking place. Cheaper telecommunication and information technology as well as the speed of international travel mean that it is now possible to offer services to international clients much more effectively than ever before.

We are fortunate in the United Kingdom that the language of business is English. We find ourselves well positioned in time zones between the United States and the Far East. All this gives UK professional services firms a competitive edge when dealing with the rest of the world. When offices in San Francisco, London and Tokyo work together, work is going on over the whole of a 24-hour cycle. Get the process right and the result is effective delivery of project work to increasingly shorter deadlines.

In recent years, many professional firms have been outsourcing functions to take advantage of reduced labour costs – particularly for routine compliance functions. In recent years, banks and other financial service business have, for example, transferred compliance functions to India and other countries.

In a world that is moving faster, one must be able to demonstrate quality and give reassurance to clients quickly. Competing effectively will mean increased promotion of global rather than national or local brands, particularly for those professional services firms that want to compete for larger or better-quality client work.

I believe that this will apply not only to multinational conglomerates but also to much smaller SME businesses seeking to expand in new markets. In my opinion, professional services firms without international capability and credibility will suffer and those firms that can truly guide their clients in developing international business will have a significant competitive advantage.

# LESSONS ON GROWTH

From our contributions on the theme of Growth, here are our top 10 lessons for marketing and business development leaders:

1. **Reasons for growth**: your growth strategy needs to be clear not only on what you are going to grow, but also why it's important and what success looks like (revenue, profit, market share, key differentiators, client portfolio and so forth).
2. **Market selection**: you will need to consider carefully the markets where you can compete, differentiate and generate superior returns. Segment your markets using clear criteria and then prioritize accordingly.
3. **Follow clients**: following your clients or growing to match their ambitions is a sensible starting point for your growth strategy, but you need to know how you are going to evaluate competing priorities for scarce resources. You must also recognize that if you don't grow with your clients, they will probably leave you.
4. **Brand clarity**: a clear and well-communicated brand that explains who you are, what you stand for and what makes you different will help attract the clients and people you will need to deliver your growth plan. It will also ease entry into new markets.
5. **Relationships**: every firm will identify different priorities to deliver its growth plan, but strong client relationship management is always likely to feature.
6. **Cross-selling and trust**: be wary of the concept and ambition of cross-selling services. Sharing clients and persuading them to buy a basket of services is not easy, whatever your business model. You need to build trust with your clients and between your teams. It should be a long-term objective built on client priorities, not a glib 'battle cry' to rally disconnected teams.
7. **Business model**: growth can be achieved in a variety of forms – organic addition of people and resources, acquisitions, mergers, alliances, networks, supplier partnerships and so forth. You need to understand the benefits to your clients and your firm of the various models in different markets and circumstances and then adapt accordingly. The model may change depending on the situation.
8. **Growth and skills**: growth is dependent on your people having strong business and client development skills. To achieve growth, focusing on these skills is as important as any other area of professional development. Ensure that they are embedded throughout the firm.
9. **Innovation and disruption**: growth is an opportunity to challenge the status quo and introduce new and disruptive services and business models.
10. **Continuity and change**: growth can and will change a firm. You need to identify and understand what you want to keep and where you want to drive change. How you retain the essence of your firm and drive clarity on what makes you different, while continuing to improve, will determine the success of your growth journey.

# THEME TWO
# Understanding

# Introduction to the Understanding theme

*If you can learn a simple trick, Scout, you'll get along a lot better with all kinds of folks. You never really understand a person until you consider things from his point of view, until you climb inside of his skin and walk around in it.* **(ATTICUS FINCH IN *TO KILL A MOCKINGBIRD*)**

This quotation – and there are many other similar examples throughout history and literature – expresses the view, often expounded in marketing theory and practice, that you can't really understand what a customer or client wants or needs without looking at their world from their perspective.

Fortunately, empathy – experiencing and identifying with the feelings, thoughts or attitudes of others – is a distinctive human trait. In a 2007 study published in *Science* magazine, scientists from the Max Planck Institute (Neighmond, 2007) looked at the respective skills of apes and toddlers. The researchers designed over two dozen tasks and tested them with over 100 chimpanzees and two-and-a-half-year-old children to determine the respective skills of the two groups.

The researchers expected that the toddlers would outperform the chimps in all tasks. To the researchers' surprise, the chimps were just as proficient in specific or physical tasks, such as counting, using a tool or remembering where something was hidden, but when it came to social skills, the toddlers came into their own and clearly outperformed the chimps. These were all tasks where successful completion required the child or ape to demonstrate, as one researcher put it, 'the ability to watch somebody else and figure out what they're trying to do – and what they want you to do'. In these tasks the toddlers would observe the researchers or other children and learn from them, while the chimps were nowhere near as proficient in demonstrating this more intuitive type of intelligence.

Social intelligence, therefore, is what really sets us apart from our closest primate neighbours, and could be considered the most distinctive feature of a human being. This is all great news for a business wanting to be more customer- or client-focused, because it shows that we have the innate ability to observe, understand and respond to others.

The chimp vs child experiment is explained further in a book by Nicholas Epley (Epley, 2014), a professor of behavioural science at the University of Chicago; he also discusses some research, conducted by his graduate students, which demonstrates another human trait that may explain why we don't always translate that social intelligence into empathetic behaviour. This research highlights everyone's egocentric sense of self-importance. It might also shed some light on why professionals – practitioners and marketers alike – may not be as perceptive as toddlers!

In a repeated experiment, a group of people was asked to enter a room, sit down and start a written test. However, one person was held back, then asked to put on a Barry Manilow T-shirt before entering the room to start the test. That person was withdrawn from the room soon after and asked if they thought the others had noticed their late arrival and the Barry Manilow T-shirt (the experiment was also run with more positive icons such as Bob Marley and Martin Luther King on the T-shirt to remove any anti-Manilow bias). Not surprisingly, those wearing the T-shirt thought that the majority of people had noticed them enter the room. How could you not notice a big Manilow fan in the room? In practice, hardly anyone ever noticed the late entrants and their T-shirts – because, of course, they were focused on the test. In short, what matters to me and what I focus on is 'me', not 'you'.

This illustrates another human trait, one where self-awareness colours your view of what other people are thinking or doing. The researchers in this experiment coined the term 'the spotlight effect' to show that everyone always thinks the spotlight is on them. This may be a learnt, rather than inherent human trait – we don't know if the toddlers or chimps would have noticed a big Barry Manilow bib – but nevertheless it shows that in practice we struggle to put our view of the world and our egocentric self-awareness to one side in order to consider truly another person's priorities.

This battle between social intelligence and self-awareness may indicate why professional firms and other businesses might profess a belief that the client's views come first, but then struggle to implement that ethos in practice. So, even if a lawyer, accountant, engineer or consultant is listening and talking to a client (remember: two ears – one mouth), what else is going through their mind? Are they thinking about their team's or personal billability (the percentage of their time currently allocated and billed to client projects)? Or the sales target they are trying to hit with this client? Or how they can work on their favourite type of project?

These are all considerations that consume professionals, individually and collectively, in firms. As qualified, technically minded people, often with impressive intellects that lead others to see them as experts or gurus, they are conditioned to think and behave as if it is their opinion that really matters. We are not trying to portray professionals as self-centred, egotistical maniacs, but we would expect the level of self-awareness to be high among professionals relative to the general population.

In these circumstances, it is hard to foresee a situation where a professional will find it easy to leave all their baggage at the door of the client's office and walk in prepared to focus entirely on an empathetic, social intelligence conversation where you really do take Atticus Finch's advice and '…climb inside of his skin and walk around in it'.

Fortunately, in this section we have three contributors who will help guide you through an ego-free conversation with your client, in terms of both the process and outcomes you should be seeking and what insights and feedback you are likely to hear from your clients. We also benefit from their personal and their firm's research, which provides clear insights as to what today's clients are really looking for.

We begin with Louise Field from the law firm Bird & Bird and Tim Nightingale from management consultants Nisus, who together outline why you should run a structured client listening programme, how to set one up and what benefits you can derive from the knowledge. We then hear from Ben Kent at management consultants Meridian West. Ben shares his firm's latest insights and research into clients' expectation of the commerciality of their professional advisers. We finish with Lisa Hart Shepherd from Acritas, the professional and financial services research firm, who also shares the best of their latest research and what that means for the professions.

# Listening, understanding and responding to clients

**04**

**LOUISE FIELD,** Head of Client Service & Insight, Bird & Bird LLP, and
**TIM NIGHTINGALE,** Founder, Nisus Consulting

**Profiles:** Louise is Head of Client Service & Insight at Bird & Bird LLP, where she has established the firm's international Key Client and Client Listening Programmes, and is responsible for driving new developments in client relationship management and client service. Louise has over 15 years' client care experience in professional and financial services, including EY and RBS.

Tim started his marketing career in advertising and sales promotion in the 1980s. He did an MBA at Cass Business School in 1990 and then became a consultant, eventually specializing in professional services. He is passionate about the central importance of understanding clients and its significance to any firm's success.

This chapter looks at the need, process and best practice around client listening. It explains why this is an essential activity in every professional services firm and how to put in place the systems and practices to ensure that those needs are understood.
It looks at:
- the barriers to establishing a client listening programme and how to overcome them;
- how a client listening programme should be structured;
- who should be involved;
- whether a programme should be qualitative, quantitative or both;
- what to do with the findings;
- how to close the loop so that both the firm and its clients benefit.

# 'Myopia Professionalosia' – barriers to client listening

Professionals are, by definition, clever people. To achieve professional status, each profession operates its own restrictive practices or barriers to entry. This ensures that standards are maintained and supply is restricted to keep quality and prices high. This strategy has served most professionals well, rewarding intensive training, hard work and long hours with excellent remuneration, especially when one rises to shareholder status as a partner.

So far so good, but restricted supply has traditionally kept the focus on maintaining the highest professional standards inward looking. Concentrating on standards meant that professionals were focused on the work, not the client or the skills needed to deliver the work. Originally, most professions actively discouraged their fee-earners and partners from focusing on clients, with almost any form of marketing at least frowned upon and, in most cases, contrary to professional standards and regulation.

You do not have to go back that many years to when the annual partner conference would involve protracted discussions, none of which directly concerned an outward-looking perspective on clients or the service clients received. One of us recalls working with a small firm of accountants some years ago. We asked one especially conservative partner what he would do if, in the course of conducting an audit, he uncovered the fact that his client's payroll system was no longer fit for purpose. Would he identify that his firm could offer something far more efficient and cost-effective? He pondered this for a moment and said: 'I wouldn't do anything at all. As an auditor, their payroll system is none of my business, so I wouldn't say anything – it's not my place to do so.'

We don't think we would get that comment as readily today, but we still believe that the professional ethic and desire to avoid selling runs deep, even when it is in the client's best interests to do so. More than 20 years after most professions succeeded in deregulating to allow firms to market themselves, there are still plenty of people for whom sales and marketing are activities to be looked down upon, that are unprofessional, if not plain undesirable.

Thankfully, a more realistic view today is that failure to embrace effective marketing and business development is likely to lead to reducing revenues and profitability. Most professionals realize that it's never about the product and always about what the client wants or needs.

This means that somebody needs to uncover those needs. Failure to do so would be short-sighted, if not negligent. We call this short-sightedness 'Myopia Professionalosia' – a common affliction among professional services organizations. We urge readers to remain alert to its threat.

Our position, then, is clear as we articulate our thoughts on client understanding and listening: clients should come first. Whether you call it 'client focus' or a 'client-centric approach' is of no matter. All professionals earn their income from providing a service to their client, and without a full understanding of that client's needs there may be a commercial exchange but there is no foundation on which to build an ongoing relationship.

We will tackle the question of how to gather these insights and who should undertake the task, but our point here is that client listening is something a lot of partners feel uncomfortable with, regarding it with suspicion if not fear. Usually this is dispelled once the report is provided, but for partners coming to this anew, there are often insecurities, which interviewers must be prepared for.

The truth is that professionally briefed and managed client listening should never be a witch-hunt against anybody. Personal criticisms of particular partners are, in our experience, relatively rare. It is about the client, the client's needs and their experience or perceptions of the firm relative to the competitors that counts. It is the foundation on which any significant relationship is founded and built.

# It's not how loud you shout, but how well you listen

Stand up in front of a room full of professionals and ask them to define marketing. Like the rest of the population, they will normally articulate things like 'advertising', 'promoting your services', 'PR', 'maximizing sales' and so on.

They are partially right, but they miss the main point. The misconception here is that marketing is solely about promotion – promoting your services to those to whom you want to sell or to anybody else who will listen. In effect, it is throwing mud at a wall in the hope that some of it will stick.

In the context of professional services, listening to and understanding clients' needs or conducting research is absolutely the bedrock of any marketing activity. It should not be confused with sales prospecting: sales exercises that are disguised as research. These are completely unprofessional, contrary to the Market Research Society's Professional Code of Conduct (Market Research Society, 2014) and, in our view, counterproductive.

If we are focusing on existing clients' needs, it goes without saying that client retention and loyalty are of primary importance. You frequently hear that it is more cost-effective to win work from existing clients than from new clients. This is no great surprise, but it simply highlights the importance of managing these relationships carefully, and a large part of that is listening.

Client listening may underpin a great deal of what the marketing and business development teams do, how they spend their budgets and their time, but it is not their responsibility alone to ensure that it is done and done well. As a colleague once observed, 'marketing is far too important to leave to the Marketing Department'.

Failure to recognize clients' needs leads firms to invest resources in marketing that are at best ineffective. The chart shown in Figure 4.1, taken from the Nisus Consulting study 'Seeing The World Through Clients' Eyes' (Nisus, 2004), highlights that in the minds of FTSE-100 general counsels, the marketing that is important to them is under-delivered, while that which is less important is over-delivered! Clearly these results will vary according to local culture, history, deregulation and so forth, but the principle is the same.

**FIGURE 4.1** The marketing paradox

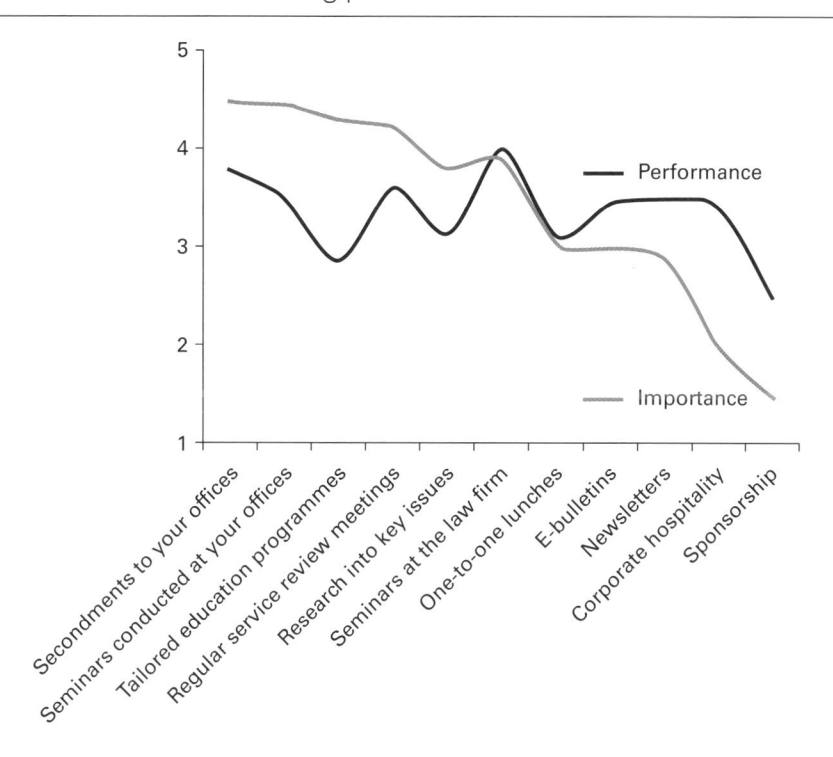

A few years ago, one of Nisus's international clients asked the firm to conduct a large survey of its UK clients. It covered private and public sector, face-to-face interviews with key clients, telephone interviews with middle managers and an electronic survey of the remaining touch points. Tim explains:

> Just as we were about to report our findings, the CEO and board of the firm released their vision and strategy for the following five years. It was very ambitious, required change, stiff targets that would move the firm up the league table in its profession. But there was a problem. When we read the five main objectives that were listed in the plan and compared them with our conclusions from our consultations with the firm's clients, it was absolutely clear that the firm was trying to change itself into something that it was not, something that clients could not possibly see it as. Innovation was important in this sector and the board wanted the firm to be a leading innovator. A good aspiration, but unfortunately the clients saw the firm as being not only far from innovative but also risk averse. There were other similar contradictions where implementing the change required was too much of a leap to be credible to clients. Smaller, more realistic and practical steps were required.
>
> The salient point here is that the board went ahead with designing and publishing their strategy before they had the results of the survey. Strategy and the clients' views were therefore seen as mutually exclusive, whereas we would suggest that any strategy that takes little or no account of clients' views is like a house built on sand.

# Setting up a listening programme

Hopefully, we have outlined a compelling case for client listening. Our next task is to work out how to do it as time- and cost-effectively as possible given the objectives we want to hit.

## *Qual vs quant*

First, we need to be clear on the approach that is going to serve us best. In research terms the line we take we can be qualitative (qual) or quantitative (quant).

The difference between qual and quant is often misconceived. If you are asked to rate something out of 10, this does not necessarily mean it is a quant study! This is a rating question and can be used in either a quant or a qual study. Similarly, asking an open question – 'What is your view on…?' – is not restricted to qual studies.

A qual study will interview a sample of clients to understand them, their motivations, preferences and so on. This group can be a cross-section and will usually be small in number. It cannot be regarded as being representative of the larger population of the firm's clients. Respondents may still be asked questions that require them to give numerical scores or ratings.

In fact, a few ratings questions at the end of a qual exercise can provide valuable confirmation of overall satisfaction and so forth, which can occasionally be hard to pin down through open-ended questions. We have both experienced interviews where individuals focus on critical feedback yet rate overall satisfaction 8 or 9 out of 10, and conversely the happy-sounding client with nothing bad to say, yet who rates a firm only 6 or 7 out of 10.

In short, a qual exercise is characterized by a smaller sample size and more in-depth questioning techniques. It cannot be deemed to be representative of a larger population, yet can facilitate greater depth of insight from a smaller audience.

A quant project takes a sample of clients that is statistically large enough to be representative of a wider population of clients. The sample will usually, but not necessarily, be selected at random. Questions can be of the tick-box variety or open ended, but typically will involve scoring. There is, however, a difficulty in business to business (B2B) for quant research, as not every client is worth the same amount to the firm. Some may bill a great deal one year and little the next. Some relationships are enormous, running into millions of pounds, others can be relatively small. Establishing what is a 'representative sample' when clients are so heterogeneous is almost impossible.

We prefer to avoid the term 'representative sample' and stick with a more commonsense 'good cross-section'. How big that cross-section needs to be is contingent on what the findings are meant to represent – one practice area in one country or the whole firm across its global offices?

The differences between qual and quant are listed in Table 4.1.

Research in professional services largely started out being qual, when a few key clients were purposefully selected and an interviewer – internal or external – was dispatched to speak to them, either face to face or by telephone.

**TABLE 4.1** The differences between qual and quant

|  | Qualitative | Quantitative |
|---|---|---|
| **Applications** | • Gaining deep insight into attitudes and motivations from a defined sample.<br>• Applied in exploring theories and generating hypotheses. | • Quantifying data and generalizing the results from a sample to a broader population.<br>• Applied in testing hypotheses. |
| **Sampling** | • Sample selection is managed, not usually random and doesn't necessarily reflect a larger population. | • Sample selection is usually random and can be said to be representative of a larger population. |
| **Data collection** | • Data are collected in a semi-structured way (face to face, telephone, focus-group interviews), using mostly open questions. | • Data are collected in a structured way (online, paper or telephone survey), using mostly closed questions. |
| **Data analysis** | • Primarily non-statistical analysis.<br>• Meaning is derived from language and requires classification into thematic categories.<br>• Results tend to be described in language. | • Primarily statistical analysis.<br>• Meaning is mostly derived from numerical data.<br>• Results shown in diagrams such as graphs and tables. |
| **Findings** | • Provides an understanding of a given situation or problem in specific cases, which may inform broader decision-making. Identifies 'actionable' client-specific insights. | • Confirms or disproves hypotheses relating to a population and may inform decision-making. |
| **Follow-up** | • Specific issues or requests raised by the clients involved. | • Broader client service initiatives, either internal (training programmes, new client service offerings) or external communications. |

We believe that there is a role for both qual and quant in professional services. They are complementary and not mutually exclusive. At Nisus, Tim spent most of his first 20 years conducting qual research, interviewing selected key clients to see what they thought of the sponsoring firm, what it could and should do better and how it compared to the competitors.

Professional services firms' progression towards globalization has demanded a more quant approach, not least because it is impractical and not cost-effective to conduct qual interviews with large samples. Face-to-face interviews provide the most depth and allow rapport to be established and, with it, trust. However, listening to only one or two people in a global company that is providing work to your offices around the world is inadequate, because the number of touch points in these relationships is increasing exponentially and qual fails to consult the majority of those working with your firm on a day-to-day basis. This is where quant can come in, with a complementary, online survey that allows all those other touch points to have their say (Figure 4.2).

**FIGURE 4.2** Qual vs quant: how to choose

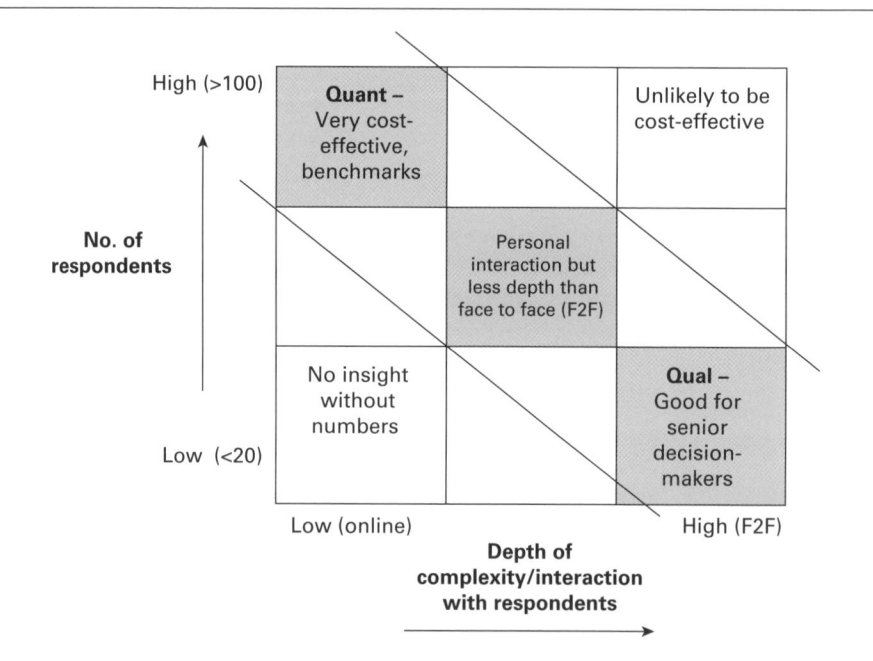

| | Low (online) | | High (F2F) |
|---|---|---|---|
| **High (>100)** | Quant – Very cost-effective, benchmarks | | Unlikely to be cost-effective |
| | | Personal interaction but less depth than face to face (F2F) | |
| **Low (<20)** | No insight without numbers | | Qual – Good for senior decision-makers |

No. of respondents (vertical axis)
Depth of complexity/interaction with respondents (horizontal axis)

## *Client listening: whose job is it anyway?*

If we accept the need to listen to clients, and know which data-collecting methods to deploy, the next step is to assign responsibility for undertaking client listening.

The simple answer to the question above is that everyone in a client team has a responsibility to listen to clients, to pick up on what clients are saying, thinking, what their needs are, how those needs are changing and, when they make disparaging remarks about your competitors, that it may be an opportunity for your firm! Ideally, listening will be a combination of a systematic and managed effort with the ad hoc and opportunistic.

There is an increasing trend to use in-house non-fee-earning staff to undertake client interviews, which can work well so long as this is not something that is tagged on to the listener's responsibilities as an afterthought. Client listening requires training on interview technique, recording data, writing up, coding, using specialist research software and so on. Sending an inexperienced or junior interviewer can leave the impression that the firm is not taking this seriously or wasting a client's time.

The need for training applies equally to fee-earners and partners, who, in our experience, tend to assume that a general conversation over lunch with minimal note-taking will suffice. These ad hoc conversations can certainly help build relationships and may deliver some useful insight, but are insufficient to be considered part of a systematic client listening project where consistency and compliance are essential. The key to any client listening is to ensure that all interviewers receive basic training, a brief as to what is required in each interview, a full understanding of the questions or topic guide and what output they need to return after the interview.

So long as these criteria are fulfilled, anybody can be sent out to see clients, with some minor caveats: it is only sensible that senior people in the firm or very experienced external interviewers are sent to the most senior clients. And if the interviewer is a partner or fee-earner, he or she should be fully independent of the team delivering services to that client.

Some clients tell us they prefer to speak to an external third party, provided they know the firm, their marketplace and how it works, and have been properly briefed on the relationship in advance. The third-party interviewer brings the advantage of having no difficulty in remaining neutral and empathizing with the client. Being defensive of the firm and colleagues is a skill that is unrequired in client listening!

The various roles and their responsibilities are shown in Figure 4.3.

## *Analysis and reporting requirements*

In undertaking any client listening exercise, a firm must decide at the outset how it wants to use the data. Setting out and agreeing the analysis and reporting requirements is essential before the fieldwork starts, to ensure that everything has been set up so the data can be cut appropriately.

A firm could ask simply for reporting on a client-by-client basis, so that each relationship partner can take away the information before sitting down with the client to draw up a mutually agreed plan. Or, for a brand study, reporting may only be required at the firm-wide level so that all data can be aggregated regardless of practice area, industry, office, region and so on. Both of us – one of us is in-house and the other an external consultant – share the belief that client listening is not a stand-alone activity, but something that should feed back into the firm's management information systems and strategic planning at every level.

**FIGURE 4.3** Responsibility for listening to clients

| Listeners | Role at client |
|---|---|
| Senior/managing partner | Senior executives only who own the relationship – GC, FD, CEO etc |
| Relationship partner | Primary relationship holder – as above or other senior manager |
| Retired partner | Primary relationship holder – as above or other senior manager |
| Associates and fee-earners in general, associates on secondment | Day-to-day contacts |
| Senior marketing and BD staff | Senior managers and day-to-day contacts |
| External research consultants | All of the above |

Every board or executive committee should be interested in capturing and then tracking a series of key performance indicators (KPIs) around client service, such as:

- client satisfaction;
- the Net Promoter Score (a feedback rating based on one question: 'How likely is it that you would recommend this company to a friend or colleague?');
- value for money;
- service delivery;
- key competitor benchmarking.

Client listening is an invaluable tool when it comes to strategic planning and looking at the firm's medium- to long-term direction of travel. It may also inform where and how marketing and business development efforts and resources should be allocated; how learning and development may be able to assist with improving service delivery skills and so on. Imagine if the voice of the client could be fed into every strategy meeting and decision-making discussion in your firm – the extent to which this occurs could significantly impact a firm's future success.

## *Whom to interview – avoiding bias and client overload*

Having selected our data-gathering methods and interviewers, where interviewers are required, the next and much more difficult task is to select our target respondents. This is habitually a difficult area for professional services firms. In our view, the fact that the relationship managers, the partners, are also the shareholders means that they inevitably carry a great deal of weight in any firm. In most we come across, surveying exercises require each partner to sign off on allowing their clients to be included in the study.

There may be very good reason for a client to be excluded, and the best person to consult on that is also the relationship partner, but therein lies a conflict and the source of potential bias. We should be selecting our respondents on the basis of objective business criteria, for example our key clients and best prospects list, or the top 50 per cent of our client list by billing over the past financial year, and so on.

Partners are naturally and understandably wary of including clients who they know to be difficult or who are likely to be critical. They do not want any fingers being pointed at them. Apply this to post-matter reviews and the bias increases exponentially. Partners have a strong incentive to put up only those deals that they know went really well, thus making them look good but denying the firm the opportunity of learning anything very much through constructive criticism. In short, there is a conflict of interest.

Firms will come to learn, as these data and the benchmarking that they facilitate become ever more important, that allowing bias to creep in undermines the integrity of the data and with it a lot of the inherent value in the exercise.

For those who come to realize the benefits of client listening on a systematic basis, it can be tempting to go overboard with research. The objective is to understand our clients, capture their views and needs, and revert to ways of meeting those needs, but with every professional adviser somewhere along the line asking that client for their opinions and, more importantly, their time; respondent fatigue is something everybody should be aware of.

As a rule of thumb, we recommend not contacting any one respondent more than once every 18 months, unless there are extenuating circumstances. Secondly, the interaction needs to be as time-effective and rewarding for the client as possible. It is easy to design 50 questions we would like answered, but this would serve only to bore and irritate our respondents.

It is far better to design 20 really good questions that follow a logical order, that facilitate engagement, discussion and even, on occasion, some amusement. This applies whether the interview is face to face or an online questionnaire. 'Keep it brief' and 'less is more' are two good tests for any questionnaire.

## *Adapting the approach – international experience*

In the past decade or so, the need to listen has extended into different regions across the world as international firms have expanded into Eastern Europe, the United States or Australasia. This presents listeners with some interesting challenges: in the same way that professional firms must strive to provide a consistent service, so interviewers will want to be consistent in their approach and questioning, while also taking full account of cultural differences. These are well documented: the Japanese are reluctant to impart bad news or be critical; Arabic nations need a long social lead-in, if not a separate pre-meeting, before any real business can be discussed; Americans and Germans tend to be far more direct than the British.

It is not just about cultural differences but regulatory ones too. Much of Western Europe is limited in what it can do in marketing and business development terms. Clients find the concept of giving feedback and talking about service provision, if not unprofessional, then completely alien. Motivating international respondents to get involved can be a demanding task and requires careful communication, a clear explanation of the ground rules, reassurance that it is not a cross-selling exercise, an explanation of what is involved, the benefits of participating, reassurance about their right to anonymity, and so on.

In addition, there are potential language problems and the need to ensure that questionnaires still work in a different language once translated. All of these complexities add another dimension for the research team, requiring extra briefing for interviewers, translation services, questionnaire piloting, analysis by region or country to look for inconsistencies, and so on.

It is, however, perfectly possible to conduct research about the firm on an international basis and compare results between countries. Between us we have conducted research in many countries in recent years in all its forms. Invariably clients are delighted to have the opportunity to provide feedback on the service – to have their say.

In markets where client listening is new, one tactic that can help is first to introduce the language of client service. Client listening tools themselves can be useful here: simple frameworks can be very helpful in translating the amorphous concept of client service into concrete elements that both professionals and clients will recognize, such as 'problem solving', 'progress updates', 'personal chemistry'.

A partner one of us worked with at a 'Big Four' accountancy firm took this idea one step further: every year he took the client satisfaction survey to his audit kick-off meeting and worked through each of the questions with his client, asking 'how can I get 10/10 from you on this question this year?' This pushed them both to really think and talk about what excellent might look like year on year.

## *Making change happen*

The only thing worse than not listening to clients is listening to clients and not following through with the requisite actions. There is always the risk that busy professionals listen attentively to a hard-hitting presentation of results, analysis and recommendations, acknowledge its value, and then go back to doing the day job, failing to make the changes necessary to strengthen and, in some cases, save a relationship.

It is all too easy for any research consultant to complete the project and supply their client with a tome of information that includes the full analysis, every data cut, every chart and reams of editorial comment. This may or may not be of interest to senior marketers, those responsible for strategy or brand, but for the most part it will be of almost no value to partners. They need to know the 'so what', the implications for the firm, its practice areas and their own individual client relationships. The average relationship partner wants to know what his takeaway is: What should he be discussing with his team? What should he be talking to the client about as a result?

A deep and meaningful client survey can have implications for a firm's strategy, highlighting a need to modify or just change it. It can shine a spotlight on specific strengths and weaknesses, or opportunities and threats. A good survey is a basis for action and change, not just introspection.

One of our clients uncovered a few home truths in its first-ever client survey. The board was shocked. The management team was taken aback. Instead of getting into a huddle or setting up a committee, they created a new department, put a senior manager in charge and initiated a road trip to communicate the findings, warts and all, to their staff.

Meetings with clients were set up that included the relationship manager and, where required, a manager from the new department. Targets were set for changing perceptions, improving scores and moving up the rankings. In short, there was a commitment made in time and resources to reappraise perceptions of their firm, their brand. Research programmes followed at 18-month intervals and progress was tracked. Unsurprisingly, that progress was good, and in four-and-a-half years the firm was viewed in an entirely different light. From being 'dull', 'middle class' and 'risk averse', it came to be seen by many as closer than all its competitors to its clients; it grew its largest multi-million-pound relationship by 20 per cent and so on and so forth. This came about simply because it listened and acted swiftly on what was heard.

**CASE STUDY**  How a top 20 law firm packages the feedback and maximizes engagement with it

In the early days at this firm, in order to build trust in the client listening programme, the relationship partner was put at the heart of deciding if/when/who should be interviewed. In many firms this model still prevails, despite its apparent shortcomings in introducing bias into the process.

Over time, as the firm's key client and client listening programmes have matured, the partnership as a whole is beginning to demand that independent client listening is done with all of the firm's key clients and that the feedback is shared, sensitively, so that all can learn. It is now clear that key client relationships 'belong' to the firm, not just to one partner, so there is an imperative to conduct a regular 'health check' and to share all feedback with management, particularly any that indicates there is a risk of losing the client.

Broader internal communication of feedback can also be undertaken effectively without attributing quotes to specific clients, so as to protect sensitivities. For instance, the firm has a monthly 'Voice of the Client' summary, with a good balance of positive and negative comments, or exploration of a particular theme using home-grown client quotes as illustration. This summary provides real insight on a regular basis.

For the key client team, we have found that full, honest communication of the client's views, warts and all, is the only way. The temptation to paraphrase or soften harsh words can be strong, but should be avoided.

## How to help effect change as a result of listening

A good survey provides insight and drives action and change on two levels: at the individual client relationship and also the firm or department level.

It is essential that all these data be first converted into insights and then to real actions. This means identifying specific actions and assigning these to the partners and relevant business services people. Client listening is not about 'nice to know' but 'need to change'.

The quality of the questioning goes a long way to being able to get the best out of it. Trained interviewers probe all vague responses until an actionable insight is identified. For example:

Interviewer: What do you think about the firm's approach to billing?

Respondent: It's OK, pretty standard really.

Interviewer: What should they do so that it is better than standard from your point of view?

Respondent: Well, sending me monthly invoices on what is on the clock for the month would help me and your cash flow. I would also like more information on the invoice about what was done and why.

## Closing the loop with the client

Anything we undertake in client listening must ultimately loop back to the client. Clients need to see us respond to their feedback, so the whole team must know what it is! Partners may prefer to share sensitive feedback verbally with associates rather than circulate a complete written report with warts and all – what matters is not which way it is approached but that it is done.

Louise's view is that where multiple contacts have been interviewed or surveyed, it is helpful for both firm and client to analyse that feedback for themes and trends and take time to consider the 'so what?' We prepare a report: what have we heard, what does this mean going forward. We then take the report to work through with the client and agree a plan. This is an area for error, as firms fail to face up to discussing the findings of research with their clients and viewing it as an opportunity rather than a threat that is best ignored.

Within our client listening programme we use outsourced online surveys for our quant and in-house in-depth telephone or face-to-face interviews for our qual. We look to blend these two approaches to give us a realistic picture of client views across the whole firm and across our key client population.

We also run projects from time to time for specific groups – for example a country, sector group or practice group. All results continually build the firm-wide picture.

# Conclusion – a brave new world?

Having worked in professional services client feedback for many years between us, the landscape has changed markedly. Whereas the vast majority of firms in the early to mid-nineties would proudly have admitted to being non-believers, today there are very few firms still in denial about the necessity of listening systematically to their clients' views.

But just as there may be very few in the bottom category, there are equally few that would qualify as being market leaders: those that are really investing in rigorous processes to ensure that they stay client focused and who select their respondents using objective business criteria, rather than the self-interested preferences of their partners. Market leaders use results as an integral part of their management information system and as a foundation to their strategic planning.

So while it appears that the professional services sector has embraced client listening, we believe that there is still new road left to travel. Clients generally want an opportunity to provide feedback and they want to see change as a result. One respondent we interviewed recently regaled how he provided the feedback, nothing happened as a result and he is now rather cynical about the investment of his time.

Any credible key client programme must have client listening at its heart, driving continuous improvement, setting or validating strategies for developing each client relationship, and building a better understanding of an individual and the organization's needs. As the custodians of a firm's clients, all client relationship partners should embrace independent client listening as an essential input: one can only think that any who do not must have something to hide.

Client relationship partners should be picking over their client reports to understand how the client views their firm, its strengths and weaknesses and where the opportunities and threats lie – so it is part of their own strategic planning as well.

Client listening needs to be managed, considered, systematic and have agreed outputs. Wherever the data are coming from – systematic or ad hoc – they need to be captured, stored and shared. They must be useful and practical, as this is not an academic exercise. We must also take care not to do client feedback to excess, not to irritate our clients, and keep it light touch, involving minimal interruption. We could regress to being non-believers and just leave our clients alone, but to do so would be recidivism of the worst kind.

To succeed in the face of severe competition means that we must outperform the competition, make our firm indispensable, and differentiate our brands. And if we can achieve a degree of positive differentiation, then and only then can we hope to avoid price competition and sustain better margins.

How we do client feedback will certainly evolve over the coming years and probably more in the direction of quant, supported or complemented by qual (as opposed to the other way round), but either way, it is here to stay, with an ever-diminishing group of non-believers.

# Closing the commerciality gap

## 05

**BEN KENT,** Managing Director, Meridian West

**Profile:** Ben is the founder director of insight-led consultancy Meridian West. Prior to launching Meridian West, Ben was a corporate lawyer, beginning his career with Freshfields. In his current role Ben advises many of the world's leading professional and financial services firms on their client engagement, and provides strategic research, consultancy and training for professional firms.

This chapter argues that there needs to be a revolution in the way that professionals deliver advice. In addition to the technical mastery that they already possess, successful professionals will need to acquire a bundle of skills we call 'commerciality' and actively demonstrate them to clients.

It is a bold assertion but the evidence is clear. The *Effective Client–Adviser Relationships* 2012 report (*Financial Times*, 2012) shows that a lack of understanding of the clients' business is the biggest factor that damages client relationships – cited by 52 per cent of clients.

So what is the best way to close the 'commerciality gap'? Since the original report, we have interviewed many more clients and professionals on the subject. This chapter shares the key findings, with a case study and top tips. It is divided into three sections:

1 Why clients are dissatisfied with professionals' commerciality.
2 How individual advisers can become more commercial by applying the seven-habit framework.
3 What professional firms can do through training and tools to develop commercially astute advisers. We will particularly focus on the role that marketing and HR departments can play in spearheading change.

# Why clients are dissatisfied with professionals' commerciality

In short, clients have become more sophisticated and have higher expectations.

It is widely recognized that across the professions, clients are becoming much more sophisticated in the way they use advisers, and this is backed up by our research. Over the past few years, client organizations have recruited senior talent from leading professional firms and are using that experience and expertise to get the best from their advisers. In-house departments have introduced more rigorous business disciplines; for example, many large legal departments now have their own chief operating officer (COO). The use of panels and procurement specialists is now widespread.

Clients are also trying to achieve more with less resource and so are less diffident and often prepared to question the value for money that they are receiving. Buyers are under pressure to justify the use of advisers to the rest of the business and need evidence that real outcomes are being achieved. They want advisers to make proactive suggestions on ways to bring down fees.

We asked clients to select what they considered to be the three biggest challenges their department will be facing over the next three years (Figure 5.1).

Clients are sometimes jaded by their experience of using professional firms. In the numerous interviews that we have carried out, we often hear clients share the following frustrations: 'They don't understand the business objectives in my experience. They assume a lot and pitch services I don't care about.'

There is no doubt that most clients respect the brainpower and technical knowledge of their accountants, lawyers and consultants, but this is no longer enough.

**FIGURE 5.1** Future challenges

**1. More complex business environment**

55% of clients say that they are managing a more risky business environment.

37% of clients say that improving communication and collaboration in the business is among their three biggest challenges.

**2. Pricing pressures**

71% of advisers say that they expect the number of advisers offering discounts to win work will increase.

31% of clients say that the procurement function will take a more active role in commissioning external advisers.

**3. More demanding clients**

80% of clients say that they will expect a more consistent level of service from professional advisers.

61% of clients say that they are trying to achieve more with less resource.

Theme 2 Understanding

In order to achieve the shift from being seen as a necessary evil to being seen as a valued business partner and trusted adviser, actively demonstrating commerciality is vital.

Commerciality is a much-used term in professional services but our research shows that many advisers are unclear on what it actually means in practice. This inspired us to create the 'seven habits of a commercial adviser' framework, which synthesizes the findings from our interviews with clients and partners to give advisers practical steps to becoming more commercial in the eyes of clients.

## The seven habits of a commercial adviser

The essence of commerciality is about providing advice to help clients maximize their profitability. Advisers can achieve this through better understanding the client's issues, understanding the context in which they are operating and delivering advice that helps them reach their goals and outcomes (Figure 5.2).

**FIGURE 5.2**  The seven habits of a commercial adviser

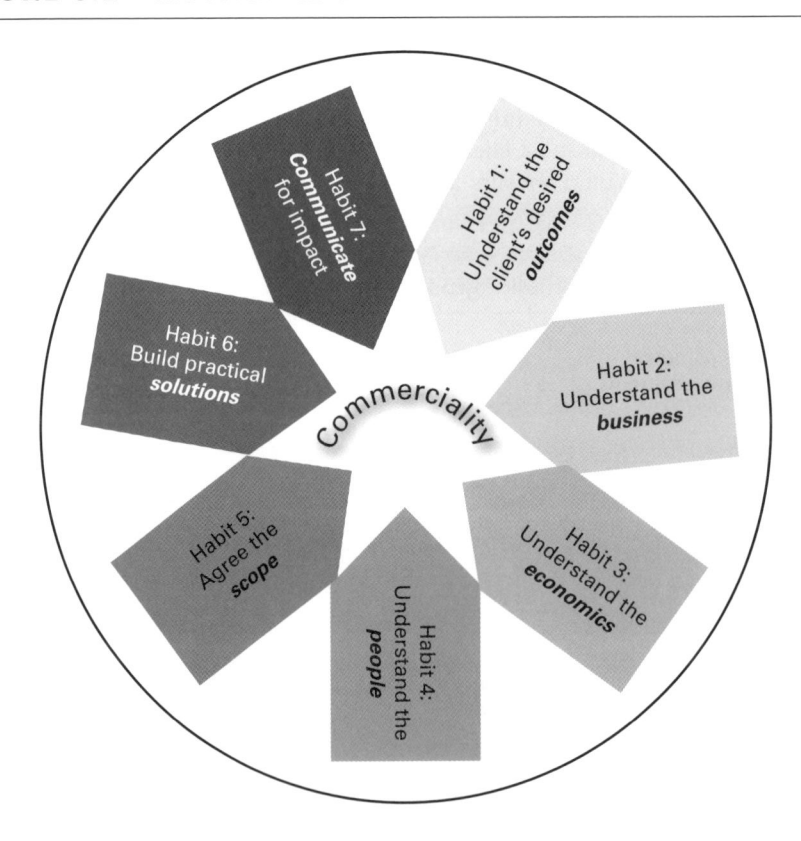

- Habit 1: Understand the client's desired *outcomes*
- Habit 2: Understand the *business*
- Habit 3: Understand the *economics*
- Habit 4: Understand the *people*
- Habit 5: Agree the *scope*
- Habit 6: Build practical *solutions*
- Habit 7: *Communicate* for impact

Commerciality

## Habit 1 – Understand the client's desired outcomes

Advisers need to change their mentality so that success is defined by achieving the client's outcomes rather than excellent inputs or outputs. Too often advisers confuse deliverables with outcomes. This mismatch arises because professional services firms tend to adopt pricing models that reward their advisers for providing deliverables, whereas clients' businesses are usually only rewarded when they achieve certain outcomes. Advisers need to focus more diligently on how their advice is used in the boardroom during the decision-making process. Professionals will need to become more adept at helping the client implement their advice.

## Habit 2 – Understand the business

The starting point for delivering really commercial advice is an in-depth understanding of the business context in which a client operates. This has increasingly become a key driver for selection and a way for firms to further differentiate themselves. When looking to instruct advisers for complex work, 40 per cent of clients cite an understanding of their business as among their top three selection criteria (*Financial Times*, 2012).

Reading financial statements and annual reports is no longer sufficient to demonstrate an in-depth understanding of a client's business. Instead, 75 per cent of clients say they expect their advisers to know about their organization's strategy and business plan, and 67 per cent expect knowledge of industry sectors and trends. Clients' expectations have changed, so how can you respond to this?

## Habit 3 – Understand the economics

Numbers are the language of business, but many professionals (especially lawyers) are tongue-tied. For example, in merger and acquisition deals, many lawyers don't really understand how the company is valued and the impact of cost or revenue synergies on the price. As a consequence, they are unable to link the due diligence they undertake with the price. They are rarely able to quantify quantum vs probability to provide a number that can then be used in price negotiations.

This lack of financial fluency puts professionals at a grave disadvantage. It excludes them from the serious C-suite conversations and it makes it difficult to justify the value of their recommendations.

A quote from the Managing Director of a European technology business captured the sentiment of many:

> In my 25 years of doing this I have met two lawyers who can add up, which means it's difficult for them to be commercial. They will delineate between that which is a commercial point and that which is a legal point and there shouldn't be that delineation. I'm not paying hundreds of pounds an hour to make all the difficult decisions. I'm paying that price for someone else to not just advise, but to make a decision.

## Habit 4 – Understand the people

Business is a social activity. Organizations are made up of people, decisions are made by people, and our clients are people.

Being able to understand the people, their styles and drivers, is fundamental to being able to navigate successfully the complex world of business and deliver success in terms of the desired outcomes. Commercial advisers are able to use tools such as stakeholder mapping. They understand that giving advice is not a logical exercise based on technical expertise. They understand and respond to clients' emotions.

## Habit 5 – Agree the scope

Clients recognize that a good scope is the key to a good project. However, many professionals have a poor reputation for scoping and managing expectations. Clients feel frustrated when things overrun or when advisers come back to them at the end of a project looking to bill for additional costs that were unforeseen.

The issue is that after the honeymoon of winning a project, advisers are keen to get cracking and are reluctant to document a plan that sets out tasks, resources, risks, roles and timelines. However, the additional time spent up front will pay dividends later in the project in terms of both efficiency and client satisfaction.

The benefits of a clear plan are great:

- It ensures that all the different stakeholders are clear about the objectives, and that work is focused on meeting them (and not 'nice to have' tasks).
- It enables you to measure success at the conclusion of the project.
- It avoids scope creep, and therefore maintains profitability.
- It maintains high levels of client satisfaction – many client complaints about professional firms are about misaligned expectations.

## Habit 6 – Build practical solutions

This is the heart of the matter – how do you solve the client's problems so that they achieve their goals?

Most professionals think that they are strong problem solvers, but unfortunately many clients think that professionals add complexity. Clients' complaints fall into two categories – those who complain that their advisers don't tell them what to do, 'they tell me the law but not what I should do', and those who complain that professionals do tell them what to do, but are too rigid.

## Habit 7 – Communicate for impact

Historically, professional advice has been known to consist of long, dense reports and letters of advice. Over the past couple of decades, business communication has become more visual, more succinct and less formal. The professions need to catch up:

- Match the communication style of your client. Do they communicate formally or informally? What language do they use? Do they communicate by PowerPoint or Word?
- Communicate in a more visual way. Increasingly, business likes to communicate with dashboards, traffic lights and even mind maps.
- Recognize that getting buy-in is a process. It can rarely be achieved with one document (however brilliant!). A better approach might include:
  - an initial debrief with the immediate client;
  - a more formal presentation to the board;
  - a workshop to agree recommendations;
  - a short presentation/video clips for staff;
  - co-present your conclusions with your immediate client.

# What firms can do to improve

So why do professionals struggle to be commercial and hence make great advisers (Figure 5.3)? The elements of commerciality are not difficult to grasp intellectually and many are common sense. The research shows, however, that commerciality runs counter to the culture and talent management processes of professional firms:

- Professional training encourages a narrow approach to problem solving. In law and accountancy, firms tend to focus on control and risk avoidance (not taking calculated risks). For example, legal training focuses on 'is there a contract, is there a breach, is there a loss, is there causation?' It does not teach young professionals to focus on how to rebuild relationships or manage reputational risk.
- Firms recruit from a narrow gene pool, usually straight from top universities. Recruiting from industry is rare. The leaders of the professional firms have usually spent their entire career at one or two professional firms, moving up the hierarchy by demonstrating technical excellence.
- Time must be chargeable. Time spent deepening relationships and getting to understand the client and industry is time wasted.
- Professionals are increasingly specialized as regulations and business get more complex. It is rare to find generalists.
- Professional firms are worried that if they give commercial advice they will be sued or contravene professional regulations. This is a particular problem for auditors.
- Their mindset means that, although well paid and intelligent, professionals are often deeply unconfident about having broad business conversations with clients.

**FIGURE 5.3** Why professionals struggle to be commercial

- Professional training encourages narrow view
- Timesheet culture
- Over-specialization
- Recruiting from same gene pool
- Liability fears
- Lack of confidence to have business conversations

# Appetite for change

Given these challenges, there needs to be a revolution in the way that professionals are trained and give advice. A cynic might argue that client complaints about a professional's lack of commerciality have been with us for many years. Historically, professional firms are not innovative: they find it hard to build partner consensus and drive through radical change. Many partners make very good money, so why change?

I am an optimist: I think there will be change and here's why:

1 Clients will drive the change. The recent downturn has given the clients buying power. There is a growing feeling that clients will no longer put up with uncommercial advice. Within the legal sphere there is also a group of leading general counsel from the big banks and major companies who are leading the charge and creating very novel ways of working. They are embracing new ways of working, eg managing legal services, hiring non-lawyers, using technology. Where they lead, others will surely follow.

2 Professionals recognize the issue – 87% of advisers say they will need to develop a more commercial skill set in addition to their technical competencies.

3 Commerciality skills are seen by professional firms as a differentiator in a competitive market. The large accountancy firms are moving more into management consultancy, and commerciality skills are even more important for these business lines than for audit or compliance services.

# Building commerciality skills

Our research identified five steps to success in building commerciality skills.

## Step 1 – Demonstrate leadership

The firms we interviewed had embraced commerciality at the highest level. Commerciality is not something that marketing, knowledge management or HR can drive forward alone. It requires a joined-up approach.

## Step 2 – Develop deep insight

The key to being a commercial adviser is to have deep insight into your clients, their sector and the wider business world. Most large professional firms have key account planning, client feedback programmes, sector groups and a knowledge management function. At some firms, budgets have been cut, but the leading firms are taking insight management to the next level. In particular, firms have focused on using technology to develop learning networks and facilitate face-to-face time with the clients.

## Step 3 – Redesign the client experience to provide more added value

Most firms now have account management programmes, but some are beginning to take programmes to the next level. Interesting initiatives we have seen include:

- providing bespoke thought leadership insights, such as client round tables;
- hiring senior-level client-facing account managers;
- having a more rigorous client on-boarding programme to ensure that the client's goals and preferences are captured;
- improving project management as a way to strip out cost;
- providing multidisciplinary/consultancy propositions;
- ensuring communication is client-friendly;
- evaluating the project's outcome.

## Step 4 – Tools and training

Training in professional services firms has traditionally been very technically focused. Firms have added some sales and client servicing skills training, but only a minority use internal or external training to develop commercial awareness. Our research has identified that informal learning is the norm.

Thankfully this is starting to change. Innovative ideas we have seen include mapping out career stages and required commerciality, and blending formal training with e-learning and social learning.

## Step 5 – Reward success

Reward mechanisms in many professional firms focus on winning new work and high personal billing rates. Focus on the billable hour is the biggest barrier to commerciality. Smart firms are addressing this issue head-on by rewarding commerciality and celebrating mentoring and knowledge-sharing.

**CASE STUDY**  BDO – making transformational change to your brand

BDO were performing well with generally positive client reviews. However, Allan Evans, the Sales and Marketing Partner, was aware that satisfaction scores had plateaued and, more crucially, that clients were getting a fundamentally different service across the firm. As Allan put it: 'There was something in the BDO DNA whereby service was part of what we were, something that we were really good at and we were proud of. It's just that everybody had a different view of what it was and what it should look like.' This meant that clients working with multiple service lines or offices had to work out how to navigate BDO rather than getting the joined-up service and consequent benefits that they were looking for.

Allan recognized that to create a strong and sustainable brand, BDO needed to change this approach. He saw an opportunity to develop a new proposition that would introduce more commonality to BDO's service delivery, allowing it to be distinct from its competition. Allan drove transformational change to the BDO brand around the concept of 'exceptional client service by empowered people'. Below he shares the key steps that enabled his success:

1 Identify the commercial opportunity – where is the gap and how will your new proposition fill it? BDO acknowledged early on that: 'We were never going to lead by being rocket scientists with technical ability, although we clearly have to be technically strong, and we didn't want to lead on price.' To identify the opportunity, they worked with external partners to conduct primary and secondary research and found that 40% of mid-market buyers of accountancy services were dissatisfied with the service they received. As Allan puts it: 'I had to demonstrate that there was a commercial opportunity and the 40% dissatisfaction gave me something.'

2 Identify the potential blockers in your organization – those with credibility with other partners who could have destabilizing influence – and get them involved as early as possible. At BDO, Allan put this at the top of his priority list: 'I had to go and find those partners that were credible with other partners but who, if I had not been able to dissuade them and bring them inside the tent, would have been a challenge to the

successful implementation.' It took a considerable amount of time, but Allan was able to convert their scepticism using the data. The fact that this research was carried out by external consultants was crucial in convincing them, 'because it's never physician heal thyself', as Allan puts it.

3  Remove surrounding messages. Having too many messages and brand statements can be confusing for staff and detracts from the power and distinctiveness of the proposition. Allan says that one of the key things they got right at BDO was: 'We got rid of lots of surrounding noise, we ditched a lot of language that was attached to our heritage.' They made it clear to their advisers that the new proposition had to take over. When it came to positioning the proposition with clients, BDO's approach was clear: 'The first thing that comes out of your mouth is exceptional client service by empowered people.'

4  Involve HR to align recognition and reward with adopting the actions behind the proposition. At BDO, it took a while for them to gauge that they should be 'more aggressive in aligning the rewards systems', as there was an assumption that advisers would understand the potential benefits to the client and 'just get it'. Allan feels that they could have been even more successful had he involved HR to a greater extent from the outset.

5  Create a learning and development (L&D) framework with a suite of training spanning classroom, online and mobile. Let people learn on their terms, including when they are on the move. At BDO, the L&D framework was based around a principle that 'aligned service to winning revenue', so fee-earners could see the benefit to the bottom line.

6  Invest in the launch – BDO chose the partner conference to cement the importance of the initiative in partners' minds. 'We took a whole partner conference over to do it and we gave them a sense of theatre and occasion and we invited clients to join us on stage. All of that said to the partners that this is not for Christmas, this is for life, so you're going to have to get on board.'

BDO is having success with the proposition internally and externally. From an external point of view, it is performing well financially and has the highest client satisfaction score in Meridian West's Mid-Market Monitor study. Moreover, others see it as a leader on client service in the professional services space. Internally, there has been considerable buy-in from staff, with 98 per cent saying that they understand the strategy and 96 per cent positively endorsing it.

However, Allan feels that consistency will be key going forward: 'I think we need to still improve all our members of staff's 365 mentality, as clients can still have a pre-Christmas experience that is not quite as good as it needs to be. I think complacency or apathy is a real thing and people do get bored, so we need to keep the energy going.'

# Conclusion – getting the balance right

So how can advisers get the balance right between technical, professional and commercial advice? In short, what are the characteristics of great advisers? In our experience, great advisers offer a combination of the following characteristics:

- They recognize that giving advice has a strong emotional element. David Maister summarizes it well: 'Many professionals approach the task of giving advice as if it were an objective, rational exercise based on their technical knowledge and expertise. Alas, giving advice is almost never an exclusively logical process. Rather, it is almost always an emotional "duet" played out between the advice giver and the client' (Maister, 1997).
- They think about the opportunities as well as the risks. Most professionals are more risk averse than business people and so need to understand the balance.
- They understand and are willing to take calculated risks. Taking risks is not a natural part of the psyche for many professionals and the training they receive is often around control. They are used to taking a rational and measured approach, but because the current business environment is so unsure, some businesses now have just got to take a risk. Professional advisers need to understand and interpret risk.
- They think about both the technical and the operational issues. Advisers need to think through how the advice will be implemented; for example, this option may save you more tax, but it may damage the company's reputation.
- They collaborate with the client to come to a decision. They act as a coach to the client to think through the issues and make a recommendation, but recognize that the client makes the final decision.
- They are not a soft touch. Great advisers ensure that the client recognizes the trade-offs associated with their chosen option. If regulations or common sense forbids a course of action, they say so.

# What legal clients want

## 06

**LISA HART SHEPHERD,** CEO, Acritas

**Profile:** Lisa established Acritas in 2002 to exclusively service the research needs of professional and financial services firms. During this time, Lisa has worked on projects with many of the world's largest law firms, devising research programmes to help clients achieve service excellence, brand strength, employee engagement and global growth. Lisa and her team at Acritas work with over 40 of the Global 100 law firms on market intelligence programmes.

Intense competition in the legal market is radically altering client–law firm relationships. The pressure on in-house counsel to become ever-more commercially minded and offer business-ready advice is altering what they need and expect of their law firms.

Although clients say that they are generally satisfied with the firms they use and that standards of expertise and service are high, only a third of clients say that they are 'delighted' with their external counsel (Acritas, 2013). Yet those firms that are able to reach this exalted position among clients enjoy:

- greater long-term loyalty;
- higher levels of recommendation;
- increased share of spend – clients who give firms a score of 9 or 10 for satisfaction spend on average 43% more of their legal budget with those firms;
- less price sensitivity.

So what is required to make the transition from competent supplier to indispensable aide? What does the extra mile look like?

In this chapter we will explore:

- what clients actually want – and effective ways of finding out what these requirements are;
- how you can customize your approach to ensure that you meet – and exceed – clients' expectations;
- why a client-focused approach is the foundation for future law firm growth.

# Capturing the client view

As part of its annual Sharplegal study, Acritas captures the views of over 2,000 general counsel (GC) in multinationals across 55 countries. This study gauges current thinking on a wide range of legal market issues among the in-house community as well as highlighting clients' changing needs over time. Conducted every year since 2007, the research reveals the pace and degree of change that has taken place in the legal market and the effect this change is having on clients' service expectations.

This chapter draws extensively on Sharplegal research findings. The advice offered is all based on feedback given by GCs from across the globe and so provides practical, pertinent ways for firms to build lasting bonds with their clients – and reap the long-term rewards of doing so.

# The value of client understanding

The importance of investing time in understanding who your client is and what they really want cannot be overstated. The first rule is never to assume that what works with one client will be successful with another. Both at the start of the relationship and throughout its course, it is important to get and maintain a thorough grasp of:

- why your client/prospect needs external support;
- what they expect of the service they are buying;
- how your contribution fits within their overall business aims;
- how your service will be measured.

Fully understanding the answers to these questions is critical to:

- winning the client's business;
- getting the relationship off to the best possible start;
- keeping the relationship strong over time;
- building your rapport to such a level that your client becomes loyal and actively recommends your firm to others.

When asked about the factors that drive loyalty during Acritas' latest Sharplegal study, the two most common themes to arise in the answers given by 2,073 GCs were 'knowledge of my business' and a 'long-standing relationship'. Although there is no magic formula for getting closer to clients and winning client loyalty, there are some broad principles, universally acknowledged to pave the way towards a trusting rapport and long-term relationship success. Central to the process is the consistent use of client intelligence. Conducting research about clients should be an ongoing process. It is a common mistake to conduct far-reaching investigations into a client's business and sector in order to win their work, only to cease active learning once the business has been won.

# Building client understanding

## *Good sector knowledge is only the start...*

Good business understanding is absolutely critical to winning and keeping clients and it is the area that GCs most frequently identify as lacking in the skills and knowledge of their external counsel. A common area in which firms frequently fall short of clients' expectations is in their interpretation of what constitutes business understanding. The firm view can differ substantially from that of the client.

Firms tend to focus on knowledge of the sector in which the client operates. In-house counsel, however, need their firm to have a multifaceted view of their business encompassing external, internal and macro-economic factors that affect both current and future growth. If the gulf between these two viewpoints is not bridged, it can readily lead to disappointment for both parties.

Firms can only really begin to impress clients when they are able to demonstrate:

- how they can offer legal advice that reflects deep sector knowledge combined with insight into the niche in which the client company operates;
- knowledge of where the company sits within that niche;
- in-depth understanding of the problems their clients face;
- commercial acumen.

For example, a firm may have a reputation for its work in banking services and assume that this knowledge will readily transfer to other areas of finance. In reality, each niche within a sector has its own specific challenges, with which even renowned sector experts may be ill-equipped to deal. Time- and budget-poor clients require concrete, concise, specific, relevant and timely advice from the outset, which is only possible with detailed understanding of how a company operates within its sector niche. This level of familiarity with the client's business also ensures that firms are able to work more quickly and effectively to deliver high-quality expertise at the client's pace – thus laying firm foundations for building long-term satisfaction and loyalty.

## *Don't overlook the in-house team's needs*

Another area frequently neglected is the internal structure of the legal department, its capabilities and pressure points, its budgeting and forecasting cycle. These factors are the ones that normally drive the need for external legal advice in the first place and should be a high priority when investigating a client's business.

Interest in getting a clear picture of what the team can and can't do in-house and the ability to find effective ways of 'plugging the gaps' by becoming an extension of the internal legal department are highly valued by GCs and effective at differentiating forward-thinking firms from the competition.

In short, law firms can derive great benefit from asking clients more questions – about every aspect of their role, their department, their business, needs, budgets and the financial constraints under which they are operating.

Probing effectively can help at every stage of the client–law firm relationship. The information you glean will:

- ensure that the solutions you offer are incisive and answer the real problems your clients are facing;
- reveal additional areas in which you may be able to cross-sell your services;
- highlight future areas of need so that you can plan ahead more effectively.

The very act of taking the time and care to get to know a client in detail speaks volumes about your approach and the level of importance you place on service. Once answers have been gathered, assimilating these data will allow you to segment the approach you take to any particular matter by finely customizing your advice to account for team size, financial factors, board priorities and so on. This attention to detail will help to ensure that your interactions with clients make a lasting impression and cement relationships.

# The client–firm relationship cycle

Building client understanding is a complex process. Like other relationships, those between clients and law firms evolve over time and the knowledge that firms require at each stage can alter quite significantly.

## Building understanding with new clients

The following guidance is based on the views of Sharplegal respondents and is designed to provide you with a checklist of actions to help you to get closer to your clients at the start of your relationship with them.

### Get to the heart of the matter
Ask in-depth questions about the needs of the in-house team as well as their business requirements. Finding the gaps in their capabilities will not only help you to tailor your services effectively but also highlight new opportunities.

Being able to put your feet in your client's shoes and look at situations from their perspective will help you to develop realistic solutions that will work within the client's constraints. This kind of forethought is highly prized by clients and will help ensure that it is your firm that stands out.

### Conduct a thorough investigation
On top of what you have learnt directly from the prospective client, it is critical to draw on as many sources of wider research as you can. These will range from formalized legal market data and reports to more personal information from LinkedIn profiles, Twitter accounts and your own in-house teams. However, it is equally important to take care in how you go on to use this research. Weaving it

through your recommendations can be extremely powerful; conversely, presenting it back in raw form can be insulting, as one Sharplegal respondent pointed out: 'They treat me like a moron. They think that I'm a dummy and they talk down to me and they think [they] know my business better than I do' (Australia, Business Services).

Thoroughly researching your prospective client's needs communicates the fact that you genuinely want to work with the prospect, that you are interested in a long-term relationship and that you are willing to 'go the extra mile'. In addition, it is a subtle, yet effective, way of providing a taste of the service the in-house team will get, should they instruct you.

### Flexible fees pay

Showing that you appreciate the budgetary pressure that in-house counsel are under and exploring ways in which you can help them to control costs are other important ways in which firms can show that they are on the client's side and have their interests foremost. Being open about pricing and providing accurate spend forecasts and flexible billing options can go a long way towards winning clients' favour and demonstrating a collaborative style of working.

### Team tactics

Trust is the foundation of any strong relationship. Nevertheless, law firms still frequently damage their chances of getting a new association off the ground by presenting a stellar team at pitch only to swap this line-up for less experienced lawyers day-to-day. Given that lack of honesty is one of the most damaging *faux pas* at the start of a relationship, misleading prospective clients about who will be working with them is a risky strategy.

### Play to your strengths

Out of eagerness to win/please, firms can easily fall into the trap of over-promising. This tactic may impress initially but it is rare that the firm's learning curve can keep pace with the expectations of a client who has been 'oversold'. The result is a bitter taste in the client's mouth and either an end to the relationship or, at best, a long, slow climb towards regaining trust. Being realistic about your firm's strengths and weaknesses instils confidence in clients, especially when you offer workable solutions that make up for any shortcomings. This approach is a very powerful way of demonstrating your honesty and confidence and lays firm foundations for the future.

### Work with, not against procurement

Although sometimes onerous, procurement can be extremely useful to in-house teams by removing the time and administrative burden that finding and instructing law firms bring. They also take in-house counsel off the hiring and firing 'frontline', offer welcome relief from having 'those difficult conversations' and bring rigour to the appointment process – traditionally an area ruled largely by familiarity over ability. GCs therefore advise firms to get to grips with the processes that the in-house legal team have to follow and under no circumstances fight against them.

## *Keeping the relationship strong long-term*

Once your initial investment has paid off and you have won the client's trust and business, relationship-building can begin in earnest. Clearly, the long-term aim is to strengthen client bonds to such an extent that your firm becomes the default choice.

The following principles, assimilated from feedback given by GCs during Sharplegal interviews, provide a good foundation for building better client understanding once the relationship has begun.

**Establish the ground rules**
A kick-off meeting is de rigueur, but the quality of the agenda for that all-important official start to the relationship can dictate its future course. A well-planned schedule that covers the matters of most importance to the client and demonstrates your commercial focus and willingness to flex to fit your client will propel the relationship to new heights. One that simply lays out your terms and way of working will serve only to sow seeds of doubt in the client's mind.

**Open the lines of communication**
Establishing a slick and efficient flow of information from in-house counsel to client team and across the firm at the outset will eliminate the need for re-briefing – which can test clients' patience and erode trust. This simple yet vital step radically reduces client frustration by ensuring that no time is wasted in repeating requests or re-briefing. This respect for client time is a simple yet highly effective way of cementing good relations, reducing the burden on clients and ensuring that in-house teams see that their firm is 'on their side' and constantly thinking of ways to make their life easier.

**Learn to read clients' signals**
It is often the small things that belie larger problems. Being sensitive to changes in the tone of communication, levels of contact and the quantity and type of work clients request can make all the difference. Early diagnosis of behavioural change is an effective way of preventing minor issues from escalating into crises.

**Watch, ask, listen, learn. Repeat**
All too often relationships get off to a flying start and then begin to falter as new priorities take over. Keeping bonds strong demands keen powers of observation, acute listening skills, sustained curiosity and eagerness to learn – throughout the life of the relationship.

**Share knowledge generously**
Exposed to a wide range of different clients with varying problems across many sectors, law firms are constantly experiencing new ways of tackling universal issues. In-house counsel say that they would value hearing from their law firm advisers how other clients, faced with similar problems, have successfully found solutions. This not only saves time, effort and money but also demonstrates that the firm has the client's best interests at heart – thereby building trust and loyalty and cementing a good working relationship.

## Don't over-promise

Once the relationship is established, realism is all-important. Billing is one area in which over-promising can backfire badly. Failing to complete a piece of work within the stated budget/timescale is more palatable for clients if the issue is flagged up in advance. Going over time and budget without warning severely compromises relationships.

## Take the long-term view

The way you act says a lot about the value you place on the relationship you have with your client. A willingness to be flexible and meet clients halfway indicates a desire for a longer-term working relationship – and is more likely to bring one about. Sticking fast to rigid structures, traditional ways of working and standard billing practices are red flags to GCs. In-house teams have had to radically alter the way they operate and serve their businesses, so they need their advisers to move with the same agility.

## Speed is of the essence

As GCs find themselves under intensifying pressure to deliver more with less, they now expect their external advisers to work to the same exacting standards. Concrete, concise, relevant and commercially sound advice – delivered quickly and consistently – is central to winning and keeping client confidence.

## Think laterally

In a world where traditional thinking still holds strong, doing something a little differently to help the client stands out. Respecting the time constraints that in-house teams face by finding time-saving solutions to their problems is an effective way of gaining favour with in-house counsel. For example, instead of inviting in-house lawyers to a seminar on environmental law, you could write a draft policy for them to customize and use across their company. This approach demonstrates your expertise in environmental law as effectively as a seminar would, but, more importantly, shows that you understand clients' pressures and provide valuable help in overcoming them.

## Think like a client

As part of our Sharplegal research, we asked in-house counsel about the areas in which they felt that lawyers needed additional training or development.

The most common response was that they needed to improve their understanding of clients' businesses and become more commercial/business savvy:

> More knowledge of our business. [In any particular area?] No, just understanding the business enables them to be more accurate with their responses.
> 
> (US, Retail/Wholesale)

> I would want them to all be quicker, more precise and get a better understanding of the business environment. The focus on customer service, not whatever garbage they learnt in law school.
> 
> (Canada, Technology/Media/Telecommunications)

The onus is clearly on law firms to invest more time and effort in getting under the skin of clients so that they can gain a thorough understanding of their needs and provide high-quality advice throughout the relationship. At a fundamental level, the larger the burden you are able to lift from clients' shoulders, the stronger the relationship is likely to become. Time invested in helping clients to look good within their organizations by solving their problems and getting through work quickly and accurately will be repaid many times over in loyalty.

## *If/when the relationship fails*

Although the ultimate aim is to ensure that no client ever feels the need to stop using your firm, it is a fact of life that clients do leave, even when the relationship is in good health. The reasons for termination of contract are wide-ranging and largely fall into two distinct camps:

### Category 1: Termination driven by market forces

This category covers the factors that directly result in the firm being dropped because of natural forces in the market rather than by actions that the firm took (or did not take). They include:

- demand issues;
- conflicts;
- consolidation/panel management issues.

### Category 2: Terminations within law firm control

This category covers the factors caused more by specific actions that the firm took (or did not take). The areas of risk in this category are of greatest concern, because in these cases there are very few second chances and they are also avoidable. They include issues relating to:

- servicing;
- attitude;
- value;
- quality.

As it can be so difficult to resurrect a relationship damaged by category two factors, the onus needs to be placed on damage limitation while the relationship is strong. Our research shows that many law firm–client bonds are weakened by issues that could have easily been avoided through more effective forward planning and better client communication – ideally through systematic feedback.

Many of the GCs we interviewed for the Sharplegal 2013 study told us that they had dropped a firm because of a specific issue that disappointed them so much that they would not work with the firm again.

The following highlights the most common watchpoints.

**Being too expensive**
Nineteen per cent of all respondents said they had fired their law firm simply because it was too expensive – the second most commonly cited reason after the work finishing. It is often the smallest items on a bill that are the most frustrating, so it is worth

looking at fees from the client's perspective. Are you charging for something that the client could have done in-house? Are there ways in which you could work more quickly and efficiently to deliver greater value for your clients? Given that the point at which a service becomes 'too expensive' is highly subjective, it is useful to look at the factors that generally fuel the perception of excessive cost.

## Value and service quality

Clients often report that when quality of service or work has fallen below par it leaves them with a perception that the firm has offered poor value and was too expensive. Another common client complaint is that they feel they are billed for every second of lawyer attention: 'I am not particularly happy with some of the service I've received in certain business and practice areas. They also invoice me every time I pick up the phone to them' (UK, Financial Services).

These issues have very negative consequences on clients' perceptions of their value within the relationship with their law firm. Clients want to feel as though their firm is investing time in achieving a good outcome, not just in achieving a good income. Indeed, Acritas' Sharplegal research shows that when measuring the value clients receive from their firms, they consider their legal spend as a whole. They tend to compare the billing practices adopted and value delivered by smaller, cheaper firms alongside those of much larger, premium global firms doing more complex work.

## Quality of advice

Clients need advice to be given in a business context. This allows them to use it in a practical way to address the business problem they are facing. Slow, incomplete or overly technical advice that requires internal resource to translate it into business-ready actions can damage the client relationship: 'Expensive and impractical. Not business-focused, too much about theory. That's what I mean about practical, they're very smart lawyers but they only think about the law and they don't know how to solve a problem creatively' (Canada, Retail/Wholesale). By altering the attitude adopted towards clients, becoming more client-focused and meeting clients halfway, law firms stand to reap the rewards of stronger relationships and reduce the chance of client dissatisfaction.

## Competitive pressure

The influence of competition runs through many areas of dissatisfaction. In an intensely competitive landscape, it is of paramount importance to understand how your firm is perceived and performing vis-à-vis the other firms your clients are working with. Any firm that has dealings with your client is contributing to the competitive environment and having an influence on the way you are perceived. Regardless of the scope or complexity of work that each of you is providing, there will be areas of the relationship, such as responsiveness, billing practices and proactive communication, which clients generally assess across the board. It is therefore important to be thinking ahead of the competition and to be the one raising standards for others to match.

## Falling short of client expectations

Gauging expectations is notoriously difficult and yet crucial to the health of any relationship. The best way of avoiding misalignment in this area is to ask clients what their expectations are for each matter, around service levels, billing, response times and communication methods – and to ask them regularly.

Clients need to feel that their lawyers are listening to them, so firms must demonstrate that they have listened by adopting an approach that aligns with clients' needs at every step. This does not necessarily involve making major changes to service delivery but just beginning with an open conversation and continuing with proactive communication and dialogue. Using the client's language and respecting their wishes are valuable actions in building trust. Offering an objective forum for clients to feed back after a matter has concluded or conducting periodic relationship reviews can strengthen understanding and build loyalty.

## *The importance of client feedback programmes in building client understanding*

Although client feedback programmes are on the increase, the rise is beginning from a very low base. In Acritas' 2010 Sharplegal study, only 27 per cent of global law firm clients said they had been asked to give formal feedback on the performance of their primary law firm. The results also revealed that 89 per cent of in-house counsel interviewed said they wanted to see improvements in the service they received from their main law firms.

The disparity between clients' willingness to talk about their requirements and law firms' reluctance to seek this information represents an immense missed opportunity. Law firms that actively implement client feedback programmes are in prime position to improve the service they deliver to their clients and to increase their client loyalty and retention levels as a result. Quality of service builds lasting relationships, drives profits and is crucial to any business, especially when operating in a competitive marketplace.

Formal client feedback is central to understanding clients' needs, aspirations and expectations. Its results also have wide-ranging applications, from improving the quality and efficiency of day-to-day meetings to providing early warning of threats to the relationship.

However, not all client feedback programmes are equally successful. The following list outlines 10 golden rules for achieving client feedback excellence:

1. **Set clear goals.** The best client feedback programmes are based on objectives that form part of a wider client service approach. Some fundamental questions worth asking before embarking on a client feedback programme include:
   - Do we really want feedback from our clients?
   - If so, how will we capture it?
   - When will we need the results?
   - How will we use the insight?
2. **Get buy-in.** The best client feedback programmes have the full support and backing of leadership. When senior management endorse the need for client engagement reviews, they commit resources to ensure the process runs smoothly. This complete backing insures against the damaging scenario of

conducting feedback research and failing to follow up on the findings – arguably worse for client relationships than not asking for feedback at all.

3 **Assign responsibility.** Embarking on any research project demands a commitment of time and energy. The most valuable programmes are led by well-briefed individuals who oversee the whole project, working to tightly defined objectives agreed by senior management. The time it takes to prepare for a research project will have been factored into the nominated person's workload and they will have a set timescale to work to.

4 **Don't cherry pick your clients.** There is a great temptation to put forward only the clients whom you think will give a glowing report. However, firms can lose faith in the value of client feedback when they unwittingly turn their research programme into an opportunity for self-congratulation – and learn little as a result. As the old adage goes, we learn most from our mistakes.

5 **It takes time.** It's possible for client feedback research to be conducted as a 'quick hit', but short-termism affects research results. The best client feedback programmes are at the heart of client service strategies and conducted with a view to the long term. It is important to plan for the various stages, including:
   - objective setting;
   - establishing a database to record results and ensuring that they are accessible to partners;
   - selecting and briefing a research partner;
   - agreeing research criteria;
   - providing lists of clients for interview;
   - conducting the interviews;
   - drafting, agreeing and executing a follow-up plan;
   - reporting to leadership and briefing relevant colleagues;
   - creating learning points for the next round of research.

6 **Appoint an expert or get some training.** It can be tempting to conduct client feedback informally, on an ad-hoc basis, as a cost- or time-saving measure. However, this rarely results in feedback of real value. The circumstances under which client interviews are conducted, as well as the method used, can make a big difference to the answers given. Clients often feel able to give the complete picture to a third party but might not be as candid when offering feedback directly to a member of the firm. It is also easy to lead and bias an interviewee, so even if you decide that budgets won't stretch to employing a research partner, it is critical to get some training in interviewing techniques to ensure that your research results are valid.

7 **Set a budget.** Conducting research requires a commitment of time and money. If your budget is very restricted, be realistic about what you can achieve and employ more economical methods, such as web surveys. Conducted consistently, over time, they can provide very valuable insight. Where budget is more plentiful, so are the options. The decision here is what the optimum mix of

research methods will be for the right level of contact. An extremely comprehensive and detailed analysis of your client servicing is possible when you combine the results of quantitative and qualitative telephone interviews with face-to-face interviews conducted among your most business-critical clients.

8. **Act on the feedback.** This should be the primary reason for conducting client feedback and must never be 'left until later'. There is no better way to waste your and your clients' time than by conducting research into their opinions only to do nothing with the responses. Smart firms place client insight at the heart of their client management programmes and build their strategies around client needs. The way in which you plan to use your research results should be considered at the outset when setting your objectives. It is also wise to have a plan in place for how you will deal with feedback – both positive and negative – and how you will communicate findings to clients and employees.

9. **Continuous improvement.** Conducting one-off research is worthwhile for testing service levels around discrete projects. However, one-off research for long-standing clients is of much less value. Gauging relationships over time helps militate against major changes in service levels that can occur when client contacts or lawyers assigned to a certain client change. Client feedback programmes are also important relationship-builders. Many clients are eager to give their opinion and welcome the opportunity to take an objective view of the health of the relationship.

10. **Make client feedback part of your culture.** This is the ultimate aim. When seeking the views of your clients becomes central to everything you do and ensuring that your services are built around clients' needs and evolving requirements, you will have achieved client feedback excellence! It is not only the client who will benefit. This win–win scenario will ensure that you are in the best possible position to prevent clients from getting itchy feet or, at worst, you will hear about the problems brewing before those feet walk away. In addition, a little-exploited yet highly lucrative side of high-quality, regular client feedback research is that you are much more likely to be the first to hear when your client has new requirements.

In addition to client feedback programmes, emotional intelligence is vital. Reading the changing signals that your clients give off can make the difference between mistakes becoming fatal or merely being written off as part of the ups and downs of the relationship. The onus is on law firms to be vigilant, ask questions regularly and act on the answers clients give.

Overall, the clients we have interviewed say that they value an effective two-way flow of communication being established early on and feedback being gathered – whether formally or informally – and acted on regularly throughout the life of the relationship.

## *Brands build business*

We have highlighted the importance of ensuring that firms understand each client's business and culture in order to win their trust and loyalty. Another crucial part in building rapport comes in the form of the law firm's brand and reputation. A strong, distinctive brand can lay foundations for understanding and act as a form of guarantee that a certain set of expectations will be fulfilled.

Choosing a recognized and well-respected law firm has the effect of reducing the risk inherent in the selection process. Well-defined brands also act as a form of shortcut, making life easier for time-pressed in-house teams who have little opportunity to seek out firms languishing in obscurity. Clients naturally gravitate towards the practices that have an established reputation for excellence in the areas in which they need support.

The promise of fulfilled expectations, as well as high levels of reassurance that the strongest brands can bring, commands a premium price that clients are willing to pay. In this way, firms that invest in developing clearly defined offerings and are accomplished at communicating them to clients and prospects are repaid many times over. Successful brands engender confidence and higher levels of client satisfaction and retention, which in turn lead to greater market share and increased profits. There is a strong correlation between the actions that law firms can take to help build their brand in the eyes of their clients and those that strengthen client relationships and understanding (Table 6.1).

## *Legal market research and competitive advantage*

In a much more competitive marketplace, law firms are finding that they have to look beyond their traditional armoury of expertise and reputation to win and retain clients' business. The cost of taking risks has become higher and forward-thinking firms are seeking ways to militate against mistakes. For many, legal market research is proving to be a central part of the answer. Law firms that have been quick to seek out market intelligence and sufficiently open-minded to take heed of its predictions have, in most cases, gained considerable ground.

Many early adopters of legal market research have secured first-mover advantage by:

- establishing offices/alliances in international growth markets before their competitors;
- spotting emerging client needs before their competitors;
- restructuring their services and approach to meet demand as it grows;
- developing flexible billing practices;
- adopting a client-focused business model.

In many cases, it is the marketing teams within firms that are ideally positioned to drive change. A client-first mindset, commercial nous and familiarity with research as a foundation for strategic planning are natural to marketers.

As such, marketers can bring great strategic value to their businesses. Encouraging the use of research as a basis for identifying clients' needs and providing advice on how best to tailor the firm's approach to meet those will reinforce the value of marketing among the firm's leadership and help to build a strong, central future position for the function within firms.

**TABLE 6.1** Important steps for improving brand health and client relationships

| DO: | DON'T: |
|---|---|
| **Lead by example**<br>Strong leadership and clear vision have the power to unite teams, accelerate growth and transform brands. Leaders who live and breathe the firm's values make it easy for the rest of the firm to follow suit and deliver the consistency of service that internationalizing clients demand. | **Wait for the market to 'return to normal'**<br>Sharplegal research shows that clients' needs now dictate the future shape of the profession. The forces of internationalization, commercialization and the quest for value are driving change that is here to stay. Failure to adjust = the risk of going bust. |
| **Research existing perceptions of the firm**<br>Your internal view can differ radically from the external opinions held of your firm. Strong brand positions are achieved only when law firms' promises meet clients' expectations. | **Overpromise**<br>Time-pressed clients place a high premium on honesty. Attempting to win extra work by exaggerating your capabilities wastes time and money, erodes trust, degrades your brand and scuppers your chances of winning any future work for which you are best suited. |
| **Invest in finding out exactly what clients need – now and in the future**<br>The fastest-growing firms are those that get close to their clients and customize their service to meet clients' anticipated needs. Law-firm brands associated with speed, service quality and value for money win loyalty. | **Assume what clients want**<br>It is easier to apply broad principles in your approach than to get to know the individual needs of clients and prospects. Yet failure to cater for your clients' specific needs simply opens the door to more flexible competitors. |
| **Constantly reinforce brand values**<br>Every single interaction that a member of a law firm has with colleagues, clients, prospects, recruits and the wider world has the power to alter perceptions of the brand. Ensuring that the firm's values are clearly understood and upheld in all communication builds brand strength. | **Let the brand grow organically**<br>The most successful brands generally start life in natural areas but thrive as a result of very careful cultivation. Brands need regular attention to keep them in shape and thriving. Anything that threatens the integrity of the core brand must be nipped in the bud. |

# LESSONS ON UNDERSTANDING

From our contributions on the theme of Understanding, here are our top 10 lessons for marketing and business development leaders:

1. **Why you need to listen:** you can uncover valuable insights into your current client relationships, market trends, future opportunities and competitor positioning just by listening to your clients better. Although most firms claim to be client-focused, evidence suggests that they are still not very good at listening.

2. **Who needs to listen:** everyone needs to listen to and understand their clients. It should be part of your culture. What you hear and how you respond should be the principal influences on strategy and decision-making in your firm.

3. **Formal listening:** understanding clients is so important that the process shouldn't be left to chance. Although you should have a firm-wide culture of listening and understanding, it is best practice to run a structured, formal client listening or feedback programme.

4. **Objectives:** be clear what you want to get out of a client listening or feedback programme. If you understand your objectives, that will help influence programme design such as who to talk to, who leads the interviews, what questions to ask, whether you adopt a qualitative or quantitative approach to questioning, and so on.

5. **Openness and engagement:** interviewing clients will be seen as a threat to some of your colleagues, particularly if something is not right in a relationship or on a project. You cannot avoid tough conversations or cherry-pick clients who will give only a positive response, but it should not be seen as a process designed to identify problems, apportion blame and right wrongs. It needs to be open, positive and forward looking.

6. **Independence:** although different people can be involved in a client conversation, you will most likely get the best response when your interviewers are independent and can interpret the client response objectively and dispassionately.

7. **Continuous improvement:** you can never say you have heard everything and can now stop listening. Clients' needs will always evolve and change, so you need to listen, understand and improve continuously.

8. **Commerciality and partnership:** different clients have varying requirements, but as a general trend they are now more demanding; they are looking for commercial business partners, not just technical advisers; and they expect

their advisers to have a full understanding of their business priorities, opportunities and constraints.

9 **Training and habits:** capabilities in listening to and understanding your clients' business needs can be taught and learnt, as can corresponding commercial skills.

10 **Action:** listening to and understanding your clients' priorities is worthless unless you then take appropriate action. If you are not going to act, after your clients give their time to tell you what they think, you are better off not asking in the first place.

# THEME THREE
## Connecting

# Introduction to the Connecting theme

> *If you build it, he will come.*
> **(THE VOICE OF LEGENDARY BASEBALL PLAYER, SHOELESS JOE JACKSON, TO KEVIN COSTNER'S CHARACTER IN THE MOVIE *FIELD OF DREAMS*)**

We often sugar-coat the past, but from today's perspective, marketing in the second half of the 20th century looks quite straightforward, especially in consumer-led businesses with chunky marketing budgets. It would certainly appear that marketing lacked the complexity and ambiguity faced by today's practitioners trying to understand and engage with the modern customer.

We may be guilty of trivializing matters, but the business of marketing then seemed to centre on working out what product or service you wished to promote and designing a communications campaign to get your message across in the best possible way. Communication was one-way, from the business to the customer (why would you be interested in hearing anything back from them?) and the media channels available for you to 'push' your message were limited. Customer choice and, maybe more significantly, access to information on that choice were restricted too. As long as you had a decent offer and pushed hard enough, you stood a good chance of success.

Even in the professions, the prevailing view was that all firms were 'market leading', however they chose to define that, and their clients depended upon their professional expertise. Marketing as a concept or investment decision was an anathema to many, but for those firms that did engage, it really just involved the process of designing communications and public relations activity to promote their chosen expertise.

Jump forward to today and the landscape on every aspect of marketing mentioned above has changed, leading to the overwhelming need to connect with your customer or client, not just send them messages that suit you.

First, on choice, it is abundantly clear that across markets the customer or client can now benefit from an explosion of choice. It may work for Kevin Costner and his 'Field of Dreams', but in business and the professions it is certainly no longer true that if you build it they will come. In the last section we looked at how it was essential that you first listen to your clients before designing or updating your product or service. Your offer must be shaped around them, not you, if you are to have any chance of standing out from the crowd.

More importantly, clients not only have choice but also have unprecedented sources of information on that choice. They no longer have to rely on you to find out what you have to offer and whether that best suits their needs. Increasingly, you and your communication channels are the least preferred options for sourcing trusted information. Why should a client have faith in what you say about yourself when there are so many other information sources and indicators? The legal sector has had the benefit of the Legal 500 and Chambers & Partners rankings for many years, and other professional sectors have similar independent guides.

Secondly, on channel, we have always had independent research, industry directories and personal references, alongside traditional media channels, to assist clients to build a portfolio of information to help them make their choice of professional adviser. But now the proliferation of information channels, many through social media, adds further to the available data points. We will all be familiar with consumer rating sites, such as TripAdvisor.com, but there are now a growing number of similar sites that allow people to rate businesses, mainly in relation to what it's like to work there, with probably glassdoor.com the best known. If a client wants to choose a professional adviser, surely they will want one where people rate their own business highly?

The significance of many of these new channels, notwithstanding the number, is that not only can you not influence the information clients find out about you, but you may not even be aware of the exchange. You are certainly no longer in control, which is a concept alien to a traditional marketer who has seen both the shaping and dissemination of company information as central to their role. It has almost defined the power and influence of a marketer in a firm. Marketers need to let go of their obsession with control and accept that they are just another player in the information exchange. They can engage and hopefully influence, but they cannot control any more.

To compound the ambiguity in the decision-making process, the rise of the formal procurement process in client organizations means that your direct client – the person who instructs your firm and judges your project performance – may not even be gathering information on you and deciding whom to appoint. He or she can probably influence the process, but may have as little control over the decision as you do.

The change in choice and channel just confirms that for our third C – communication – marketers have to accept finally that it is not a one-way street. Marketers cannot invest all their efforts and resources in a campaign to push out information and messages and expect success. They have to aim and want to connect with their clients and facilitate a genuine two-way conversation whenever and wherever the client chooses. Note that it is not for the marketer to decide the channel here. As individuals, let alone as teams, clients expect to be able to engage through multiple channels – face to face, video, social, online – and sometimes all of these regarding the same topic or project.

A firm can still try to initiate a conversation and pick a preferred topic and channel, but it is the client's choice whether to connect. The good news for professional services firms is that in a world of ever-increasing communications traffic, the value of great content rises to a premium. Today, you need to be saying something really interesting and topical for anyone even to notice.

Professional services firms, with all the brainpower and ingenuity they command, are gold mines of rich content. Pity the poor proverbial widget manufacturer trying to find something valuable and topical to say. However, firms have a great track record of neither using that content in a creative, engaging and timely manner, nor thinking first about what the client may want to hear.

In this section, we explore the concept of connecting in terms of what it means today, especially in a world increasingly dominated by digital media, and look at a number of examples where firms have used great content, shaped to address a client need, to engage in a conversation that addresses a client issue and ultimately leads to new business.

In the following chapters we have contributions from Nick Masters at PwC, who challenges us to think about whom you and your clients really trust, and what that means for your communications strategy. We also hear from Alastair Beddow at Meridian West and Dale Bryce at APSMA, who both bring new ideas and insight to the growing trend for 'thought leadership' in professional services marketing communication.

# From communities to cohorts

07

**NICK MASTERS,** Head of Online, PwC

**Profile:** Formerly a print journalist, Nick has been involved in online communications since building his first site in 1995. He was a founder of a start-up venture during the dot-com boom in 1998, but has spent the past decade at PwC, where he is currently global head of online.

In this chapter we discuss the need to create new marketing and communications approaches based on a wider market shift in the way clients search for, accept and consume business information both from organizations and also from each other.

## Why marketing isn't working

If the definition of madness is repeatedly doing the same thing and expecting different results, many marketers must be starting to question their sanity, as their tried and trusted methods begin failing to deliver familiar outcomes. After years of steady growth, e-mail marketing response has fallen off a cliff, search advertising spend is rising without comparative increases in leads, traditional PR impact is waning and core website traffic is softening. Even mobile apps – where they exist – are demanding ever-greater levels of nurturing and refinement just to stand still.

Given that the bulk of 'digital' marketers work in organizations still rooted in a legacy analogue world, this is doubly disturbing: first, because their reporting is clearly going to show up these changing trends over time; and secondly, because having just won around challenging stakeholders to a new way of thinking and acting, the sands have shifted again, and a new set of ideas have to be argued through and stakeholder support sought. This time around, however, the stakes are somewhat higher. The changes that digital technologies are now infusing into the business landscape are far more fundamental and deep-rooted than previously, and therefore require a much greater level of understanding and subsequent reaction by businesses.

To stand a realistic chance of adapting to meet these challenges, companies have to make a basic break with their past. However, the gap between a problem and its solution is nearly always further than it seems, because in the words of the old joke, 'if you want to get there, I wouldn't start here'.

Through design, apathy or happenstance, most organizations look at the world from the inside out. While essential to the success of the business, customers are viewed as external to it, and therefore to be accommodated rather than integral to its processes. And this is where the problem starts in an interconnected world.

## What this has changed

Many tracts have been written about the travails of high-profile brands at the hands of their ruthless digital competition, but most miss a fundamental point. It's not so much the technologies that drag down the incumbent but their thinking, despite this being easier and cheaper to change. The best way to understand the implications of the changes is to consider an example that we can all recognize.

For many years our holidays were booked through high-street travel agencies. We turned up at their shops with an idea of where we wanted to go and a budget, and let them do the rest. We ended up going where we wanted or where we could afford. It was a relatively painless, fast, efficient and all-encompassing process, especially where package tours where involved.

Over the past decade this scenario has changed dramatically, as we now spend our time researching our breaks online. We do this because we can now choose new and exciting destinations through search engines, book flights on airlines we've not heard of, and visit multiple sites by any means of transport necessary as we travel between locations of our choosing.

As a result, generally, we spend more time and money now on tailoring our holidays than we used to do through the travel agencies. It flies in the face of the received wisdom of digital (speed, efficiency and cost) but has rapidly become the norm. The reason for this is that we are now in charge of our own content and information needs and, as a result, will invest the time, money and resources in ensuring that we get what we want, when we want it.

From an industry perspective, this encapsulates both challenge and opportunity simultaneously. Ensuring that you are part of a customer's deliberation process now requires a much greater reach than – in this instance – just the travel agents. But that is only one dimension to the problem. Getting known is one thing, but being taken into serious consideration is another.

It may sound perverse, but the concept of a truly interactive internet is a relatively recent phenomenon. While packets of data have happily been pinging backwards and forwards around the wired network since it began, the concept of user interaction only really came to prominence in the mid- to late 2000s in what was then known as Web 2.0.

Since then, for various fairly obvious reasons, all of this activity has tended to be categorized as social media, which is something of a catch-all to define those places and instances where we as customers, consumers, stakeholders or interested onlookers can input into a public discussion. The power and importance of this shift are that it allows us to talk about what we choose, where and when it suits us.

## How mobility drives activity

A major driving factor in this specific development is the unprecedented rise in availability of mobile devices such as smartphones and tablets. In 2014, over 62 per cent of UK adults owned a smartphone, the market having doubled in the past 10 years (Ofcom, 2014). Similarly, the number of tablet computer owners also doubled in 2013, from 12 per cent in 2012 to 29 per cent in 2013 (over 70 per cent of tablets are assumed to be Apple iPads). In the same year (according to the same study), we passed a long-awaited tipping point where more smartphones were in use than PCs. Now users are able – and likely – to consume, share and comment on information at any point of their choosing, in terms of both time and geography. The ubiquity of mobile is so all-encompassing that it has also thrown up its own challenges. Can content created for PCs be properly consumed in this environment, particularly phones, which are a lot more challenging than tablets?

And some challenges are not just presentational, but also functional. Peak times for engaging with online information on mobile devices is not, as expected, in commuting periods and lunchtime, but is between 10 pm and 11 pm. This offers organizations the challenge of structuring themselves to be ready to deal with queries at unsociable hours. If your clients are engaged with content and each other at the end of the day, should you be ready and available at the same time?

## Pros and cons of change

Isn't this all going to create a world of ever-greater noise, where anybody can comment on anything, and where we all get lost in the welter of confusion and conflicting messages that surround every experience or idea? Not according to internet consultant and commentator Clay Shirky, whose response is: 'It's not information overload. It's filter failure' (Shirky, 2008).

Quite simply, we have to learn to deal with the abundance of information that is coming our way, for no other reason than that it is in our own objective interests to do so. We have to begin to curate our own needs and requirements, as we cannot rely on the traditional outlets and sources to deliver on our behalf.

For years, our information came predominantly from the printed press or broadcast media. They sifted through everything they knew and filtered it based on the demographic of their specialism or perceived audience. But now newspapers and magazines are fast disappearing and broadcasters are increasingly struggling to deal with the problem of throughput themselves. Interestingly, both devote much of their time and space to information generated by social media – another case of the media eating itself, just one piece at a time.

Business leaders have invariably grown up with the national newspaper as a daily staple and were probably quite clear about their personal preference. But now they can – and do – have access to all these titles and more, conveniently packaged up through a sophisticated RSS reader (such as Flipbook or Feedly) or more simply on followed Twitter feeds.

Consuming more information in less time, in your chosen environment, is what makes social media so powerful. But it is also increasingly in our own interests to decide where to source our information from – whom we trust, essentially – to prevent things from becoming overwhelming. And lots of us are increasingly adept at this task. Just look at how we already segment ourselves. According to the same Ofcom report, in the UK the average person spends over 24 hours a week online, which is heading towards a working week. Within that expansive period, a quarter of all time is spent on just four or five social media sites. This is more time given over to the social aspect than almost any other part of our lives.

While the plethora of sources makes this more challenging in many ways, it also offers more diversity. Instinctively we look for those that reinforce our accepted ideas and opinions, but it's increasingly impossible to avoid the wider discourse and debate. If nothing else, the matrix of sharing and interconnectivity opens us up to more sources, ideas, individuals and organizations, many of which were unknown to us previously.

With both our personal and professional lives now open to these opportunities, we find ourselves taking a similar approach to both. Individually, we fail to discriminate between the two, and we will happily use either, where it is useful or expedient to do so. This is all great, unless you are charged with communicating the messages of one organization to another, in search of further business.

If our audience (ie us) is individually starting to control and curate our own information needs, and increasingly trust those with whom we choose to connect, how do those traditional models of companies identifying, targeting and tracking their targets stack up in a networked world?

## Disrupting the disruptors – the flight from communities

Quite simply, our personal adoption of disruptive technologies is, perversely, disrupting a function (marketing) that has always prided itself on being disruptive. For a long time now, marketers have been 'warming up leads', 'creating communities' and 'executing engagement strategies'. Many of these activities, though, are no longer credible because the exchange of information between individuals within any specific personal network (cohort) is regarded as more trustworthy or actionable. If one person is recommended to do something by somebody else in their network (even if it's just to read a particular article), it's more likely that it will happen than if compelled to do so by a random e-mail.

It might be convenient for a large organization to ascribe attributes to their clients and targets and call these 'communities', but in an age where we are all bombarded with information, unless what we are sending out is clearly actionable and of immediate interest to the recipient, it will be rejected and ignored. Aggregating content into products, based on such broad assumptions, is increasingly difficult to justify in a world where information flows so freely.

In the wider social context, this is not a new phenomenon. In his paper first published in German in 1887, 'Community and society', sociologist Ferdinand Tönnies

(Tönnies, 2003) identified the shift from smaller communities, which were regarded as definable unitary entities, to a more urban society comprised of fragmented networks of association, or cohorts. Crucially, such associations differed through being made from personal choice rather than external ascription, strengthening an individual's trust in their specific cohorts rather than the arbitrary groups (communities) to which it was assumed they belonged.

This is where it all gets interesting. Businesses require structure and organization to operate efficiently, but also to measure and manage that efficiency. As such, it makes sense for areas of knowledge and expertise to be grouped together internally, and similarly it makes sense to rationalize the marketplace into discrete areas that can be targeted through marketing, business development and sales activity.

However, there is an increasing mismatch between the structured groups used to target individuals and their view of how they wish to find, accept and consume that information. As information becomes an increasingly key commodity in business decision-making, it is imperative that we all understand the nature of this change and operationally adapt to its processes to meet the needs of a world where information is more readily distributed *through* cohorts rather than *to* communities: where communities are defined as structured and defined groups where predominant communication originates one-way from centre to constituents (one to many); and cohorts are unstructured groups, which are self-replicating, and where responsibility for information dissemination shifts to the individuals (many to many).

So how do we begin to move towards 'cohort marketing'? The good news is that a crucial element of it is relatively straightforward – just start creating and distributing useful and relevant content. However, to achieve this aim we have to start to think of information as a utility rather than a support mechanism.

In this model:

- Access to information online means that clients and users can be less loyal. They are guided by who best answers their information needs. Furthermore, they are more likely to trust information recommended within their networks.
- No organization can guarantee to get its messages in front of a desired or targeted audience anymore, as users decide on their own sources.
- Google will be a major factor in deciding the reach and therefore the success of your activities. With various studies showing that Google is used for the vast majority of business search traffic and most business decisions are partially researched online, its dominance in the B2B search market is almost total.

## Cohort market – the content dynamic

Despite this shift, content has continued to be devalued, partly because it has become a commodity and partly because its role is so ill-defined. Much of what we see today is borne out of the last major information revolution in the mid- to late 1980s, when desktop publishing technology (DTP) allowed organizations to emulate the processes of the mass media and produce their own print-based publications.

This development allowed organizations to create and distribute a myriad of attractive and branded print products to their clients and targets. While DTP brought production costs under control, in order to overcome the expenditure and difficulties associated with distribution (postage, administration and so on) companies continued to borrow from the mass media model by aggregating multiple pieces of content together into magazine- or newsletter-style products aimed at the defined communities. The bigger the community, the more content could be packaged together, and the bigger the savings in distribution. This approach is still the norm in many organizations that support sizeable resourcing of print-oriented production. It also dominates thinking around the commissioning of content.

But the market now demands that information is stripped back to its core messaging and is readily available as a unique article, be it a publication, article, comment, white paper, video, webcast, podcast or whatever. This is how the material is indexed, this is how it is searched and this is how it is found. While businesses continue to bundle content together in ready-made packages, the bulk of its intellectual value is lost.

Just as DTP allowed companies to diversify into print publishing, the continued increase in computational power and broadband bandwidth has created an environment where video and audio products are almost as easy to create, edit and distribute as print documents. Despite all this and the evidence of mobile activity outpacing traditional PC-based web browsing, the PDF file format remains as popular as ever. Again, this continues to be based on organizational structure and the ease of production rather than user demand. So, just ask yourself this question: when was the last time you read a PDF on your phone?

We also know that users consume content one piece at a time, and they do not necessarily know or care about the provenance of the information, as long as they trust its referring source. This is what undermines the business model of traditional newspaper publishers. They are now competing with each other on a story-by-story basis and cannot rely on discounts in cover price to shore up a title.

Similarly, companies can no longer rely just on their brand image, size or reach. Clients and targets may initially think of looking to organizations for their information needs, but businesses can no longer rely on that response. It is far easier to type a query into a search engine and find the answer to the question on your mind.

In this way, aggregation of content into a greater whole actively damages the chances of it being found and read online, particularly if you use content to distribute thinking and look for client engagement. Our 'cohort marketing' model needs to be adjusted to one that sweats every asset produced to ensure that the maximum value can be extracted.

This is best done by publishing information individually, in multiple formats, via multiple channels to the widest possible audience. As the user experience continues to diversify towards video and audio, personal blogs, social networks and so on, the onus is going to be on firms, as information providers, to connect with the audience on their terms.

If you are investigating a question and you are predisposed towards watching videos rather than reading documents, you'll choose a YouTube link over Wikipedia. Similarly, if you think someone in your network will know the answer to a question, you may well ask them via Facebook, Twitter or LinkedIn. As a result, it is crucial that we ensure our content is as portable, mobile and shareable as possible.

## Network behaviours are now a social norm

The basic challenge here is simple enough – in an information-rich environment, how do we best reach our clients? This brings us back to the central importance of networks.

This means not just populating our own online properties but using third-party channels. Why start a blog to discuss a business challenge when a LinkedIn group is already doing just this – where anyone can go and join the conversation?

You have to be where your clients are, if you want to talk to them. And now you have to communicate with them via their preferred methods. We may consider this pampering, but they are calling the shots more than ever, and we need to respond to that change. Established business methodologies still group people together based on some form of market segmentation, but the fragmented nature of people's roles and lives means that these ascribed groups are not necessarily understood or recognized by those target groups.

While a fan of Manchester United is as likely to live in Shanghai as in Salford, it is equally true that organizations can no longer generalize about clients based on a single criterion. However, two individuals connected – even indirectly – via a cohort are more likely to take notice of recommendations, referrals or advice based on that network.

It might be convenient for a large organization to ascribe clients and targets to groups or communities but, in an age where we are all bombarded with information, unless what we are sending them is strictly targeted and clearly actionable, it will be rejected and ignored. And when this has happened once, it tends to become a habit. Aggregating content into products, based on such broad assumptions, is increasingly difficult to justify in a world where information flows so freely.

It is still necessary to create original ideas and communicate them, but on an opt-in basis, not an ascribed one. Firms should build networks around ideas, themes and issues, not assumed communities of interest. It is important to be opinionated and succinct, and it is important that our content is available to be consumed by our clients where and when they want it.

## Why you need your employees to be engaged

Where possible, organizations can use their own employees to become the advocates for their products and services. By using these engaged employees, companies can increase not only their reach but also their impact.

When employees are engaged, they are much more likely to actively share information with others. In this way, engaged employees become brand advocates using social media tools.

Research published by Technorati indicates that your employees can reach an audience that is up to 10 times larger than the one your brand is currently reaching (Social Chorus, 2014), and acceptance of a recommendation is on average around 70 per cent higher through personal recommendation as opposed to unsolicited communication (Technorati, 2013). All brands are affected by this client discussion on social media and employees can play a crucial role in bringing a real face to that discussion, not least because we all now trust individual recommendations more than those that come from a brand itself.

If firms encourage employees to become engaged with their cohort groups, they can build a team of positive and effective brand advocates. Then, not only are engaged employees twice as productive, but they can be responsible for up to 80 per cent of your clients' overall brand satisfaction. Enabling employees to become a channel to market will also help them to create their own cohort groups on both the organization's and their own behalf. This in itself will greatly increase the impact of any given activity.

Clearly, cohorts and communities can often be one and the same thing, in the same way that in the natural world, fish form shoals with different types of fish (cohorts), but also form schools with the same species of fish (communities). Where this simplifies the task of producing and distributing information, this should be encouraged and seen as a bonus, rather than an excuse not to change.

## Honing content

**CASE STUDY**  PwC

The fact that this change has largely already occurred is relatively easy to test. A while ago at PwC, we published a traditional print-style publication (PDF format), which had been going for a number of years and had an associated mailing list (supposedly of clients and targets). We published the document as normal and sent an e-mail to the ascribed mailing list. Simultaneously, we also broke the document into a number of discrete parts – written, video, graphic and data – and distributed these individually on the website and via social links.

The outcome was startling. The content was viewed much more often in its broken-down forms (by a factor of over 700 per cent) and most of the users supplied information about themselves in exchange for access. Video views were also up by over 500 per cent, with the vast bulk of the traffic delivered via search and social links.

The increase in views was striking, but the real story was the data. Not only did the user-supplied data far outstrip the number of clients on our mailing list, but also the cross-over between the two was below 10 per cent. This did not indicate a problem with our lists, but highlighted a much more important development. This outcome showed that our clients are most interested in content when it is relevant to their needs. Our tendency as marketers and communicators is to force the issue and encourage clients to engage with content when we publish it – irrespective of whether or not it coincides with their interests.

Locating the intersection of what somebody is interested in and what you are talking about is an inexact science – but if you address the issues on the mind of the audience you are trying to reach, in the language they choose, and make it available where they are likely to look, your chances of success will increase.

Do this consistently over time, and you'll find that your content does find a home. Furthermore, it may often not be the one that you originally intended.

## Communities to cohorts – a conclusion

The all-pervading nature of cohort networks has created a communications environment that is more challenging than ever. To begin to address the new orthodoxy, it's important to understand that existing publishing models are as outdated and flawed as much as they are also now inefficient and wasteful.

These models need to be reviewed to address the challenges in commissioning, producing and distributing content. Similarly, it is crucial to accept accelerated adoption of mobile-enabled technologies in the most mutually beneficial way possible. All organizations must gear up to support a multi-channel media strategy in terms of both production and distribution of content through external channels – without limiting the scope of that content's reach.

Possibly the biggest challenge is to dismantle programmes aimed at communities of interest in favour of a theme- and issue-based approach – cohort marketing – which can be ramped up based on user engagement, feedback and take-up. This will require the development of a rapid response approach to content creation, which allows for deployment of some resources to react to the market demand.

Only by combining a market-led approach to content creation and active cohort distribution through engaged employees will organizations begin to make sense of the challenges of communicating in the mobile-led digital age. Failure to do so will not lead to overnight catastrophe, but it will certainly test the limits of teams charged with making this a reality of your clients. This is especially true when your clients are ready to do much of it for you, anyway.

# Thought leadership

08

## transforming insights into opportunities

**ALASTAIR BEDDOW,** Associate Director, Meridian West

**Profile:** Alastair is Associate Director at Meridian West. He works with professional and financial services firms of all sizes to develop engaging, differentiated and successful client strategies, business development initiatives and thought leadership campaigns. He has published widely on issues relating to professional services account management, business development and thought leadership.

Succeeding in business sometimes feels like treading water: you expend so much energy trying to stay afloat that you don't propel yourself forward. Senior business decision-makers face on a daily basis a myriad of challenges that threaten both their forward motion and their ability to manage day-to-day tasks. Their agenda is packed with concerns as diverse as spotting strategic opportunities, implementing operational changes and grappling with regulatory uncertainty.

This chapter looks at how firms can address some of these business challenges through the application of thought leadership. It explores the practical steps that those responsible for marketing and business development at advisory firms can take to make their thought leadership outputs as relevant, useful and engaging as possible. It will give direction to those approaching thought leadership for the first time, as well as providing guidance for others with a track record of thought leadership on how to maximize success and support genuine business development.

## The business challenge

An example exemplifies the current pressure on business leaders and how thought leadership can help. Jennifer is the Finance Director of a mid-sized engineering business who wants to fund its aggressive expansion plans by listing the business on AIM, but she and her fellow directors have no experience of listing on an exchange. If Jennifer was to type 'listing on AIM' into a search engine, what would she find? The first page of Google results could provide links to the London Stock Exchange website, a couple of press articles and reports from professional advisers.

This illustrates how thought leadership can help individuals reframe their business challenges: how do I list my business on AIM and what can I learn from others who have done so before me? Often thought leadership is the vehicle through which individuals have their first interaction with an external advisory firm. Thought leadership can help move clients and potential clients through the sales process towards a paid-for instruction, and is particularly helpful for confirming a firm's credentials on a topical business issue.

## Definition of thought leadership

Professional firms are repositories of interested, engaged and intelligent individuals who have points of view on the issues of the day. Yet, time and again, clients of these firms cite significant frustrations that this knowledge is difficult to tap into without calling up a fee-earner and facing the prospect of a bill for a 20-minute phone call. Thought leadership provides a way for a professional firm to showcase this insight and expertise in an easily digestible format. With this in mind, I define thought leadership as:

> A research-based publication or campaign on a subject of current interest, produced with the aim of attracting media coverage, building a firm's brand and providing opportunities to engage a wide range of external and internal audiences including clients, prospects and colleagues.

This definition is purposefully broad. The most effective thought leadership supports not just brand-building and PR coverage, but genuine business development activity. It offers a hook for a business conversation, giving a firm's fee-earners the confidence to discuss the issues at the forefront of their clients' minds supported with evidence taken from research in the market. Thought leadership can provide a crutch for those fee-earners who need it, taking the fear factor out of providing a view on a non-technical subject.

The definition of thought leadership has also widened in line with new ways of consuming content. Online short-form content, such as blogs, videos and infographics, has proliferated alongside long-form PDF reports to satisfy the requirements of time-poor executives. As the range of material considered as thought leadership snowballs, a drive towards quality (rather than quantity) will be increasingly important for professional firms to differentiate their ideas. Firms that want to maximize their return on thought leadership spending are now opting for a more commercially engaged model of thought leadership, which drives business development and is better integrated with other forms of client engagement.

**FIGURE 8.1** Five simple criteria for assessing excellence in thought leadership

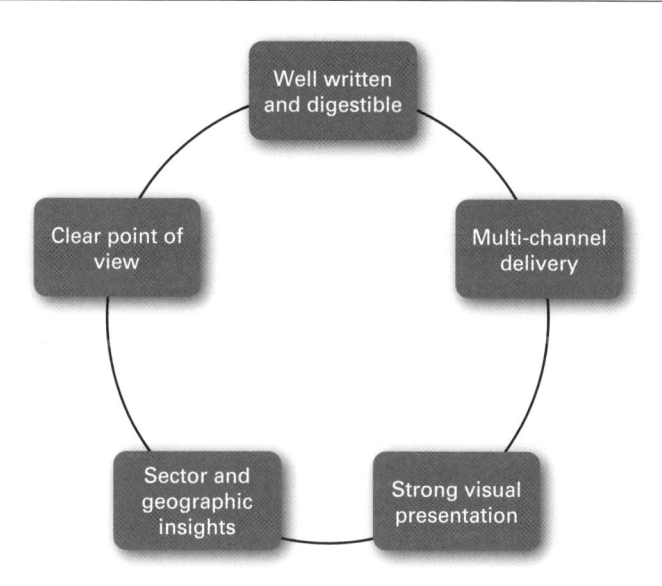

```
              Well written
            and digestible

Clear point of                    Multi-channel
    view                            delivery


        Sector and      Strong visual
        geographic      presentation
         insights
```

# Five criteria for excellence in thought leadership

Every day, professional firms around the world release hundreds of pieces of thought leadership. What separates the good from the great (Figure 8.1)?

1 **Well-written and digestible:** it sounds obvious, but excellent thought leadership needs to read well; it is surprising just how much material fails to engage because ideas are poorly communicated. Effective thought leadership makes judicious use of the material available, including concise summaries and easy-to-digest takeaway points. The tone should be practical rather than academic, commercial rather than technical.

2 **Multi-channel delivery:** the campaigns that engage the widest audiences are those that cater for different ways of consuming content. An inventive online roll-out strategy helps to showcase a firm's experts in multiple settings. Recycling content across multiple delivery channels is a time-efficient way for marketers to enhance the reach of any campaign.

3 **Strong visual presentation:** don't underestimate the power of visual appeal. This does not simply mean having an attractive front cover, though striking visual representation of the themes of a report can definitely help. The presentation of data should excite the reader and not distract from the key messages. Visual frameworks help create proprietary intellectual property (IP) and add to the eye-appeal on the page.

4 **Sector and geographic insights:** effective thought leadership personalizes insights as much as possible to different audiences. Articulating sector and geographic perspectives on macro-issues through case studies or expert views is a useful way of showing the relevance of ideas and concepts to each reader.

5 **Clear point of view:** poor thought leadership offers a series of facts with little context or interpretation; it describes issues and problems without considering solutions. Effective thought leadership, on the other hand, provides a clear call to action, highlighting the 'so what?' in any research. Having a firm's experts provide a point of view on issues demonstrates expertise and credibility. Focusing on the practical implications of a thought leadership topic provides hooks for business development conversations.

These five attributes set the bar high for excellent thought leadership. For this reason, many leading professional firms have deliberately adopted strategies of doing more through less: choosing to undertake fewer, but better executed, campaigns that reach a wider audience and have a much clearer impact on business development and sales. This can make the difference between a firm having a small amount of successful thought leadership that is actively used, and a lot of thought leadership that sits on a shelf gathering dust.

**CASE STUDY**  PwC's 'Breakthrough innovation and growth'

In the autumn of 2013, PwC launched a global thought leadership campaign, 'Breakthrough innovation and growth' (PwC, 2013). It was one of the largest campaigns of its kind launched by PwC and was based on over 1,750 interviews with senior C-suite individuals in more than 25 countries. PwC published a report exploring the changing dynamics of innovation, with practical examples and case studies illustrating how any organization can enhance and refine its innovation capabilities.

'This campaign was crucial for establishing a clear link between the PwC brand and innovation', said Sarah McQuaid, PwC's Global Marketing Director for Consulting and Deals, who coordinated the campaign. 'To support this positioning we took three clear decisions up front: to articulate the business benefit of enhanced innovation capability, to showcase PwC's range of experts in innovation and related fields, and to extend the innovation conversation with our clients beyond the one-off hit of the global launch.'

The report was based on extensive primary research, so PwC was able to model the link between superior innovation practices and revenue uplift. The leading 20 per cent of innovators surveyed had enjoyed faster growth rates, a point made clear on the front cover of the report. 'To grab the attention of the reader, we put our central finding on the front cover. $250 billion is a figure that tends to make the C-suite sit up and listen,' says Sarah.

Another benefit of undertaking such a comprehensive piece of research is that it created networks internally within PwC that had not existed previously. 'Innovation is a multifaceted topic. By drawing out perspectives on issues as diverse as tax, organizational design, people management and supply chain, we were able to connect individuals within PwC who might not have previously worked together', added Sarah. 'This has ultimately enabled us to offer a more coordinated service to our clients.'

'Breakthrough innovation and growth' provided a springboard for multiple spin-off thought leadership pieces exploring innovation within different industry sectors or geographies. 'The global campaign was led by a small group of stakeholders centrally, but individual sector and territory teams within PwC then had autonomy to take the research and produce thought leadership outputs that would help them best engage directly with their own clients and markets', says Sarah.

For PwC, the investment of time and resource has yielded a successful campaign with a long shelf life. Over a year after the global launch, sector and country teams continued to publish their own spin-off collateral. The global campaign has also generated videos, blogs, online diagnostic tools and opportunities for PwC experts to speak at conferences and in the media.

The lessons for success from this campaign were:

- Provide hooks for readers by clearly articulating business benefit.
- Extend the shelf life of a campaign by tailoring to multiple audiences.
- Leverage insights over multiple delivery channels.
- Use thought leadership as a platform to create internal networks.

## Making the business case for thought leadership

With marketing budgets under intense scrutiny and with difficult decisions to be made about where to prioritize resources, how can marketers best convince a sceptical partnership or executive committee that a thought leadership budget is money well spent?

First, consider your ambition and scale. Not every thought leadership campaign needs to be as extensive as PwC's 'Breakthrough innovation and growth'. Significant impact can be achieved with a more modest budget. Organizations undertaking thought leadership for the first time should be realistic; it is much easier to make the case for increased budget in year two following a small but successful campaign in year one.

Second, any professional firm that is truly in touch with its clients will recognize that there is a need for thought leadership. Research undertaken by Meridian West has shown that 90 per cent of clients of professional firms say thought leadership and white papers are beneficial for improving the quality of the advice and service received by external advisers (Financial Times, Meridian West, MPF, 2012). Two-thirds (67 per cent) of clients say it is essential for their advisers to understand industry sector issues and trends to deliver successful advice. The voice of clients is clear: thought leadership plays a role in shortlisting which advisers to work with, and in deepening client–adviser relationships in the long term.

Third, and most importantly: thought leadership is not vanity publishing. Frankly, it is a waste of resources to create a campaign just so that your firm can be seen to be talking about the topics that matter. Instead, thought leadership is a worthwhile investment when it supports business development. The chairman of a FTSE 100 company recently told me that he finds it remarkable that firms seem to be waiting for their phones to ring; he, and many executives like him, are far more willing to have commercially minded conversations than professionals realize. The boardroom door is open to advisers, and the firms with relevant and insightful things to say will be able to get their foot through it ahead of their competitors.

## The perfect thought leadership plan – working from the outcome backwards

Behind every successful campaign is a well-thought-through plan outlining the strategic rationale for undertaking the campaign and the tactical approaches that will engage external and internal audiences. The perfect campaign plan works from the outcome backwards. Only by building consensus on the outcome is it possible to gain agreement on the kinds of outputs and research methodologies necessary to meet objectives.

Too often, marketers dive into drafting research questions without properly considering their intended outcome. As Laurie Young neatly observes in his book *Thought Leadership*, 'ambiguity of purpose will dilute the impact of any thought leadership. It will lack consistency, insight and ambition' (Young, 2013: 147). Marketers can avoid 'ambiguity of purpose' by thinking through the following questions:

- What would a successful campaign look like for your clients, potential clients and internal audiences?
- What products and services are fee-earners trying to sell to clients off the back of the campaign?
- In which market segments do you want to focus your business development activities?
- Are there particular client organizations or individuals that you want to target through the campaign – what issues are furthest up their agenda?
- How do fee-earners prefer to use thought leadership with their clients?
- Which fee-earners will take the lead on using thought leadership with clients and communicating the messages to colleagues internally?
- Which research methodologies will give you sufficiently robust insights to support your proposed campaign roll-out activities?

- Which topic areas will resonate most with your target audience and provide the hooks for business development conversations?

Increasingly, marketers are assigning metrics to define thought leadership success. Putting metrics in place at the beginning of a campaign helps focus minds on the outcome and provides greater direction later on during the research, design and analysis phases. A mix of hard and soft measurements can be used, ranging from firm-wide brand-building (coverage in the national and trade presses, online analytics and search engine optimization, and brand awareness and reputation) to individual fee-earner engagement (opportunities to speak at industry events, social media and LinkedIn connections, face-to-face meetings with clients) and financial metrics (sales leads generated, contribution to revenue).

## Choosing the best campaign topic

Choosing the right topic area is perhaps the singularly most important decision during any campaign. A useful starting point is to gather together a small group of internal stakeholders to oversee the project: they should be given clear responsibility for providing input on the research themes and giving a perspective on the research findings. This input can be provided on a one-on-one basis or, often more effectively, by having all stakeholders meet together to discuss the issues.

At this early stage, you can focus on what group members have heard through their recent conversations with clients. What issues are clients currently preoccupied with? In which areas do clients need most help? What issues are coming up on the horizon that clients haven't properly considered yet? These open questions should yield some fruitful topics that might lend themselves to a thought leadership campaign. Having an open discussion up front ensures that people are bought-in to the direction of the campaign and feel that their suggestions have been considered.

In general terms, thought leadership themes can be divided into three broad areas: *growth* (where are the opportunities for revenue generation?); *efficiency* (how can businesses remove cost and increase productivity?); and *risk* (what issues might derail growth ambitions?). Table 8.1 maps out how these themes can be further sub-divided in a 'Megatrends Map' – a framework developed by Meridian West. Growth, for example, encompasses topics as broad as innovation, merger and acquisition (M&A) activity and emerging markets.

The extent to which these themes resonate will differ between sectors (financial services, pharmaceuticals and public sector organizations all have very different priorities) and between different functional roles (what concerns a CFO most will be different from an HR director or general counsel). It is worth considering these multiple dimensions to understand how different audiences will receive a topic area, and how it links to the different service propositions offered by your firm.

To hone the topic area further, it can be helpful to review competitor outputs to understand what similar firms have recently published. Although a thought leadership campaign does not have to be unique to be effective, it is wise to avoid substantially repeating what has already been published without offering a new angle on the material. During the ideas generation phase, some firms run their topic

**TABLE 8.1** Meridian West 'Megatrends Map' for thought leadership topics

| Maximizing opportunities for sustainable, profitable growth |||
| --- | --- | --- |
| **The Growth Agenda** | **The Efficiency Agenda** | **The Risk Agenda** |
| 1. Growth through innovation<br>2. M&A opportunities<br>3. Emerging markets<br>4. Financing growth<br>5. Digitization | 6. Operational efficiency<br>7. Supply chain<br>8. Collaboration<br>9. Attracting and incentivizing talent<br>10. Fiscal considerations | 11. Macroeconomic volatility<br>12. Regulatory burden<br>13. Changing customer demand<br>14. Disruptive competitors<br>15. Governance and reporting |

ideas by a small number of clients to sense-check and shape the themes. Sometimes this is done informally; on other occasions, firms have formal client innovation panels established to co-create ideas for thought leadership campaigns and other client initiatives.

With the topic honed, the internal stakeholder group can develop thought leadership hypotheses. These are ideas that can be validated or disproven through research, such as 'Most businesses are not prepared for the impact of forthcoming EU tax reforms' or 'The majority of businesses will adopt Cloud technology within three years'. These hypotheses begin to give a narrative structure to thought leadership ideas, and provide greater clarity on the story angles that may work better for press coverage or business development. Drafting research questions is much easier when there is consensus on the themes and hypotheses to explore.

**CASE STUDY**  Buzzacott's 'Dispelling seven myths about auto-enrolment'

Pension auto-enrolment is an issue that impacts all organizations in the UK, regardless of size or sector, and so is a topic that lends itself well to thought leadership. 'We noticed that much had been published speculating about the potential impact of auto-enrolment when the legislation was first announced', says Kimberly Bradshaw, Managing Director of Buzzacott's HR Consultancy practice. 'However, relatively little had been published subsequently, so we decided there was an opportunity to produce thought leadership on auto-enrolment targeted at Buzzacott's key market: SMEs and not-for-profit organizations in the UK.'

In spring and summer 2014, Buzzacott undertook research among 100 organizations, contrasting the experiences of larger organizations that had already implemented auto-enrolment regulations with smaller organizations that were still grappling with implementation or had not even begun planning for auto-enrolment. 'The research provided an opportunity to bring together various experts within Buzzacott's Employment Solutions Team – across pensions, payroll, and HR strategy – to present a joined-up view on the implications of auto-enrolment', says Kimberly. A group of senior stakeholders from each of these teams formed an editorial board. They were closely involved in shaping the direction of the research, contributing their perspectives and offering a view on the issues that would resonate most with clients.

Once the research had been carried out, the group was again asked to provide reaction to the research findings. Kimberly sat down individually with members of the editorial board to capture their views and document the practical steps that organizations can take at each point in the auto-enrolment process. 'Although everybody offered their perspective based on their particular area of expertise, what we are ultimately showcasing through the campaign is a collective Buzzacott point of view on the issues', says Kimberly.

In addition to publishing a report, Buzzacott invited clients to an event to launch the campaign. Each of the stakeholders was given responsibility for presenting some of the key research headlines, and Buzzacott's managing partner gave an introduction. 'Because the topic resonated with so many of our clients, the event was very quickly over-subscribed', says Kimberly. The research will now form a core element of the Buzzacott team's interactions with both existing and potential clients over the coming months.

The lessons learnt from this campaign were:

- Involve an editorial committee at key stages in campaign development.

- Use gap analysis to uncover the differences in experience between different market segments.

- Engage clients both online and offline.

- Create a practically-focused report with insights, perspectives and a clear call to action.

## Conducting research and synthesizing data

Research is the backbone of all thought leadership campaigns. While thought leadership insights can be collected in a variety of ways, the most effective campaigns often blend two or more of the following approaches:

- **Online:** online research can be a cost-effective way to gather insight from a wide audience. Pulse polls – half-a-dozen questions that can be answered in just a few minutes – provide a useful snapshot on topical issues. Instant diagnostics and benchmarking studies are also popular means of collecting data online. However, response rates can be low if online research is not positioned or executed properly.
- **Telephone:** telephone research allows for more detailed, nuanced conversations than online research, but it is more costly to execute. Insight from telephone research will usually lead to richer analysis and commentary.
- **Face to face:** face-to-face research allows for more discursive conversations that get into the detail of a given topic. It is particularly useful for generating case studies that can be used in thought leadership collateral.
- **Desk research:** often a lot can be gained by synthesizing or reanalysing existing data sources collected through desk research. Data on corporate deals or stock market performance, for example, can all be used to support research hypotheses.

The best thought leadership synthesizes the findings from these various research strands and weaves them into a compelling narrative, with a clear call to action, supported by robust data analysis. What is most often lacking in thought leadership produced today is a clear, forward-looking point of view on the issues, and intelligent segmentation of data to explore underlying trends and implications for different market groups. Simple frameworks and checklists of practical points or questions for readers to consider can turn an academic discussion of business issues into genuinely useful thought leadership.

**CASE STUDY** Allen & Overy's 'Unbundling a market: the appetite for new legal services'

Not every piece of thought leadership necessarily starts life as a thought leadership campaign; sometimes thought leadership opportunities can arise out of existing strategic research initiatives. In late 2013, Allen & Overy decided to undertake research about the changing needs of buyers of legal services and how the appetite for new legal services would evolve over the medium term. The primary objective of the research was to provide robust market data to support Allen & Overy's own hypotheses about the opportunities for growth in the legal sector and insight about the firm's market positioning. The evidence collected would contribute to a debate about future strategy at the firm's annual partner conference.

Allen & Overy gathered insights from 200 general counsel and heads of legal services at multinational corporates and banks around the world. 'We quickly realized that through this research we were collecting insights that would be highly valuable to our clients, and so it made sense to share the findings back with them', says Michael Michaelides, Associate Director of Business Development at Allen & Overy. The ability to benchmark their views against their peers and to get a first look at trends shaping the market was a powerful incentive to encourage individuals to participate in the research.

A report called 'Unbundling a market: the appetite for new legal services', summarizing the main points from Allen & Overy's strategic research, was released in summer 2014, and is supported by a microsite on the Allen & Overy website (Allen & Overy, 2014). In video content released to support Allen & Overy's 2014 Annual Report, the firm's managing partner and senior partner discuss findings from the research. Each piece of campaign collateral showcases the firm's perspective on the critical issues and Allen & Overy's response to an evolving legal services market. The thought leadership material provides practical questions for readers to consider, based on the approaches of the most innovative legal departments.

In addition, the thought leadership insights have been shared with the firm's account management and business development teams. 'We organized an internal ideas-sharing session so that account teams could quickly get up to speed with the key messages for their clients. We invited along one of the participants from the research and the internal partner sponsor to explain their perspective on the issues', says Michael.

'Unbundling a market' struck a chord with its audience as it became one of the most downloaded legal briefings on www.legalweek.com for August 2014. The lessons from this thought leadership experience were:

- Spot opportunities to create thought leadership collateral from other client insight initiatives.
- Provide a clear point of view on issues dominating the client agenda.
- Share knowledge internally to help account managers use research effectively with clients.

# Effective thought leadership roll-out – don't fall at the final hurdle

After the initial outcome-planning and topic development phases, the roll-out of a thought leadership campaign is likely to be the most time-intensive aspect for marketers. Yet this is too often neglected: it is easy to forget that the intended outcome of thought leadership is not to produce a glossy report, but to engage clients and start business development conversations. Unfortunately, just generating interesting and insightful collateral will not guarantee that business development opportunities follow. At the point of campaign launch, energy levels and momentum have often reached their peak, so how can marketers overcome the final hurdle to implementing a successful campaign?

The easiest next step is to think about how thought leadership material already generated can be recycled into bite-size or 'snackable' content, such as LinkedIn posts, blogs or infographics. Reusing existing material in different channels is an effective way to maximize reach among different client groups. The example of PwC's 'Breakthrough innovation and growth' campaign (see above) illustrates that planning for a staggered multi-channel roll-out can significantly extend the shelf life of a campaign.

One of the most significant trends in thought leadership in recent years has been the rebalancing of the push–pull dynamic. Historically, firms have pushed thought leadership to all their clients via mass mail-outs, in the hope that by spamming enough people at least a small proportion will be interested, open an e-mail, glance at a report and request a follow-up. But it is almost impossible to predict which contacts will engage this way; common sense suggests that this is not the most efficient way of engaging clients. It sends out the signal that the firm isn't interested in understanding the nuances of an individual's business; it is left up to the person receiving the thought leadership to infer how it may be relevant to them.

Instead, professional firms are beginning to adopt techniques that allow for greater personalization. Research by ITSMA (Information Technology Services Marketing Association) suggests that almost half of clients (48 per cent) say they are more likely to consider firms that personalize content marketing to address their specific business issues (ITSMA, 2014). A simple way to achieve this is by having fee-earners contact their clients directly to promote relevant thought leadership collateral. Brief personalized e-mails (using editable templates pre-scripted by a marketer) work well, as do quick phone calls or informal catch-ups over coffee with clients to discuss the issues. In my experience, these personalized approaches can yield up to 10 times as many positive responses as generic mail-outs.

Personalization need not be an onerous process. Getting fee-earners onside up front, and asking them to nominate a manageable number of contacts to follow up directly (say between 6 and 10), can be the best way of ensuring that they resist the temptation to mass-mail their contacts or, worse, to disengage completely. Those who have not been directly involved in shaping a campaign may require additional encouragement: short tablet-friendly resource packs summarizing research headlines with prompts for conversations can help fee-earners understand how thought leadership collateral could be useful for their interactions with clients. Another tip is to task senior associates or senior managers (ie non-partners) with setting up client meetings to share thought leadership insights. They are often more hungry to do so because they are at a stage of their career where deepening and developing their own relationships with clients are key attributes required for promotion.

Technology can also increase the efficiency of personalization: online diagnostic or benchmarking tools, whereby individuals interact with data or compare their answers to thought leadership questions with those of their peers, is a useful way of helping individuals understand the application of thought leadership ideas to their own business context. The best examples of these online tools work where firms share enough valuable insight to sustain the interest of a client, but withhold some information to encourage the client to request a follow-up meeting. This rebalances the push–pull dynamic in favour of the client actively supplying information about their needs and preferences and proactively initiating the next steps in the sales cycle. With any online roll-out, the guiding principle should be to understand how it will help move a client from an online engagement with a firm's thought leadership collateral to an offline business development conversation.

## The future for thought leadership

This chapter has outlined how thought leadership has evolved over the past five years to become a vital tool for genuine business development and relationship-building within professional firms. What trends will shape the development of thought leadership over the next five years? Five areas that will grow in importance are suggested below:

1 **Bespoke content:** firms will expend less energy producing generic content; instead, they will adopt more personalized delivery models for their thought leadership. Online diagnostics, benchmarking and data analytics tools will move into the mainstream as the required technology becomes more intuitive and accessible. Professional firms will follow the lead of B2C organizations such as Amazon or TfL (Transport for London), which already include a high degree of personalization in their marketing communication. Sceptical fee-earners will be won around to the benefits of using thought leadership with clients on a more personal basis. This will soften the line between thought leadership and advice, and should lead to more open, commercially minded conversations between clients and advisers and deeper, long-term relationships.

2 **Growth agenda:** thought leadership has been dominated by risk and efficiency issues as businesses looked for insight to help them survive difficult economic conditions. The growth agenda will bounce back strongly as economic conditions become more favourable and businesses look at ways of using their cash reserves to fuel rapid growth. Risk will remain important, however, as new-found optimism is tempered by caution and uncertainty. Selecting thought leadership topics that reflect, and even anticipate, the changing zeitgeist is important for maximizing client engagement.

3 **Account management:** thought leadership has traditionally been viewed as a separate activity from account management in professional services firms. Yet the boundaries between the two will become increasingly blurred as thought leadership and insights are delivered in more personalized, bespoke ways to clients. A virtuous circle occurs, where thought leadership topics are used to shape the agenda of client account review meetings, and client concerns are fed back into the development of future thought leadership initiatives. This will empower account managers in professional firms (especially those in non-fee-earning roles) to take greater responsibility for sharing market insight with clients.

4 **Curating content:** finding relevant and interesting thought leadership on many professional firms' websites is currently a nightmare: content is hidden away and search functionality is poor. In future, firms will need to give more thought to how their collateral is curated; again, simple lessons can be learnt from B2C organizations such as Amazon or Apple about how users navigate online information. Some professional firms have created more prominent insights libraries on their websites, with more intuitive search and recommendation functionality. Other firms have bolstered the resources available to fee-earners internally. One leading executive search firm, for example, curates customizable business development packs to accompany thought leadership campaigns. This allows fee-earners to easily download executive summary reports, PowerPoint decks and e-mail templates that they can edit and share with their clients and targets. More firms will follow these examples.

5 **ROI tracking:** better technology, more accurate measurement and greater client engagement will lead to more sophisticated return on investment (ROI) tracking. Social media and other online tracking will allow marketers to identify the common attributes of their most successful campaigns and begin to replicate success. It will be easier to demonstrate the top-line impact of thought leadership and hence justify budget. With better information available, marketers should aim to integrate this with customer relationship management (CRM) and client account data to track individual client preferences, downloads and interaction with thought leadership.

## In conclusion – secrets of a successful campaign

Thought leadership at its heart is about packaging up what the most commercially savvy professionals already do on a daily basis: sharing perspectives on issues dominating the agenda of their clients, with a view to helping clients make sense of the issues for their own business. For busy executives trying to tread water and keep an eye on strategic opportunities and risks, external perspectives (especially those supported by robust research and case studies) are incredibly helpful and cement the relationship between client and adviser.

There are no real secrets to successful thought leadership, because the sheer variety of content and delivery channels means that each firm is able to tailor its approach to work for its own purposes. However, to ensure that a campaign is as successful as possible, it is worth remembering these three tips:

1 Focus on the outcome at the beginning to form a consensus about campaign objectives and how thought leadership will be used.

2 Maintain the involvement of a core group of fee-earners throughout to develop a clear point of view on the issues and ensure buy-in.

3 Save some time and energy for the roll-out phase, because this is where thought leadership has maximum impact for both clients and advisory firms.

# Conversation is king
## connecting thought leadership and sales

**DALE BRYCE,** President, Asia-Pacific Professional Services Marketing Association (APSMA)

**Profile:** Dale chairs a board at APSMA dedicated to the provision of a professional development and engagement network for sales, business development, marketing and communications practitioners working for the leading professional services firms in Asia Pacific. He has more than 20 years' services marketing experience. Now with consulting engineering firm Entura, his career also includes positions with Sinclair Knight Merz (now part of Jacobs), King & Wood Mallesons, the Port of Melbourne Corporation and Lloyd's Register.

While content marketing is the topic du jour in an age of social media, more serious consideration should be given to another C-word – conversation. Selling a service requires the establishment of a relationship. This is especially the case in professional services, as recognized through descriptors of some fee-earners as 'trusted advisers'.

Professional services marketers have a key role to play in acting as a catalyst to conversations with clients. In this chapter we will explore how compelling content should be seen not as an end in itself, but as a social lubricant for client engagement and conversations.

In particular, we will see how 'thought leadership', consciously combined with the Challenger Sale (Dixon and Adamson, 2013) process, can act as a tangible demonstration of both expertise and care for a client. Thought leadership – seen as the preserve of marketing – and sales are often kept apart in firms, seen as different processes aiming to achieve contrasting outcomes, but this could not be further from the truth.

Success here requires marketers to be leaders and facilitators of change, pursuits, content generation, client engagement and the implementation of an integrated sales framework. You should expect to be challenged yourself along the way, but, if you can connect the dots, the rewards, both personal and professional, can be plentiful.

## Thought leadership and the Challenger Sale model

I believe that the professional services marketer can, indeed must, act as a discipline specialist, relationship guide and client champion by linking 'thought leadership' with the Challenger Sale process.

Joel Kurtzman is widely credited with creating the phrase 'thought leader' in the mid-1990s, while he was Founding Editor of the Booz & Co magazine *strategy + business*. From this origin, the phrase 'thought leadership' has been warped and confused with magazine content alone. In a BusinessLife.com article accessed in June 2013, Kutzman refined the definition when he said: 'For me, a true thought leader has to have some new important ideas that are worth sharing and that have real application.'

Thankfully now, within most firms, thought leadership is no longer seen as something pushed out into the ether by the marketing team. Rather it is recognized as a means of integrating marketing communications, business development and sales.

In contrast, Matthew Dixon and Brent Adamson in their book *The Challenger Sale* (Dixon and Adamson, 2013) proposed that success in complex B2B sales comes through teaching, tailoring and taking control. Teaching, they say, best takes the form of a challenge, based on a deep understanding of a client's business. The best sales people, Dixon and Adamson propose, are not afraid to share even potentially controversial views.

In the context of professional services, the Challenger Sale model has real application, given that many fee-earners will at times feel compelled to bring particular issues forward to clients. If they don't, they could even be deemed to be negligent. To teach and to tailor requires individual engagement with a client, and this is best done via a conversation, face to face and one to one.

Thought leadership campaigns can be the catalyst for those challenging conversations.

## Left brain vs right brain

The difference between left- and right-brain thinking is now well known. The right-brain–left-brain theory originated in the work of Roger W Sperry, who was awarded the Nobel Prize in Physiology or Medicine in 1981. While studying the effects of epilepsy, Sperry discovered how the human brain's hemispheres operate both independently and in concert with each other (Sperry, 2003).

In general, the left hemisphere is in charge of carrying out logic and exact mathematical computations. When you need to retrieve a fact, your left brain pulls it from your memory. The right hemisphere is mainly in charge of rough estimations and comparisons and makes sense of what we see. It plays a role in interpreting context and a person's tone.

Success in a competitive professional services market requires whole-brain thinking. Although it is fair to say that professional services firms are dominated by left-brain thinking, logic, exactness and computation, we know that there must also be right-brain engagement with the client in an effort to build a relationship based on trust and context.

## Content as a social lubricant

Professional services marketers often have to deal with fee-earners who resist and avoid making personal contact with clients, happy to wait for the arrival of the next 'Request For Tender' or, at the other extreme, approaching the client with a blunt 'sell what you make' proposition.

All the data and client verbatim I have seen reinforce the fact that clients want their service providers to bring forward valuable ideas. They actually want well-thought-through, unsolicited proposals that could potentially solve their problems. As Matthew Dixon, Karen Freeman and Nicholas Toman said in their ironically titled article 'Stop trying to delight your customers' (Dixon, Freeman and Toman, 2010), 'To really win their loyalty, forget the bells and whistles and just solve their problems.'

This confirms that a thought leadership approach can be used as a legitimate reason to contact clients and engage in a deeper conversation about likely challenges and issues. The right content, framed in the right way, can indeed be a catalyst to a conversation with a client and work-winning.

### *Of course, content can build brand too*

The basis of a content marketing approach is often to build brand and reputation and this is, of course, a very valuable thing. Content marketing combined with digital strategy can be very powerful, especially for a new firm in new markets when reputations need to be built.

Great content can do all of this and more. 'More' equates to taking the next step through the sales funnel, in fostering and enabling face-to-face, genuine engagement between fee-earner and client. Imagine being famous for not only your content but also your client focus, partnership approach and proactivity in bringing forward valuable ideas. Imagine your go-to-market strategy being the basis of your brand.

## The marketer as choreographer

The role of a marketer in professional services firms is a challenging one. This is what makes it so interesting. If we revel in our potential difference and don't mimic the traits of our fee-earners, marketers can use a combination of left- and right-brain thinking to facilitate and choreograph the sales process.

We know that the more our people get in front of clients, the more they will win work. As marketers, we can provide the reason for that meeting of minds. Models such as the Challenger Sale process, combined with content marketing approaches, can help marketers to teach, tailor and take control within their firms, to help build reputations and win work.

## *Drive the change*

Sales and marketing within professional services firms is really all about change management. Good marketers have empathy for their (internal and external) clients. Every fee-earner is concerned about winning work. So, I would encourage you not to talk about thought leadership, but instead about winning work. You will then have a greater chance of gaining everyone's attention and leading the agenda.

You should be talking about work-winning as a process, where instead of the weight of effort being at the end, for example documenting the bid, you are looking to re-weight the process towards the front-end, where thought leadership sits. And you should be looking to do all of this for the same cost of sale or less, while also increasing your win rates.

Proactively pursuing the work you want to win, rather than reactively responding to a competitive Request For Tender, is now standard sales process thinking. This is thinking that allows time to consider and combine a more strategic, thought leadership and Challenger Sale approach.

If this looks a difficult shift with your firm, think about which areas of practice are going to be more amenable to a change in approach. I recommend you work initially with a small coalition of the willing, rather than trying to 'boil the ocean' of the whole firm. You can even de-risk the process if you like, and call it a pilot. If you first trial this different approach and it succeeds, others will soon want to come on board.

Questions you should be asking before piloting this approach are:

- Which part of the business is going to be most amenable to change?
- Who needs to win work the most?
- Which team is already most flexible in their thinking?

## *Pursue the work*

Just as you have now selected who you want to work with, get your fee-earners to do the same. If we are going to break out of the bid cycle, we need to get our teams to think ahead, and dream about the work they would really like to win. Which clients and sectors will present the greatest opportunities? You might need to workshop this with them and agree selection criteria too.

Once you have a coterie of opportunities the team is keen to win, drill down further. Who are the decision-makers? Do we know them already? Think job titles as well as people's names. Now think about the issues affecting them. What are their problems now and in the near future? Can we genuinely help them? This is again standard sales process thinking – and thinking that can set the context of a thought leadership programme that aims to engage clients and build reputations that can win work.

Questions to ask include:

- What work do we want to win?
- Who are the people most affected by particular problems?
- Do we have the capability to make their pain go away?
- What do we want to be famous for?

## *Draft the content*

With the context set, issues-rich content can be drafted, with a group of target clients and their specific issues in mind. This is also where the marketing group can come together as a team with a common objective – business development and communications practitioners working in unison.

Journalism skills can help to shape a compelling narrative, in plain English. Client-oriented language is key here, as is simplifying complexity. Most technical practitioners are used to drafting long technical papers to impress their peers and address complex matters in detail. We ask too much of many of them suddenly to switch and draft a snappy piece of client-focused communication.

The ideal is a combination of technical accuracy and well-honed presentation. Often it is best to sit a corporate writer down with the technical expert to extract the most compelling ideas and narrative about a particular challenge facing a sector now and into the near future. The writer can then do what he or she is good at, ensuring time for sign-off by the relevant practice leader for technical accuracy. If your firm does not have in-house corporate writing resources, hire a freelancer. You will save time and money in the long run, and get what you need to drive the sales process.

At this point there is often concern about giving away valuable intellectual property. As always, it is a question of balance; there needs to be enough in the piece to be valuable and credible to a client, while at the same time keeping to its purpose, as a catalyst to a conversation with a client. If we think again of the Challenger Sale process, the focus here should be on the 'teaching', with the 'tailoring' and 'taking control' coming later in the sales process.

In my experience, short (1,500-word) articles work well, especially in terms of being fast to market. Short video interviews also allow the opportunity to bring the issue, and thought leader, to life. And if a thought leader is dedicated enough to the cause, longer-form reports or books too have a real place in the thought leadership armoury.

Whatever the format, content is the bullet in the battle to engage the client. The question then becomes how best to fire that bullet, and ensure it hits the right target.

Questions to ask include:

- What is the real issue at hand here?
- What is new, and what does it mean to the client?
- Who are we promoting as the thought leader?

- Who is best to actually draft content?
- How can we make content generation easy for the practitioner?

## *Engage the client*

If we know that content is not an end in itself, we have to think about how to reach prospective clients, and what to do after that. If we have run a client-focused process, we will also know how our clients want to be reached.

All digital mechanisms have a role to play here, social media as well as the old-fashioned e-mail campaign, subject to meeting the requirements of privacy legislation, of course. Interestingly, some now argue for the return of the hard-copy magazine, as a means of cutting through the increasing digital noise.

Firms will also be familiar with the running of client seminars and boardroom lunches. If you have a honed and compelling narrative in written form, it is easy to verbalize the story at an event or thought leadership forum.

These broadcast methods allow the building of brand awareness and relevance, of the firm and individual practitioners, but a narrowcast, client-focused approach is, however, key to the sale itself. How then to get in front of clients, face to face, and preferably one to one? We need to remember that while clients may not want to be sold to, they do want someone to solve their problems. And they actually do want their professional services firm to think about them, and proactively bring forward valuable ideas, relevant to their business success.

The obvious thing to say is that we can really target the clients we want to work with by just contacting them direct. A proactive follow-up after the dispatch of thought leadership content, offering some free time with a thought leader to discuss a particular issue, makes this a more compelling approach, especially if focused on a client not a firm.

So, who makes the call? Ideally, it should be the practice leader or relationship manager within the business who contacts the client to seek a meeting. We know that this can often be a challenge in professional services, with practitioners often fearful of doing anything that may be construed as cold calling, at least in their minds. If this is an obstacle, real or imagined, the marketer should consider making the call, with permission from the relevant relationship manager.

However it is achieved, a list of client visits needs to be compiled. The point of thought leadership content is to make this process easier. Only in a meeting can a tailored conversation take place with a client. And remember, this is all about solving the client's problem, not providing the opportunity for the nominated thought leaders to give a one-way lecture designed to showcase their brilliance.

Key to the success of this meeting is to set the scene with a client, outlining the issue as you see it, genuinely expressing concern for the client, given the challenge at hand. It is important then to allow the client to respond, outline their particular take on the issue, for them as individuals, and for their business. Only then can the practitioner begin to 'tailor' his or her thinking. All clients are not the same, and they appreciate being treated as individuals.

The fact that you have provided a tailored gift of thought leadership to particular clients will be well regarded. All that needs to be done now is to ask for the work.

Questions to ask include:

- How do we best broadcast the firm's thinking on an issue, and build profile for particular practitioners?
- How do we best then connect with target clients face to face and preferably one to one?
- Who is best to contact the client direct, offering tailored client briefings?
- Who is best to coach and prepare the thought leader on how best to engage with a client, to ensure a genuine two-way exchange of ideas?

## *Ask for the work*

All of this preparation is for nothing unless we ask for the work. Great thought leadership content will indeed generate leads and you will need to be prepared to manage incoming calls. Some of these opportunities will be great, others not. At the same time, we need to remain focused on our beginning, when we prioritized the work we wanted to win. At some point, you need to ask for the work you really want to win, as confronting as this may be to some practitioners.

As usual, it is all in the preparation. Having used thought leadership to provoke the client's response to a particular issue, the next step is to think about how best to frame a feasibility study or unsolicited proposal.

In a complex world, it is likely that a tailored response may require an internal workshop with a range of practitioners to brainstorm the best solution and next steps. A collaborative workshop with the client is also a compelling idea, and according to some sales practitioners, a potential 'billable event' in itself.

Either way, a proposal needs to be developed and put to the client, preferably in a proactive, unsolicited manner. At the same time, we are all conscious of the increasing power of the procurement team within client organizations. Depending on the size of the proposal, and their organizational protocols, a formal, competitive process of appointment may be required. Even if this is the case, your firm will be in the best position by having been proactive in initiating the ideas in the first place.

Questions to ask include:

- How do we best ask for the work, and when?
- Who is best to ask for the work, and do they need help or coaching?
- Are we clear what we are offering?
- Can we solve the client's particular problem as they have articulated it?
- Can we involve the client in the development of the solution?
- Could a solutions workshop itself be a 'billable event'?

## *Leverage your content*

As you work with your expanding internal 'community of the willing', you will over time generate an archive of thought leadership material. Make the most of it, and look for recycling opportunities.

At the very least, I strongly recommend that you build an archive within the framework of the firm's website. It is likely that posting content to the internet will assist in digital distribution. At the same time, take the opportunity of making your firm's website a resource for issues-rich content available to all. Key words and other search engine optimization techniques are also well worth considering.

With our new-found focus on client issues, it is ironic that we can sometimes forget the broader, internal market. All firm practitioners are busy people focused on building their own practice. As such, sometimes they are not completely aware of the capabilities within their firm. Thought leadership circulation lists should include internal distribution to build awareness and encourage cross-selling approaches. And you can begin to enjoy what may become a common comment within your firm: 'I didn't know we did that!'

Thought leadership content itself can also be used to support relevant bids, through inclusion in the appendices of proposal documents, reinforcing the broader value proposition.Questions to ask include:

- How can we leverage a growing archive of thought leadership content?
- Can we make the archive available on the firm's website, for all to see and search for?
- How do we best circulate content internally?

## CASE STUDY  *Insight Trading*

The book *Insight Trading* was written by Nick Fleming and Susanne Cooper in collaboration with a team of marketers and thought leaders at engineering firm Sinclair Knight Merz (SKM – now part of Jacobs) to facilitate a dialogue with key clients about more sustainable approaches to infrastructure projects (Fleming and Cooper, 2013).

SKM took a broad view of sustainability, noting that it required analysis of the economic, social and environment context of projects. A 2010 study (United Nations Global Compact, 2010) involving some of the world's most progressive CEOs revealed that they felt the factors central to creating a sustainable enterprise should be fully integrated into the strategy and operations of a company. However, half of the CEOs surveyed cited complexity of implementation as the most significant barrier to success. The problem for business leaders was to bridge the 'policy–practice gap' – the gap between vision and strategy and practical, on-the-ground action and results.

The authors recognized that a change in mindsets and behaviours was required. The book addressed key technology issues, overall intent, questioning techniques, systems, collaboration, tools and reporting.

Advance copies of the book were dispatched to clients in advance of an international road show. This gift then opened the door for the authors to meet with CEOs and other members of the C-suite. Fleming and Cooper arranged meetings that would have been difficult to organize without the book and indeed that SKM client managers were unable to achieve on their own.

CEOs were not only curious to meet with Fleming and Cooper, but also keen to discuss their problems and potential approaches to solving them. The book ensured that the authors' calls to clients were not cold, but red hot.

*Insight Trading* won work for SKM because it demonstrated that the firm's approach to helping clients was to solve their problems. The book provided a means of combining solutions development with an improved client experience, and built business partnerships along the way.

## Conversation is king – a summary

As professional services marketers we have the privilege of working with some very smart people – people who are trusted advisers to a range of clients. Our challenge then is to influence influential people. In attempting to drive change and a sophisticated thought-leadership-based sales process, we must ourselves become trusted advisers, walking the talk on thought leadership, relationship-building and value creation.

Thought leadership is a powerful and proactive approach to connecting firms and practitioners with their clients. It is also a practical methodology for connecting sales, business development and communications practitioners and processes to build brand awareness, brand relevance and win the work we want to win.

My top lessons are:

- Content marketing is great for building reputations for new firms in new markets.
- Combining content marketing and digital strategy is indeed powerful.
- The real point of content marketing in professional services should be to facilitate deeper engagement between fee-earner and client – conversation is king!
- The Challenger Sale process equals teaching, tailoring and taking control. Thought leadership should be seen as teaching.
- Clients value the bringing forward of valuable ideas. They just want service providers to solve their problems.
- Professional services marketers can build brand and facilitate relationship-building and sales by helping fee-earners to focus on client problems and proactively bringing forward tailored solutions, not selling what firms happen to make.
- You too can be a thought leader, adding value to your (internal) clients and helping them win the work they want to win.

Success requires marketers and business developers to hone their influencing skills and be robust and resilient. If they can do this, the rewards, personally and professionally, can be plentiful for everyone involved. Go ahead – seize the day!

# LESSONS ON CONNECTING

From our contributions on the theme of Connecting, here are our top 10 lessons for marketing and business development leaders:

1. **Opportunity:** in a world where high-quality content is needed to cut through the noise and trusted sources are increasingly valued, professional services firms have a privileged opportunity to build brand, increase authority and establish leadership.
2. **New mindset:** be prepared to ditch many of the traditional marketing models for 'pushing' communications out into the market. You should now be developing conversations and engaging in two-way exchanges with your key audiences, not 'shouting' at them.
3. **Client control:** marketers need to accept that they are no longer in control. The client chooses with whom to engage, where and on what.
4. **Trusted source:** recognize that trust, timing and context are as important as the message. You may have a great message, but if your audience doesn't trust the source or is not looking to engage right now, your efforts will go to waste.
5. **Employee engagement:** the route to your target audience will increasingly be through your employees. Peer-to-peer communication, where individuals trust and engage with others interested in similar topics, is the new model. Make sure your employees are engaged, identify your thought leaders and make sure your content is easy to access, share and curate.
6. **Channel choice:** clients expect to be able to access content where and whenever they choose. Multi-channel conversations and content consumption are the new norm. Even if you're not using a channel, don't assume there isn't a conversation there that concerns you.
7. **Thought leadership's purpose:** thought leadership content offers an excellent opportunity to engage a client and stimulate a conversation, but it needs a purpose and should instigate action. Make sure it answers the 'so what?' question.
8. **Thought leadership and sales:** thought leadership and sales are on the same continuum; they are not separate activities. Marketers are positioned perfectly to connect the two. Make sure every thought leadership conversation and activity is connected to the objective of winning work with target clients and markets.
9. **Bespoke content:** who are you trying to connect with and how can you engage best on their terms? Answer that question first and then design your content and conversation. Consider bespoke content for a particular audience on a major pursuit or sales opportunity.
10. **Engaging content:** your content must be original, thought provoking and action-oriented, but it also needs to be engaging, visually strong, digestible and easy to share. It should also come in a variety of forms, not just an article: videos, podcasts, infographics, blogs, social media posts, seminars, webcasts, discussion forums and so forth.

# THEME FOUR
## Relationships

# Introduction to the Relationships theme

> *A relationship, I think, is like a shark. You know? It has to constantly move forward or it dies. And I think what we got on our hands is a dead shark.* **(WOODY ALLEN IN THE FILM *ANNIE HALL*)**

A dictionary definition of a relationship is 'an emotional or other connection between people'. Relationship is a word and status we use in our everyday lives that has been hijacked and is now a buzzword or jargon in marketing and across the business world to describe any connection, fleeting or otherwise, between a brand or product and its customers.

In our personal lives we are very guarded about whom we admit to having relationships with – family, life partners, friends… Would you include anyone else? We think most people would probably stop there if they were talking about themselves and their personal life.

If we move into the business world and stretch the definition a bit, how many people would you say you have a good relationship with: some of your colleagues, a few other contacts, hopefully some clients…? The world of social media – Facebook, Twitter, LinkedIn – allows you to maintain contacts and 'friends' in a way it was previously difficult or very time consuming to do, but would you say you have a relationship with all of them? Is there an emotional connection, as per our standard definition?

We all know what a relationship looks like. It's a two-way process where both parties invest time and effort over the long term and seek mutual benefit. You are keen to see the other person get as much out of every exchange as you do. In fact, there will be occasions where one party gets nothing other than the satisfaction that the other party is happy. It is not a relationship if it's just one-way traffic, or if one party doesn't want to put in the time or if any exchange delivers benefit to only one side. While we may not all identify with Woody Allen's idea of connecting relationships with moving sharks, the idea of progression being important to a relationship holds true, especially in business.

In recent years, the explosion of social media has expanded the language and thinking about relationships. Whether it is Facebook, Twitter, LinkedIn or numerous others, the opportunity to develop, maintain or find new relationships online has never been easier. However, new media has not extended the circle of relationships we hold close and value dearly; it has just made it easier to maintain a wider group of contacts. It demonstrates that a contact is not a relationship.

This is all great news for a professional services firm. Pity the poor marketer who is trying to jump on the relationship bandwagon and so has to instigate a complicated and expensive marketing campaign to ensure that customers feel committed and connected to their product, beyond what is available with the latest deal or offer. Can you have a relationship with an inanimate object?

There was a day when you could develop a relationship with your bank manager, or maybe the staff in the local branch, but banks have moved away from that because, despite professing to want relationships with their customers, it is now inefficient to invest extended one-to-one time in every individual looking for a financial services product. We are happy to be proved wrong, but we don't think it is possible to claim that a call centre can feature in any relationship.

On the whole, professional services firms are different. They have far fewer customers than a bank or almost all business to consumer companies. Client concentration – the percentage of revenue or profit a firm takes from its major clients – means that there are relatively few organizations that are important to them and the number of important decision-makers and contacts within each client company is limited. It is not only desirable but also efficient and effective to invest time and effort into those relationships.

Typically, that effort in relationship development in professional services firms was the preserve of partners, directors or senior management. 'Investing in the relationship' was also code for 'can we get some tickets to the cricket/rugby/opera… [insert the name of the partner's favourite pastime]'. It was not a disciplined and well-considered approach that either the individuals in question or the firm looked at in the same way as if they were attempting to develop a personal relationship.

Central to the conundrum of relationship development in a professional services firm is the question of who owns the relationship. As defined earlier, relationships exist between people, not inanimate objects, so there cannot be a good connection between a firm and the client organization without real relationships between people in the respective businesses.

We have, however, always bristled slightly when a partner or director of a firm talks about 'my client', especially when it means that the individual is restricting access and acting as gatekeeper to benefit their own individual status and interests. It is always reminiscent of a teenager reluctant to see their new romance talk to any of their friends for fear of being dumped for someone more charming and better looking! We want everybody in a professional services firm to invest in, but be open about, client relationships, but then always talk about 'our client', not 'my client'.

One route to success for any firm, in particular if there is high client concentration, is to broaden out the client relationship. The cost of acquiring new clients means that you are probably more likely to sell a new service to, and make money from, an existing client. We hate the term 'cross-selling' – the concept of selling an ever-increasing bundle of services to the same client organization – because it looks at the benefit from only the firm's perspective, not the client's too. Where is the mutual benefit of a good relationship in the concept of cross-selling?

In a business context, a relationship that depends on two people alone is fragile. Unlike families, you can escape your firm even if you are a partner, and client contacts are equally or more likely to jump ship for pastures new. In addition, whether or not the partner/director and main client contact are bosom buddies – went to the same school, are mutual alumni, holiday together in Tuscany – the service the client buys and experiences is not delivered by that one person.

For the benefit of all concerned, a broader team-based approach, where a range of people from the firm know and develop relationships with their counterparts at the client organization, is a much healthier approach. The term in relationship management jargon that is frequently used is 'zippered', to illustrate that the connection between two organizations doesn't fail if two teeth in the zip fail.

Not every relationship will succeed; we wouldn't be human if they did, and they won't work just because you take someone to the rugby every now and then. You need to invest in the relationship just as you would with a life partner or friend. Moreover, you must consider carefully what the other party is getting from the relationship, not just the benefit to you – so junk the 'cross-selling' terminology!

Into this emotional and fragile rollercoaster of relationship management steps the brave marketer and business developer. In some instances they aim to establish and own relationships directly, but they are more likely to facilitate and manage the process so that it works better than it would if everyone behaved like a group of hormonal teenagers.

In this theme we will hear from three experts who all have the experience, and probably bear the scars, of managing and developing a client relationship programme in their firms: Gillian Sutherland from the infrastructure and support services firm AECOM, Susan D'aish from lawyers MacRoberts and Dan O'Day from Thomson Reuters.

# The importance of client relationship management

**GILLIAN SUTHERLAND,** Director, Global Key Account Management
Buildings + Places, AECOM

**Profile:** Gillian is the Director leading the Global Key Account Management Programme for Buildings + Places, one of four businesses in AECOM, an integrated infrastructure and support services firm providing architectural, engineering and project-related services. Gillian has over 30 years' experience in marketing and business development, predominantly in the professional services field. Her roles have encompassed all aspects of marketing and business development, including client management and sales, pursuits and bidding, brand and communications.

In this chapter we look at the importance of client management for professional services firms. In particular, we consider why a firm should establish a client management programme and how to do that successfully. We follow a four-step process, from analysis of the current client base, through setting objectives and identifying clients to designing the programme. We also look at systems support for a programme and the likely issues and challenges a programme will face.

## The primacy of relationships

Having spent most of my professional life in professional services firms, in law, construction and property, I have observed similar behaviours across the professions. However, there are also differences between types of organization: in particular, partnerships and corporate organizations.

Professional firms are about people. There is no product, so we are selling our people and their expertise or the service they offer. We are selling our intellectual property to people within our client organizations, and therefore relationships are of fundamental importance.

Anyone who has studied marketing knows the expression 'the customer is king'. This is absolutely true for a professional organization and we achieve customer satisfaction through excellence in relationship management and service delivery. Therefore the management, care and development of client relationships are at the heart of what we are about. Ignore this at your peril.

The challenge is to deliver a benefit to your organization and to the client, often described as 'win–win', through the investment in a client management programme. As with everything across the marketing spectrum, it is essential to measure the success of a programme, which can be challenging. It usually takes time to see a significant return, as some measures of success are 'soft', and difficult to measure.

With each relationship the ultimate objective is to move from being a provider of services to having a partnership with a client where you are working collaboratively, adding value to the client's business, not just an individual project, and getting work without having to compete or bid. Remember, however, that the relationship will always be commercial, so customer satisfaction remains vital.

Figure 10.1 shows the stages of development in a client-to-adviser relationship.

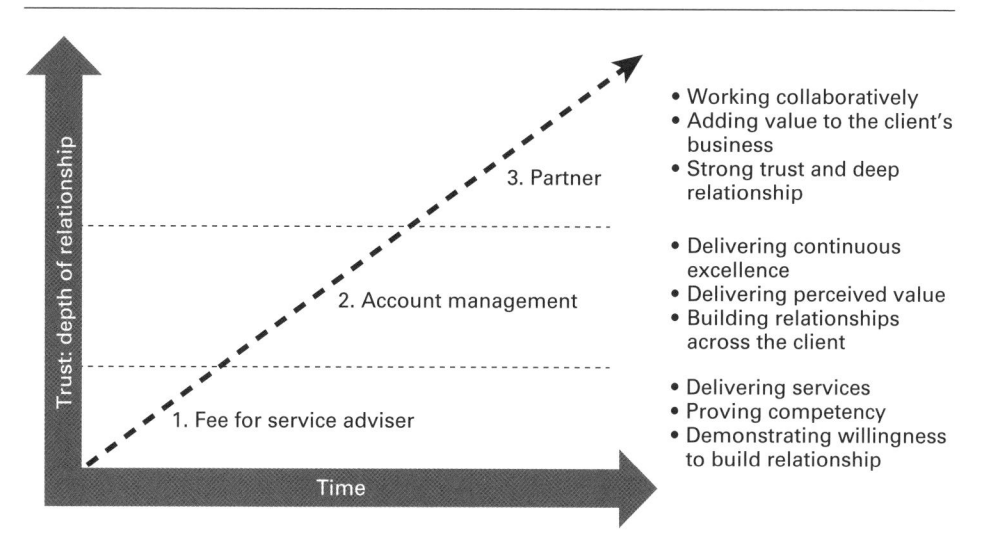

**FIGURE 10.1** Stages of development in a client-to-adviser relationship

- Working collaboratively
- Adding value to the client's business
- Strong trust and deep relationship

3. Partner

- Delivering continuous excellence
- Delivering perceived value
- Building relationships across the client

2. Account management

- Delivering services
- Proving competency
- Demonstrating willingness to build relationship

1. Fee for service adviser

Time

Trust: depth of relationship

## *Important aspects of relationships*

If you think about significant relationships in your life that you have with people who supply you with services – your hairdresser, a favourite restaurant, your accountant – you will know that trust is the most important ingredient in that relationship.

David Maister's trust equation (Maister, Green and Galford, 2000) demonstrates the chief aspects of trust, where credibility, reliability and intimacy are positive trust builders, but self-orientation can decrease that trust. More specifically:

- Credibility is about being credible on a subject area.
- Reliability has to do with being dependable on delivery.
- Intimacy refers to giving confidence that a client will be safe with you, eg you will not violate confidentiality or embarrass the client.
- Self-orientation refers to how 'selfish' your motives are.

I have found that professionals can relate to how this works in their client relationships. Self-orientation is a critical factor here – a client manager with high self-orientation is thinking about what they can get out of the relationship, whereas a client manager with low self-orientation will be most interested in how they can help the client meet both their business and their individual needs.

One-on-one relationships are built on, and thrive on, trust. When you look at the number of relationships that you are involved in across a client organization, the interrelationships can make this complex. This is particularly so in a large client organization or a global business. The more complex the client, the more people involved in the buying group and influencing group, the more complex the relationship. Figure 10.2 illustrates how relationships work in many client situations.

**FIGURE 10.2** How client relationships work

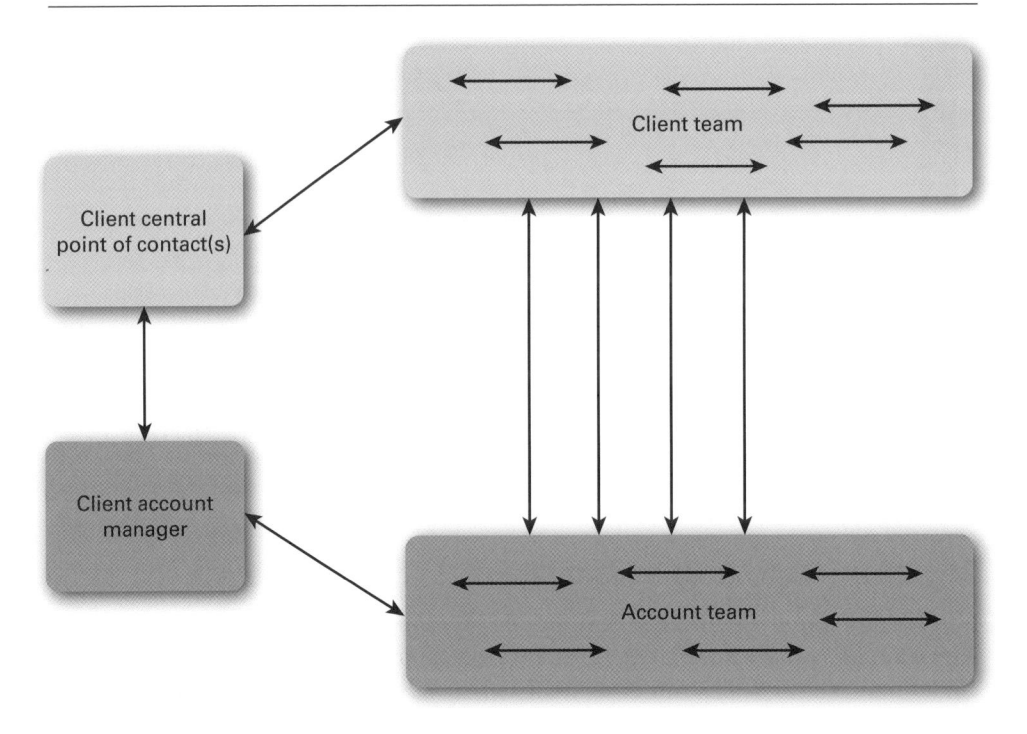

The reality is that the relationship is never just on two people who lead each side of the relationship. To build a strong business-to-business relationship the teams need to be well connected and each individual relationship well managed. This means that the relationship is built on firm foundations and is strong across all aspects of the client and supplier teams. This should, to some extent, mitigate losing a relationship with a key client if the lead manager leaves the business. However, it should be noted that the strong personal relationships built with the client could be very personality and individual focused, so you need to avoid losing a key account manager where he or she is central to the relationship. This means that client management has to be paired with good people management and talent retention. It goes without saying that the account managers should be your 'stars' and should be people whom your firm wants to nurture and to keep.

Given that relationships are personality driven, it is important to ensure that the key people – account manager and the top team – are people who are a good personality fit with the equivalent people in the client organization. They also need to understand the personalities in the client team and know how to interact best with their personality types. This is particularly relevant at the beginning of the relationship and in early meetings with the client. Getting your account teams to do some simple personality profiling of themselves and their contacts helps them to understand who is best placed to look after whom and also how to approach different personality types in client meetings.

# Achieving a successful programme

A major argument for setting up a client programme is to focus on what you have, that is, relationships that have already been developed. Various studies show that the cost of acquiring a new client far outweighs that of developing an existing client. Many firms could grow organically just by mining their existing client base and this would be more cost- and time-efficient than chasing new clients.

Professionals are naturally passionate about their clients, but they sometimes lack the ability to organize themselves to get the most out of what they already have. They often need help to develop some of the softer skills around sales and business development that they find quite difficult. Professionals are trained to know the answer and to tell the client what to do; relationship development and sales focuses on asking the client about their business and their issues in order to deliver a relevant solution, which is counter to the training of most professionals.

## *Setting up the programme*

Because professionals are naturally client focused, winning the argument for setting up a client programme is not usually a problem. The difficulty occurs when the programme appears to run out of steam and senior people start to ask what the business is getting out of it and, indeed, what the clients are getting out of it. The most common reason is a lack of definition of what the business wants to achieve from the programme, which is why defining and agreeing this at the beginning is so important.

All too often, organizations simply decide they need to have a better client focus or happier clients or they need to grow their relationships. They typically ask their business development team to take on the task, or they recruit someone or they ask someone in the business who is 'good with clients' to take on the role. The instruction is vague and there are no clear objectives of what the organization wants to achieve and how clients will benefit. Having clear goals is crucial to the success of the programme. The following steps provide a guide to the process.

## Step 1: analysis of current client base

Analysis of your current client base allows you to understand what you have at present. Understanding the current shape of your business, the number and size of your clients and how they are distributed will help you to work out what you want it to look like and therefore what type of programme you should embark on. Does the Pareto principle, or 80:20 rule as it is often known, apply, or is it more extreme? I have often found, having done the analysis, that the distribution is nearer to 90:10, where 90 per cent of the firm's business comes from just 10 per cent of the clients. There is then a long tail of very small clients. In addition, it is valuable to analyse the profit margin to see if there is any correlation between size of the client, size of the work and the profit margin achieved.

This type of analysis will help you to work out where you want to focus your efforts and what your objectives should be.

## Step 2: setting objectives

Having understood your current client base and asked some questions around what the ideal would look like, where there are risks and where there is work to be done, you should now be able to set clear objectives for the programme and to communicate them to the business.

Examples of the types of objective you may have are detailed below. These could be combined or stepped, for example effect cultural change and develop key clients:

- Sales led: to increase profitable work:
  - to get more profitable business from a selected group of clients;
  - to increase business gained from business units not currently working with the client or doing very little with the client (cross-selling);
  - to increase business from different geographical locations (cross-selling).
- Client care led: to improve client satisfaction, which leads to increased repeat business:
  - to gain feedback in order to measure satisfaction with service delivery and relationship management;
  - to ensure that account managers are properly matched to identified clients;
  - to increase repeat business percentage.

- Culture change led: to achieve a client-focused culture:
  - to ensure that all senior executives are trained in how to manage and develop clients;
  - to reduce risk and reduce emphasis on one or two large clients;
  - to broaden the programme and achieve an overall focus on client management and client development across all areas of the firm;
  - to create a 'firm way' of dealing with clients.
- Key client programme: to increase attention on the top clients and potential clients to move these from transaction to relationship based:
  - to increase business with large or potentially large clients and those who align with the firm's strategic goals;
  - to create dedicated, well-trained account managers to manage the key clients of the firm;
  - to develop deep, long-term relationships with key clients.

## Step 3: identify clients

Whatever the goal, you will need to select carefully the clients to include on the programme. It is also critical that you have the right account managers for the selected clients. So, time spent on client and account manager selection is a good investment, as this will have a major impact on the success of the programme.

One useful way to help you work out which clients to consider is to score the attractiveness to the firm of developing the client relationship and your competitive advantage (Table 10.1).

Having scored the client, you can now see that those who score highly on both measures should be the first clients to include in the programme. It also highlights any actions that may be required; for example, there may be an attractive client with whom you think you could work to improve your competitive advantage.

There is, of course, more than one way to do client selection. Where the objective is around cultural change, getting senior executives to nominate clients for the programme as a first step works well. They need to be provided with the selection criteria so that they are able to score the client and validate their inclusion in the programme. This approach immediately achieves buy-in from the senior people in the business and identifies those partners and directors who are serious and enthusiastic about developing their clients, which means that you are starting with a team of senior executives who are bought into the concept.

## Step 4: programme design

A methodical approach here works best, particularly where you are dealing with quite large clients, which means that you have a fairly complex client organization and internal team set-up. This allows everyone involved to understand the order of events and to keep up with what is happening on an account.

Figure 10.3 shows a design for a client relationship management programme:

1 **Account selection:** we have already discussed how to select the clients for the programme. Targets and KPIs need to be agreed for each account on the programme. These should reflect the overall objective of the programme, but

**TABLE 10.1** Selection criteria for identifying relationship clients

| Client attractiveness | | Score |
|---|---|---|
| Available spend | Clients who spend appropriate/large amounts on our types of services | |
| Revenue potential | Clients where we have the potential to earn good revenue | |
| Crown jewels | Long-term repeat clients whose income is crucial to the long-term health of the business | |
| Strategic importance | Clients who assist us to achieve our strategic goals | |
| Profit potential | New and existing clients where there is potential for profitable growth | |
| Referral | Clients who attract referral business (blue-chip clients in our chosen markets) | |

| Competitive advantage | | Score |
|---|---|---|
| Areas of expertise | We have the expertise/range of services that the client needs | |
| Sector specialisms | We have sector experts who really understand the client's business environment | |
| Geographical compatibility | We have the appropriate geographical spread to service the client | |
| Cultural fit | We have similar cultures | |
| Current relationship strength | We have good or developing relationships with decision-makers and influencers | |
| Size of current account | We have a reasonable level of income upon which to grow the account | |
| Total score | | |

there may also be some client-specific KPIs that are appropriate. As always, these need to be SMART (specific, measurable, achievable, realistic and time-bound). Buy-in from the executive team should be sought.

2 **Account team:** it is vital to the success of an account that the right account lead is appointed. The success or failure of client accounts tends to reflect the suitability of account leads, around either their relationship with the client or their ability to manage clients. A clear role description is required. It is also good practice to support the account leader, who is usually a partner or director, with a 'driver', who is typically someone at associate or manager level. It is this person's job to ensure that actions are completed and momentum maintained. This is a good career move for someone looking to make partner or director and will provide him or her with invaluable experience.

3 **Account plan:** the client plan can often be regarded as an administrative function. This should not be the case. A client plan should be approached in the same way as a good strategic plan, backed up with thorough research and used on an ongoing basis. In order to ensure that the process is as admin free as possible, it is good to ensure that there is no repetition. Clients can be managed through their plans with no need to produce any other notes or information – it should all be in the plan. The plan should be user-friendly and all the team must have access to it. For some parts of your programme, 'light plans' may be suitable. These should be in the same format as the full plan but with less information, usually more implementation focused. If the format is the same it can be extended easily. This is suitable for clients who are not complex or perhaps are not likely to require the time and resource but who still need a managed approach. My preferred approach to planning, particularly on local clients (it is usually too difficult with diverse global relationships), is to augment the internal and desk research with some feedback from the client prior to working with the team to put the plan together. Then the plan can be based on client feedback, including their objectives and issues.

4 **Meetings and momentum:** as with any activity that is outside the chargeable arena, it is important to have structure in order to maintain momentum. Either weekly or monthly client team meetings work well, with set agendas focused around the action plan, the pipeline and the relationship. This will ensure that actions are carried out and next steps identified.

5 **Account performance measurement:** monthly or quarterly reporting to the board or management team keeps the leaders of the business appraised of progress and any issues that have arisen that you may need help with. Quarterly reviews with the account lead and team are also required to monitor overall progress with individual accounts. Adjustments to the programme may be required.

6 **Client feedback:** client feedback is a topic in its own right. It is an essential part of the programme. Many firms fall back on online feedback either on individual transactions and projects or on the overall relationship, for

example the Net Promoter Score. This type of feedback is good and essential, but the really valuable feedback is the face-to-face type that is undertaken by either a senior marketer or an independent reviewer with two or three senior decision-makers from the client. This gives you some real insight into performance to date, but also a better understanding of what the client is looking for in the future.

## *Measurement criteria – what does success look like?*

If you have clear objectives for the programme, it should not be difficult to work out how to measure success. It is vital, in order to maintain momentum and to increase buy-in to the programme, that you are able to demonstrate success in a clear and quantifiable way.

It can take a number of years to achieve a substantial change in this area, so it is important that you have some way of measuring progress along the way. In addition, there will be some corrective actions that may be required and you will only know what those are if you have some data to guide you. My research shows that it can take up to five years to move a client relationship from service provider to partner.

There are a number of key areas of measurement that should be monitored on a monthly basis:

- revenue;
- profit margin;
- work in progress;
- wins;
- pipeline;
- cross-selling.

In addition, you may have set key performance indicators (KPIs) for the overall programme that should be monitored on a regular basis.

## *Systems to support the programme*

There is often a misconception that a client relationship management (CRM) system is client management. This is not the case, but a good, firm-wide CRM system is required to support the programme, as is a firm-wide finance system that is capable of reporting by client. The systems either need to talk to each other or there should be a clear demarcation line between the systems so that it is clear when a project or matter moves from the sales/CRM system to the finance system.

A CRM system should:

- contain information on the client, the contacts and any activities that have taken place with the client and the individual contacts;
- run the pipeline and track movement through the pipeline, showing when a project or matter moves from a lead through to a pursuit or from a bid through to a win;

**FIGURE 10.3** A design for a client relationship management programme

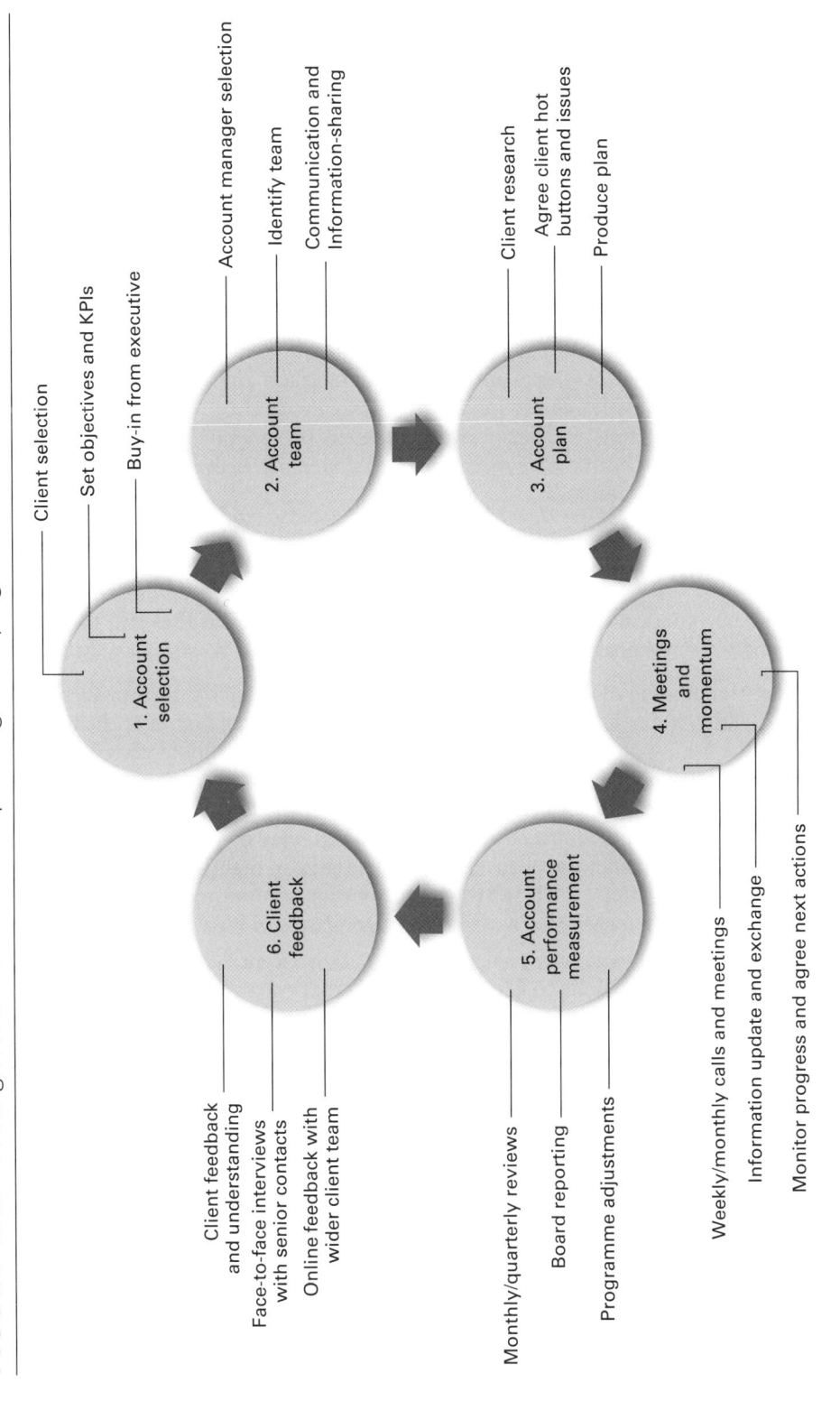

- Client selection
- Set objectives and KPIs
- Buy-in from executive

**1. Account selection**

- Account manager selection
- Identify team
- Communication and Information-sharing

**2. Account team**

- Client research
- Agree client hot buttons and issues
- Produce plan

**3. Account plan**

- Weekly/monthly calls and meetings
- Information update and exchange
- Monitor progress and agree next actions

**4. Meetings and momentum**

- Monthly/quarterly reviews
- Board reporting
- Programme adjustments

**5. Account performance measurement**

- Client feedback and understanding
- Face-to-face interviews with senior contacts
- Online feedback with wider client team

**6. Client feedback**

- contain meaningful reports in relation to both the client account and the pipeline;
- be capable of managing activities such as events and mailings;
- ideally provide additional capabilities for sharing information – such as a social networking area for fast knowledge exchange – and the ability to store documentation about a client. Sometimes independent products are used, but the more connected the systems the better the take-up and use across the business.

The finance system should be capable of reporting by client, which means bundling all activities into single client accounts. Understanding the whole picture around income and profit by client across the whole firm provides the essential backdrop to deciding on the right strategy for the programme. Understanding the picture around the subsequent key accounts and the ability to track and report on progress with these accounts enables you to monitor the progress of the programme.

Finally, marketing and business development professionals need to have a good understanding of both the finance and CRM systems in order to run an effective and commercial programme.

## *Issues and challenges*

From my experience, the most likely issues and challenges a firm will face in establishing a client management programme are:

- **Maintaining momentum:** most teams set off enthusiastically but then get on with the day job and momentum can be lost. Having buy-in at the top level in the firm, with good account leads and good drivers, should ensure that this does not happen. In addition, success will motivate the teams, so if the right clients have been selected (where there is a realistic chance of success) and there are opportunities to follow up on and regular wins, the team will be enthused to achieve more. Other things that can maintain pace are wider communications, such as award schemes for account managers and teams or reporting internally on successes and good behaviours.
- **Benefit to clients:** often client programmes are centred on what the organization wants to get out of them and are geared towards increasing business. A good programme should benefit both the organization and the client. The best programmes include the client in the planning process, the actions and the feedback. Ideally the client should know that it is included on the programme, should have input to the plan and should influence the way the account progresses. If the aim is to achieve a closer partnership with the client, open conversations and joint involvement in the plan are the right way forward. Many clients operate their own programmes and are therefore very familiar with the concept; indeed, many larger clients now positively ask for a 'partnering' approach. Marketing and business development professionals can play a role in encouraging partners and directors to be more open with their clients. The best way to achieve this is to have direct contact with the client, initiate conversations and ask questions around areas that partners and directors may find difficult.

- **Training and coaching:** during their professional training, professionals are rarely trained to sell or to manage and develop client relationships. It is therefore not surprising that they often find this part of their role very challenging. Training and coaching are essential elements of the marketing and business development role. They can be delivered either by the team or through outside organizations and should encompass building relationships, managing accounts, sales skills development and winning bids.
- **Global vs local:** managing and developing global clients is complex. Both the client organization and your business will have complexity to overcome and work with. In both cases there is usually a tension between central departments and local delivery. Resolving this requires good contacts across the client organization and a good team set-up across your own organization with people who are collaborative. Finding resources to deliver across the globe in places where you may not have them and delivering globally in a consistent way are both challenges that take up the time of the account team. Persuading local businesses to focus resources on global clients, or clients of another internal business unit, is difficult, owing to the financial conflict between winning work for their business unit and getting work for another business area or the firm globally. The KPIs of the business unit often stand in the way of developing global clients.

    Executive sponsorship is imperative to encourage the right internal behaviours but alignment to strategy is also crucial; this could mean having to tell a client that you cannot help them in a particular country, or revising the strategy to accommodate a specific client. A major global client of the firm could help to drive your strategy. Open and honest conversations with clients about what you can deliver, and where, help to overcome any issues. Clients appreciate honesty and do not expect an organization to be able to deliver everything everywhere. Working with local clients can be more straightforward. The client is in one geographical area, there are no cultural issues, it is much easier to engage with the client on a regular basis and the team is all in one geographical area, usually working within the same profit centre. There are usually fewer delivery issues and therefore progress can be faster. In all cases, IT systems can assist with sharing information and with communication. CRM systems, internal chat sites and file-share systems all add to communication across global and local teams, but can be particularly useful for global accounts.
- **Lack of buy-in and 'we do this anyway, don't we':** many partners or directors believe that they have, and indeed often do have, good relationships with their clients and cannot see the need to have a formal approach. For those clients who fit the criteria, there is always more that can be done to improve the overall relationship, to widen it, develop more business and bring more value to the client. It is really important that the client lead sees this process as helping them to develop the relationship rather than see it as a threat. For marketing and business development (BD) teams, working closely with the account lead is imperative. In extreme circumstances I have seen major clients lost owing to the lead not allowing a formal client management approach.

This is due either to there being a problem that the lead knows about or, more often, to the lead not having a wide enough understanding of the client's business, what the client needs and what is coming up over the horizon for the client. Again, building the internal relationship with the client lead and supporting them is imperative to gain their trust to allow you to help with the client.

As I have said before, and cannot stress enough, executive buy-in is crucial to get a programme up, running and maintaining momentum. If the board and management team are not totally and proactively supportive of the programme, it will fail.

## Future trends

So what are the trends that are likely to develop over the next few years?

- **Dedicated account leads:** I think there will be an increase in professional firms' appetite to allocate dedicated account managers for large clients or to work on a number of clients. These are likely to do little or no fee-earning work but will concentrate on managing the client relationship at senior levels, manage the team and ensure that the plan is developed and implemented.

    Will and should these people be from a technical background or from a sales, business development or industry background? In reality any of these options can work. I favour having account managers who are from either a technical or an industry background, using sales and business development professionals to cover a wider programme of clients. This way, you can leverage the sales expertise across a larger number of accounts. Typically, I think one account manager can manage up to five accounts, depending on the size, but if you limit sales professionals to a maximum of five clients you are limiting the impact they could have by up-skilling a greater number of account leads.

- **Increased client expectations:** most clients operate their own client or customer programmes, so they are coming to expect it from their advisers. Most sophisticated or large client organizations are completely comfortable with the account management approach and are keen to engage. I believe that this trend will continue. Professional services firms that work with major organizations cannot afford to ignore this trend, as competitors will be doing it.

- **Reward and recognition:** most professional firms expect partners and directors to undertake account work on a voluntary basis and their salaries and bonuses are not directly linked to the work they do in this area. In the future, I think that performance management, including reward and recognition, for senior executives will continue to become more targeted on specific objectives and that client management will be one of the key areas.

Marketing and business development professionals must anticipate future trends and consider how their own firm could adapt. Each firm is different and the ability to influence the future direction of the firm is part of the role of the director or head of marketing and business development. To introduce something substantially different requires strong influencing skills and a well-thought-through plan with back-up evidence to support a proposal. When developing a new approach, starting with a small and enthusiastic part of the firm will allow you to test and amend the proposal. Enthusiastic sponsors are always the early adopters.

## Conclusion – success factors for client management programmes

In summary, the four aspects of a successful client programme are:

- **Executive sponsorship** and buy-in are essential; without these, you will be sure to fail.
- **Clear objectives** for the programme must be agreed at the outset so that you can measure progress.
- **Getting the client involved** and really understanding your client is the only way to a true partnership approach.
- **Measuring progress and reporting** on it will help you to maintain momentum, ensure that everyone involved stays focused on the objectives and allow you to demonstrate to the executive that the programme is a success and is achieving its objectives.

# Developing internal and external relationships

## 11

**SUSAN D'AISH,** Business Relationship Director, MacRoberts LLP

**Profile:** Susan is a chartered marketer and qualified coach, with over 18 years' experience working within professional services. Susan works with firms to develop business plans for new income generation and strategic growth. She has successfully transformed business cultures around client and account management, resulting in multi-million-pound increases in turnover.

If you take a step back and look at a business from a distance, it is clear that no business works in isolation. Essential to any business's success are the performance of, and relationships with, key stakeholders, including customers, financiers and professional services providers. Relationships between these stakeholders are a key success factor for any business. It is little wonder, then, that when asked why firms chose to work with a particular firm, relationships with key individuals are cited as the number one reason.

In this chapter on relationships, we'll look at why they are so important in the context of marketing professional services, and their impact on a business's long-term resilience and profitability. We'll explore building good relationships and trust internally, and ways to manage differences in values, priorities and motivators.

The chapter's main focus will be on developing client relationships at a firm-wide level. We'll look at case studies and guidance for managing client relationships, through the good times and the bad, and share some examples of common challenges, how to overcome them and the positive outcomes they can have on the professional services firm.

Over the past 20 years, the dominance of traditional transactional marketing models has given way to relationship marketing, particularly among professional

**TABLE 11.1** Differences between transactional and relationship marketing

| Transactional marketing | Relationship marketing |
| --- | --- |
| Focus on short-term return | Focus on long-term return |
| High volume, lower value | Lower volume, high value |
| Focus on technical features | Focus on delivering client goals |
| Limited client interaction | High client interaction |
| Little or no client feedback | Client feedback integral to process |

services firms (Table 11.1 shows the differences between transactional and relationship marketing). While transaction marketing may still have a place within some business-to-consumer (B2C) firms, successful promotion of professional services hinges on excellent relationship marketing. Maintaining and growing work from existing clients is for most firms more efficient and more sustainable than having a high turnover of transactional clients.

The legacy of historic restrictions around the marketing of professional services has meant that, traditionally, firms have grown through carefully cultivated and managed relationships – managed or, in most cases, zealously guarded. To be honest, many professionals are managing, not from an entirely altruistic client-first perspective, but rather from the perspective of 'what rewards do I get from this relationship and how can I protect my rewards?'.

We will talk a great deal about trust throughout this chapter. Without trust, it is impossible to break the mindset of individual service providers looking after their specialist area, rather than the actual needs of their client. Before widening a client relationship firm-wide, the client partner needs to trust that their colleagues will provide the same standard of service, and that they won't undercut the firm's pricing arrangements with the client.

The relationship marketing approach also requires trust that all firm members are committed to the relationship for the long term, rather than to short-term transactional gain. Reciprocity may not occur instantaneously, and individuals need to trust that a relationship marketing approach will bring increased opportunity in the long term.

The age of social media has made it even easier to establish connections that have the potential to be developed to meaningful client relationships. It is surprising, therefore, how many professionals fail to harness the full potential of this relationship facilitator. For many, it is a numbers game of adding contacts, but to little end. The jewel in social media's crown is the ease with which you can communicate relevant information of value to contacts to stimulate their engagement, and to share networks to assist in expanding your clients' wider relationships.

# Importance of good relationships

One of my first tasks as a professional services marketer was to go on an expedition in search of the firm's utopian USP (unique selling point). I conducted research of senior managers and leaders throughout the business, asking why our clients chose to work with us. The responses were consistent: we were a collection of specialists in niche areas who could offer expertise in areas that our competitors couldn't. I then met with several of our best clients and asked the same question. Their responses were in stark contrast. Each client cited the quality of relationship with key individuals as the reason they worked with us, and for most, it was the thing they valued above all else.

Up to this point we had procrastinated on key client management, agonizing over whether certain clients should be given key status, how we should manage data, what would we communicate to staff around key client management – you name it, we pondered it. Gaining consensus across a large number of senior managers can prove something of a challenge within professional services, and the longer we debated the finer details, the longer we put off key client management in practice.

Another stumbling block was the absence of a sophisticated client relationship management (CRM) system. Many of the firm's directors felt that we couldn't or shouldn't embed key client management until we had purchased the right CRM programme. What was the point in putting effort into client management if we didn't have the tools to manage information? In my opinion this missed the point of CRM. CRM is a process, an ethos, a culture – thinking that CRM was reliant on expensive software prevented us from making any progress. We may not get from zero to ten immediately on the scale of CRM, but what would it take to get us to a five or six?

From our starting point of having little or no client management processes, I believed that developing client plans using simple Excel or Word documents, and communicating through SharePoint, an existing and inexpensive knowledge-sharing platform, were infinitely preferable to doing nothing. The key to successful relationship management is to get buy-in to the process and the behaviours required. If people are not going to record client intelligence to improve our quality of corporate relationship using simple systems, it's unlikely that they will do so using expensive software.

We first used our directors to make a compelling case for getting started with our key client management programme, imperfect though it may be. To further illustrate the point, and to help our internal stakeholders to empathize with our clients, we asked them to consider their own behaviour as clients. We asked them to think of factors they would consider when choosing a transatlantic airline, if the cost for each flight was identical. Among the most common factors identified were customer service, comfort, ease of booking and punctuality.

We then gently explained that engine performance, wingspan, or pilot qualifications featured nowhere on their lists. Technical competence is taken as a given, they said – airlines wouldn't be in business if their technical credentials weren't up to the mark. Slowly, the penny dropped. What clients value in receipt of professional services is how they feel throughout the process, how easily they can communicate with their service provider and whether we deliver what we say we will. Factors around personal relationships and customer service were key to our success.

This raised a few important questions. What were we doing to ensure that all our staff excelled at developing good relationships? How were we rewarding relationship-driven successes such as referral of new clients? How were we developing relationships at firm-wide level, to protect and grow clients who were loyal to key individuals?

In my experience, training and performance management all too often overlook the role of good relationships in organizational performance. Performance in professional services firms is almost exclusively measured on an individual level against individual outputs. What this overlooks is the potential gap between high-performing individuals and high-performing teams.

One way to address this at senior level is through key client management. Forming multi-service teams from across all parts of a business to protect and grow key clients drives improved relationships internally. Teams that are measured and rewarded in accordance with the successful growth of their respective client will be motivated to work interdependently with colleagues, setting the tone for firm cultures that are centred on good relationship-building.

Part of our key client management process was to map existing relationships with the client and to identify gaps, either by service or geography, where we did not have strong relationships with key individuals and influencers within the client's team. Relying on just one point of contact, the client-care partner, is a high-risk strategy for client management. Should that partner be hit by a bus, retire or leave the firm, we would have little to fall back on. This highlights the importance of encouraging good relationship-building at all levels throughout the business, and not just leaving it to a few individuals who we might think are naturally good at it.

Emotional Quotient, or EQ, is a relatively new measure of an individual's emotional and social intelligence (Stein and Book, 2000). It goes some way towards explaining why many senior managers and partners are naturals when it comes to forming good relationships, but many aren't. The ability to obtain a professional qualification is attributed to Intelligence Quotient, or IQ, a number representing a person's reasoning ability. Emotional Intelligence, however, assesses an individual's skills in key emotional and social realms, including self-perception, self-expression, interpersonal, decision-making and stress management, all key factors in developing and sustaining good relationships. While some senior professionals may be certified geniuses, it doesn't necessarily follow that they will be a firm's best choice as client relationship partner. As our client insights showed, clients will generally value a good relationship over the most technically brilliant advice.

In order to grow relationships at firm-wide level, successful teamwork is essential. In Stephen Covey's acclaimed book *The Seven Habits of Highly Effective People* (Covey, 1989), he describes how the key to successful teams is the ability to move your team from dependence to independence and finally to interdependence.

In moving from independence to interdependence, a firm can harness the power of a group of professionals to develop successful internal and client relationships in order to further their collective aims. Fundamental behaviours or 'habits' include:

- think win–win, a concept any successful negotiator will recognize;
- seek first to understand, then to be understood – the importance of listening before speaking;
- synergize – creative cooperation will form new solutions to problems.

At the heart of this transition to interdependence is trust. As Covey puts it, 'Trust is the glue of life. It's the most essential ingredient in effective communication. It's the foundation principle that holds all relationships.'

## Building internal relationships

Whether as a sole marketing professional working with a team of fee-earners, or as a member of a wider marketing and business development team, we achieve optimum performance when we work effectively as a team. Successful teams understand how they relate to their external stakeholders and have a shared desire to overcome problems and challenges. Often, the key challenge for professional services marketers will be to demonstrate their value as a member of a team. Without overcoming this hurdle, the value that a marketing professional or marketing department can add to the firm is limited. For this reason, getting our own house in order and starting with developing internal relationships is the foundation for developing excellent client relationships.

One of the most noticeable differences I observed when moving from an engineering professional services firm to a law firm was the difference in staff motivation and behaviours. The marketing challenges were almost identical: the need to improve cross-selling, understand our clients and their purchase models better and improve our client information management, to name a few. In theory, I thought that following a similar approach to achieving success in one firm was likely to bring similar positive outcomes if applied to the new firm.

It didn't take me long to realize that building successful relationships and teams within a partnership differed from the same process within a shareholder-driven plc. Organizational characteristics, such as how performance is reviewed and how success is measured and rewarded, and how failures are dealt with, have enormous impact on the attitude of individuals to change and to risk, and consequently on their behaviour.

A common human characteristic that presents a challenge to implementing change is the fear of failure. It is this fear that often underlies resistance to marketing initiatives. While the enthusiastic marketer's natural instinct may be to go straight to the tried and tested solution, this approach misses the opportunity to deliver a collaborative solution, involving the wider team, that generates buy-in to the process.

Before embarking on implementing a new strategy to address marketing challenges, it is essential to understand individuals' expectations, motivations, the culture they work in, their perceived barriers to success and their personal vision for business improvement, as well as understanding the firm's overall vision and objectives.

In order to fully engage the whole firm in the marketing process, it's not enough for marketers to know what needs to be done and to communicate that to the wider firm. This misses the important steps of:

- determining where individuals want to get to for themselves and as a firm;
- fully understanding what creates resistance to the marketing process;
- identifying what solutions have been tried before and why they may have failed;

- exploring what approaches individuals would like to try;
- agreeing a course of action that involves input from each individual, as well as the marketers.

Readers of Sir John Whitmore's *Coaching for Performance* (Whitmore, 2002) will recognize the GROW model approach to these steps. Outlining the goals, understanding the existing status quo, exploring options and agreeing the course of action, if carried out collectively, will greatly enhance internal trust-building and the chances of success.

Putting these principles into practice, we developed our marketing strategy in close collaboration with partners and their service teams. We carried out one-to-one meetings with each partner to discuss their individual experiences, successes and failures and in what areas they felt we would get a good return on marketing investment. We then held team meetings to discuss common themes and to agree consensus on our key clients, target markets and strategy for growth.

For each service area, we drafted a strategy document based on the individual and team discussion and circulated this back to the teams for comment. Testing our understanding of what was said and what was meant proved insightful, and it was surprising how many changes were made to the draft. Seeing thoughts expressed in a formal plan resulted in several 'what I meant was' responses. Once the team were happy with the strategy, we began a series of regular meetings to agree specific actions to be undertaken by each of the team members, including the marketing team, that would enable everyone to reach their agreed objectives. This allowed the team to work more transparently, and to start to build stronger relationships through frequent dialogue and understanding of how each person was contributing to overall goals.

Testing understanding is a vital step to ensure that both parties are on the same page and to grow trust by dispelling any misunderstandings as early as possible. Reflecting on your understanding of what is being communicated can be done verbally at meetings or in written form as a follow-up to discussions.

The importance of communication in developing relationships cannot be underestimated. Agreeing roles and responsibilities from the outset will provide clarity around expectations. Having a plan or guide to refer back to minimizes the scope for misunderstanding or ambiguity around expectations, both internally and with clients. 'Fail to plan, plan to fail' will ring in the ears of any marketer who has tried to integrate marketing and business development initiatives with professional services teams. Too much of my early career was spent in business development meetings that were little more than talking shops.

It is almost impossible to over-communicate while matters are progressing. We can leave the impression that nothing is being done if we don't acknowledge how we are taking actions forward. When we anticipate delays, it is best to communicate this as early as possible, to allow other stakeholders to plan accordingly and to manage the impact of delays. I have found this to be a common theme during client feedback reviews. They identified that the best relationships were with individuals who communicated. Clients could accept hearing bad news if they were informed at the earliest possible opportunity. It was the nasty surprises and last-minute letdowns that damaged a relationship. The same is true of marketing professionals communicating with their internal clients. Developing good relationships hinges on trust, transparency and shared understanding.

## Influencing strategies

Part of developing mutually beneficial client relationships is the ability to influence the client to purchase. The words 'selling' and 'salesperson' are rarely commonplace terms in professional services firms as, to some, selling can suggest applying pressure to purchase, something to be rightly wary of.

Influencing, however, is the ability to communicate with the client in a way that generates synergy with that client. It results in a win–win outcome where both the professional services provider and the client feel that they have a mutual understanding and objective.

Without influencing, it may be possible to sell services to a client, although the client is likely to reflect back on the transaction with some degree of negative feeling of having been pressurized or manipulated. This is likely to jeopardize the development of a long-term client relationship. Effective influencing will generate the desire from the client to purchase from the professional services provider willingly, and with positive feeling towards the professional services provider.

While it may be easy to influence someone of similar vision and motivators to our own, it won't always be the case that prospective clients share our priorities and values. Understanding and developing effective influencing strategies make it easier to build trust with prospective clients and to build a mutually beneficial relationship, in spite of commercial and personal differences.

Reflecting on successful as well as unsuccessful client approaches has highlighted recurring factors that contribute to influencing, including:

- liking;
- reciprocity;
- consistency;
- authority.

Perhaps the most obvious influencing factor is **liking**. It seems obvious that clients are far more likely to be influenced by somebody they like. Professional services firms sometimes overlook this factor if client-care partners are assigned based on seniority or circumstance of the first service purchased by the client.

An interesting observation that we made during our client feedback exercise was that the individual relationship that the client most valued was not always the relationship with the client-care partner we had assigned to them. While they were not dissatisfied with their client-care partners, there were clear indicators that there may be others on the team who were better placed as the key client contact. This could be down to the individual's style of communication, proactivity in delivery or shared interests outside of work.

We made some corresponding changes to our client-care partners and the results were not disappointing. By matching individuals where the client most valued the relationship had the dual benefit of the client feeling heard and valued, as well as the new client-care partner being energized to develop the account. The new client-care partners were extremely proactive in seeking out new opportunities to take to their clients and the result was an increase in business generated by these clients by up to 30 per cent in the first year.

This highlights a second key factor in influencing – **reciprocity**. It's no longer enough for professional services firms to wait for instruction from clients; we are now expected to understand their plans for growth and to seek out and communicate opportunities. Reciprocity is no longer a case of a professional providing a service in return for a fee. With so many firms competing for a limited pool of work, those that will influence a client to purchase are the firms that take something of value to the client to further the client's aims, rather than just their own.

Reciprocity achieves best results when it is planned and coordinated. Many successful professional services firms have seen the benefit of developing a referrals plan as part of their key client management programme. This allows the firm to track and identify which referrals bring value to the client, and can be a good basis for maintaining regular dialogue with clients when business is slow. Reciprocity is also essential to generating referrals from other professional services providers.

Another key factor to influencing is **consistency** – doing what you say you will. One of the biggest barriers to cross-selling is the concern that another individual or team within the firm may not undertake successfully what the client-care partner pledged to the client, eroding credibility owing to lack of consistency of service level.

It is challenging for any global professional services firm to achieve consistency of service across multiple geographical areas, skills and individuals. One way that has been successful in meeting this challenge is to develop a working charter for key clients, outlining the client's objectives and preferences, the professional services firm's commitment, agreed ways of working, fee bands, and procedures for addressing any conflicts, should they arise. Embedding this charter into client management systems and job-opening procedures ensures that a firm can demonstrate consistency of service to their clients.

Consistency plays a significant factor in moving a relationship to a working partnership. If a client actually commits to using a firm on the next opportunity, they are more likely to do so, having expressed that intent. Good communication between firm and client is important in order that there is no misunderstanding of intent on either side.

A client is more likely to want to engage with an expert than with an inexperienced consultant, the key influencing strategy here being **authority**. Authority can be demonstrated by qualifications, written articles and practical experience, and is at its most effective when a firm or individual can clearly demonstrate the value that this authority can bring to a prospective client. Anything less could be seen as bragging.

# Repairing damaged relationships

Bill Gates said: 'Your most unhappy customers are your greatest source of learning' (Gates, 1999). With the best intent and planning, sometimes things go wrong and we find that our clients are not as delighted with us as we would like. Regardless of whether the issue was not of our making, professional services marketers are often called upon to smooth troubled waters.

I recall several instances shortly after I had joined a new firm when I made contact with one of the firm's top clients and was presented with a less than flattering view of the firm. Not only was the firm not addressing the negative perception, they weren't even aware of it. In this instance, we were fortunate to have the opportunity to repair the relationship. I'll wager that there were countless others where clients turned to other professionals, rather than report and repair the breakdown.

Providing clients with the opportunity to provide frank feedback will capture most if not all early warning signs of damage to the relationship. At global engineering consultancy WSP, we carried out a programme of detailed client feedback meetings with key stakeholders in our top client firms. Any issues that were raised were then embedded in key client plans and their remedy was agreed and progress communicated regularly with the clients. The result was increased client retention. We intentionally did not use these feedback interviews to try to identify new opportunities to work with the client, though this was a frequent outcome of the discussions. Clients valued the fact that the meetings were about how we could work best together, rather than a soft sell.

Perception versus reality is an important concept when dealing with damaged relationships. Professionals' natural instinct is to defend or justify why an action was carried out in a particular way. Regardless of whether we did the best for the client, if the client does not perceive that to be so, the relationship will start to fail.

How we communicate is likely to be transmitted more loudly than usual in hostile or conflict situations. It's important when resolving conflict to be mindful of all aspects of communication: body language, pace of conversation, intonation and language.

The first time I received very negative client feedback, it was transmitted by telephone. Though there was the temptation to resolve things then and there, it was fundamental to preserving the relationship that I arranged a face-to-face meeting to discuss the concerns in detail with the aggrieved client. This allowed us the opportunity to gather as many facts as possible around the matter and, importantly, it enabled a much richer conversation with the client. Though still aggrieved at the meeting, the meeting lacked the hostility that the phone call had, setting the tone for a more even-tempered discussion with a successful resolution as the objective.

It was by no means a quick fix – we developed a corrective action plan with the client, clearly outlining what, how and by when we would address their concerns. These actions were embedded in performance management plans for their respective owners, and reviewed regularly at face-to-face meetings. Each milestone in the plan gave us the opportunity to report back positively to the client and by the time the last action had been completed, we had developed a much stronger relationship than we had prior to when the issue had arisen. The client became a key ally, promoting us within their own business, and we saw a sustained increase in instructions from then onwards.

Good preparation is critical to a successful negotiation or conflict resolution. Outlining your expected outcomes from the discussion, what areas can be conceded and what is non-negotiable helps the professional services firm to understand the boundaries within which to conduct a win–win negotiation. It is also helpful to think these factors through from the other party's perspective – what are they likely to want and how could we successfully accommodate that? It may be appropriate to consider the consequences if a mutually agreeable resolution cannot be found.

A large degree of emotional intelligence is required in repairing damaged relationships. I found it helpful to take an EQ 'temperature check' before undertaking each client feedback meeting by asking myself:

- Am I having a bad day at work and can I be certain that this won't spill over in my approach to the discussion?
- Am I prepared to listen without interruption to understand fully what is being communicated?
- Am I confident that I won't convey any frustration or stress when presented with negative feedback?

If the answer to any of these questions was 'no', I took the necessary steps, from a few deep breaths, a walk around the block, re-reading my notes on effective listening, to, in extreme circumstances, rescheduling the meeting until such time as I could answer 'yes' to these questions.

## Conclusion

There are several points to take from this chapter that will help today's business development and marketing professionals in their careers:

- Professional services firms in today's market need to be far more than technical experts. They need to be proficient communicators and relationship-builders as clients now expect to receive excellent service, transactional marketing having given way to relationship-based marketing.
- Professionals, accounts directors, business developers and marketers must work together as client-focused teams to deliver exceptional client service. Client relationships should be measured and rewarded at team level, to ensure succession and resilience during staff changes. Successful teamwork relies on good internal relationships and trust.
- Professionals and marketers need to see themselves through their clients' eyes. How the service is delivered is more valuable than intellectual ability. How the client perceives us is truth for our client. We need to ensure that their perception matches our aspirations of excellent customer service.
- While CRM software helps facilitate good relationship management, it is behaviours and client activity that achieve results. Planning is essential. Business developers and marketers have so much to be responsive to that CRM must be just that – managed.
- Firm organizational structure influences culture and individual behaviour and attitude to risk. Business development and marketing teams must understand and adapt to their internal stakeholders to achieve buy-in and success.

- Client development strategy will have greatest chance of success if developed collaboratively with partners, rather than delivered to them. Honing good influencing skills will lead to mutually satisfactory relationships, both internally and with clients.

While this chapter may state the obvious to many professional services providers, it is my experience through discussions with a diverse range of professional services providers that a large percentage of professional services firms have difficulty in applying many of the relationship principles outlined. I hope that the examples provided will assist and inspire other marketing and business development professionals to try new approaches and to generate successful outcomes through enriching client relationships.

# The primacy of relationships
## how and why clients choose

**12**

**DAN O'DAY,** Vice President, Thomson Reuters Elite

**Profile:** Dan is Vice President of Operations at Thomson Reuters Elite, where he is the general manager of several business units, including Business Development. Dan's career has focused on improving the operations and efficiency of professional services firms through the use of technology. Prior to joining Elite, Dan practised law and worked in both small and large firms. He is licensed to practise law in the state of California and received his JD and MBA from Pepperdine University.

This chapter explores how and why a client chooses their professional services advisers and considers the primacy of relationships in those decisions.

Working for a company with the resources of Thomson Reuters has provided me with considerable insight into how companies purchase professional services. In particular, we have done significant research into how legal services are purchased. In this chapter I will be using some of this information and enhancing it with my own experience both as a lawyer and as a vendor of business development software to professional services firms.

The chapter will focus on the legal sector, but I believe that the lessons are relevant across the professions, including accountants, engineers, forensic scientists and economists. All of these professions are similar in their focus on the value of the individual and their knowledge and skills.

As outlined in the introduction to this book, that value proposition for these firms has expanded from deep domain expertise and now includes knowledge and understanding of the client's business and their needs. We will look at how your firm can use that knowledge and understanding to influence a buyer's decision and either reinforce or overcome the primacy of existing relationships.

## Marketing the individual

One of the striking things about law firm marketing that separates it from most corporate marketing is how poorly the firms differentiate themselves. If you want to experience this for yourself, take five pitch books from five peer firms in the same area of practice and remove all occurrences of the firm name. Now try to identify which firm submitted each pitch book.

To further emphasize this point, take each pitch book and separate out the material about the client and the client's needs from the material about the firm and the firm's lawyers, history and expertise. The material about the firm will take up significantly more space than the material about the client. The emphasis is often on the individuals at the firm and their expertise. Regularly the professional biographies make up the bulk of the pitch book.

As a marketing professional this approach to a pitch makes sense because general counsel hire lawyers, not law firms, when purchasing legal services. The number one factor in choosing a lawyer for a new matter is whether the client enjoys working with that person. It is only occasionally when a client is presented with a new type of case that they will look outside of the people they usually work with. Even in this case they will most likely go to existing counsel they enjoy working with for a referral. Thus, relationships are of primary importance to new business development. This includes relationships with clients, prospects, and even other counsel who may refer work to the lawyer.

## Market segmentation

Despite the significance of the individuals and their relationships, there is value in the firm name. The one critical thing the firm name does to differentiate its lawyers is place them in a tier of peer firms. Our research confirms my own experience that corporate counsel think of law firms in tiers. Most corporate counsel think of their legal firms as qualifying for one of three tiers. Marketing your firm fully depends on you knowing which tier your firm is in. Marketing outside your tier is unlikely to produce results in the form of new business. It would be like Fiat marketing to the very wealthy or Rolls-Royce marketing to the middle class.

The first tier includes firms that excel in everyday commodity work. This is where price and efficiency are paramount. These firms not only have the lowest hourly rates, but they are also expected to produce the work in fewer billable hours than a high-end firm. They are seen as the value firms. The work quality is sufficient for most routine matters when the amount at risk is under a certain threshold. These firms are most competitive when there is a high volume of similar work to be performed. They have developed workflows and procedures to deal with this work in a quick and effective manner. They often invest in technology to automate steps that are done manually at most other firms.

In the second tier are firms that are used when the work is complex, but still under a certain level of risk. This includes both corporate transactions and certain types of litigation. At most companies this is the majority of the work that is sent to firms. They are looking for competent counsel, but not a firm that commands a huge premium for its work. This part of the market is also undergoing a transformation, with many firms merging to gain market share. Work moves around in this market more than in the other tiers.

At the top are those firms that command the high-value work. This is large litigation, big mergers and acquisitions, and some specialized tax and regulatory work. As one general counsel put it to me, 'in these cases my board members need to already know the firm has expertise in this area or they will question my selection'. In these cases the firms are typically those seen regularly in the *Wall Street Journal* or *Financial Times* articles. In the UK market they have a name and are known as the 'magic circle' firms. In Australia there is the 'big six' and in the United States there are the 'white shoe firms' (albeit this term applies more broadly and has a less well-defined membership).

This market segmentation is where relationships reach their limit. No matter how strong the relationships, clients rarely allow firms to submit proposals for work outside their tier. On occasion, and in particular during the recession, firms in the top tier offer to perform work at a lower tier to keep people busy. These tend to be temporary relationships and are rarely sustainable because of the negative impact that such actions have on profitability. Some firms in this tier have made the strategic decision to shrink a little to keep rates at a premium.

Corporate counsel who propose that the work be done by a firm in the wrong tier know that they are putting their careers at risk. They will likely be questioned on the selection and if things don't go well their judgement will be questioned. This can take the form of a bad outcome or of an inflated bill, which does not meet the budget. Naturally, corporate counsel are risk averse and in our interviews we did not find anyone who was willing to take that type of reputational risk.

It should be noted that tiers are not universal to the firm brand. They vary by region and practice area. For example, the 'magic circle' firms do not have the same reputation when it comes to US banking that they do for EU banking. In addition, international law-firm mergers have created global firms that have different tier profiles in different markets.

## Corporate counsel are conflicted about change

It is not surprising that relationships are so critical. In talking to corporate counsel I consistently hear that they like to work with people who have complementary work styles. Some like to work through things in a challenge and response mode. Others like to have it presented to them in more of a dissertation style. Responsiveness is universally cited as a key factor. Clients want availability and expect a quick response, even if that response is 'I will get back to you'. Responsiveness is no longer a differentiator. It is a baseline expectation.

There are a lot of headlines about corporate counsel driving change in firms. In some cases they are pushing for better budgets and more legal project management; in other cases they want fixed-fee and capped-fee arrangements. Regularly they are pushing firms to think about efficiency, where historically firms focused on effectiveness, and often they are asking their outside counsel to think before filing an extra motion that has a slim chance of success.

Yet in all this drive for change they still enjoy working the way they always have, and they want to work with people they like. The push for change comes on top of the fundamental aspects of the relationship. They want the work to go to the people they like and will often help those firms with which they have a relationship to pitch for the business. As one marketing director wisely advised, 'even if the RFP says do not contact us, you should contact them. It is always helpful.'

## Firms can no longer assume that business will keep coming

In today's competitive market it is critical that a firm does not assume they will win the business on relationship alone. In particular, if it is for a large volume of work there will be many people in the selection process. This is where they need to leverage their relationships to navigate the request for proposal (RFP) process and steer the responses towards a favourable outcome. For example, if the company has made legal project management (LPM) a critical component, the RFP response needs to come back with more than just a paragraph or two on it. Come back with an actual plan on how this work will be managed. In other words, treat the RFP like you would the legal work itself.

Firms often lead the pitch with their experience. In the corporate world, experience means efficiency. An experience pitch that is often followed up by what they see as reinventing the wheel frustrates clients. For example, if your firm pitches experience in doing mineral rights agreements in a particular jurisdiction and you are hired to do that work, the corporate client wants your partner to ask him the 10 relevant variables and produce the agreement in no time. He does not want a back-and-forth dialogue with multiple drafts and various clauses coming in and out of the agreement. At the end of a matter run in this way, clients often feel that almost any lawyer could have done similar work and the experience the partner brought did not provide the value they were seeking.

Experience needs to be captured in a way that makes it reusable. Most firms have developed several knowledge management initiatives in an effort to achieve this goal. The vast majority of these initiatives fail to produce the desired results. This is one area where the UK firms have had more success than the firms in the United States. This is a direct result of the willingness of the UK firms to dedicate the resources, including lawyers, needed to make these projects a success. The US firms often focus on passive solutions and technologies to help with this, and inevitably end up falling short of expectations.

## Value of relationships often exceeds value of experience

As discussed above, experience is what firms believe they are selling, yet when they look to bring in lateral partners it is not what they are buying. As one partner put it: 'When I get a call from a recruiter, I am only asked two questions. What is your book of business? And how portable is it?' He went on to lament that 'they never ask about my experience or qualifications'. That is because the real value of lawyers is their relationships. It is an unfortunate fact that their book of business and its portability are the best measure of the value of those relationships. This fact is not lost on partners and they treasure both their book of business and the underlying relationships.

The critical value of the relationship has also created one of the largest obstacles to cross-selling professional services. There are two concerns that are most often stated. The first and most common concern is that another partner will not provide the same level of service and this will cause the client to lose trust in the referring partner. The second, less commonly said aloud, is that the partner could lose control of the relationship and that would reduce their value to the firm and the marketplace.

## Why a CRM system is not a solution

A firm's real asset is the value of all of its relationships in total. Most professional services firms have recognized this and deployed customer relationship management (CRM) tools. It is also no secret that most of these projects have failed to deliver the promised return on investment. This is because most CRM tools require the active involvement of the people that own the relationship, and it is only human nature that people both do the minimum to get by and jealously guard items of great value. This is a significant barrier to overcome.

Our research (based on mining Microsoft Exchange at approximately 100 firms and corporations) shows that fewer than 20 per cent of relationships ever make it into the CRM tool. Even the data that make it into the system are not kept up to date. Even when contacts are entered correctly, the accuracy of the information fades quickly. It could be anything – a title, address, phone number; all of it changes – even names and sometimes genders. Just think of the number of fields you have in Outlook and most CRM systems have far more than that.

This problem is not just experienced at professional services companies. Even in corporate environments, such as Thomson Reuters, contact details end up in the CRM system because they are needed for some other reason, not to benefit the relationship itself. For example, they are added because someone needs to be invited to an event or perhaps because they are required to get an expense report paid. In fact, after an initial burst of activity surrounding a CRM implementation, it is quite common that its primary use devolves to managing newsletter subscriptions and the annual holiday-card mailing.

On top of this, lawyers are particularly adverse to the idea that they are in sales. Any comparison to sales people is seen as derogatory. Expecting them to keep a CRM system up to date is seen as unnecessary work and their time too valuable for that kind of task.

That said, lawyers are the primary rainmakers for their firms, and therefore must assume business development or sales activities. These may be mostly related to developing and maintaining good relationships with clients, potential clients and referring counsel. They may also be related to making pitches, responding to RFPs and crafting profitable alternative fee agreements.

All large firms and most small ones have put in place tools to help lawyers with these tasks; however, adoption and use of these tools and technologies remains largely up to the lawyers themselves. This presents an interesting conundrum: most lawyers have at least a profile on LinkedIn and a bio published in one or more online databases; many tweet, blog or make other use of social media, yet few could name the CRM tools their own firm uses daily. This is because they understand the fundamental principle that the relationship is key. They do what they have to do to manage their own relationships, and are not interested in, or motivated to risk them by, exposure to a larger audience.

Another area where firms fall critically short of corporations is in win/loss analysis. Most firms do not have good data on what percentage of pitches they win vs lose, and when they do lose them, tracking the reasons for losing in order to look for trends. These data can be extremely valuable to stemming market loss and growing the firm. As a marketing professional, this is an area where you could make a real impact on the firm by simply following up with the partner after the RFP and pitch cycle to see what happened.

Naturally, there are tools to address these issues, and they are getting better at doing so despite lawyers' natural predilections to avoid them. These tools allow people within a firm to see who has relationships with clients they want to meet or who has the specific knowledge required to make a referral. There are other tools that aggregate data about a client to enable better pitches and more accurately understand a client's business goals and issues.

## The importance of delivering value

As stated above, clients are under pressure to focus on efficiency. This move to value is a fundamental change for a profession that was previously measured on effectiveness. Lawyers have been trained to focus on the outcome. The final determination or settlement was how they have been measured and what they have been trained to excel at in law school. Winning the argument was more important than the time invested in it.

Another term for efficiency is value. Much has been written about this over the past few years, and the Association of Corporate Counsel (ACC) has instituted a very popular (among corporate counsel at least) programme known as the ACC Value Challenge. They have published several handbooks on subjects such as value-based fees, value-based staffing, value-based relationships with outside counsel, and legal project management. The trick for law firms is to figure out or define what value means for a particular matter in the client's eyes. Is it a quick resolution? Lower cost? Shared risk? There are many pitfalls in assuming that value is a fixed quantity, and this is where good relationships and close collaboration prove their worth.

So, if relationships are so valuable, how do law firms ever get new clients? Our research indicates that there are four reasons why corporate counsel would hire you over another firm:

1. **Argue for quality:** deliver better results at the same price as their current law firm. That is easy to say but hard to do. You typically get only one chance to prove yourself in this scenario. References and testimonials are crucial to this pitch.
2. **It's time to upgrade:** a growing company has outgrown its current, smaller firm. You must demonstrate that your firm has the experience and capacity to deal with matters that the smaller firm cannot. Highlight your advantages, whether they are practice groups more aligned with the company's needs, compatible office locations, and so forth.
3. **Cost efficiency:** we offer the same quality you get today at a better price. Firms are challenged to do this every day. You will need to show the client how you will achieve this goal, and you will have to show your partners how you can do this and be profitable at the same time.
4. **Trust relationship:** we will continue to deliver the quality you get today. You know us and can rely on us. General counsel want stability, predictability and reliability in the lawyers and firms they hire. Performing good work at a reasonable price is a sure recipe for success.

# Winning new business with relationships

Given the limited opportunities for new business, it is critical the partners at your firm be prepared to take advantage when those opportunities arrive. There are two common ways to dislodge an entrenched competitor (outside of the still popular lateral hire method). One is to leverage some already existing business into a much larger opportunity with the client; the second is to develop a relationship so compelling that the prospect thinks it may be time for a change.

One of the first principles to understand in building relationships and trust is never to disparage your competition. This is particularly challenging for individuals who are naturally critical, as most lawyers are. Negative commentary on your competitor only provides them with credibility and can give the impression you are threatened by them. It can also make the firm or partner look petty and small. This can be particularly difficult when the firm is asked to review the work of another firm. Unless that work looks like serious malpractice, the response should start with the positive elements of the work, followed by areas for improvement, and be summed up with a statement that it is good work that could be even better.

Another area to watch with relationships is entertainment. This is an area where the clients themselves say: stop asking about lunches and dinners and just talk about your work and its relevance to them. Talk to them about current issues that impact their business. Clients that can be influenced by corporate entertainment are few and far between. These days, many companies have clear limits on what can be accepted from vendors to prevent this type of bias.

Work relationships are best started on a professional footing and can then move to become more social over time. As a marketing professional it is best to organize events around content for prospective clients. You may want to make it a breakfast or lunch for the convenience of work schedules, but you should still focus on the content rather than the food. Topical webinars targeting specific issues for specific industries also work well to introduce the firm's expertise. For existing clients some events, for example golf days, are good ways to help maintain the relationship, but no matter the event it is important that there is some substantive business content.

It can take years to wean a client away from another firm, so success is about being consistent. The frequency depends on the nature of the relationship and what you have to offer. As a general rule, only contact the prospective client when you have something that is both relevant and new. If more than three months go by without contact, the relationship partner needs to look for a reason. Just checking in is not a reason.

If your marketing responsibilities include new business development, you can add value by reminding the partners to keep the relationships going. They are busy people and easily distracted. Track the date of their last exchange (there are tools to automate this). When the relationship starts to stall, help them reach out. Find something relevant for them to latch onto. If the relationship is strong, at some point that corporate counsel will call back and start talking about a 'situation' and the business will open up from there.

## Conclusion – the importance of trust

We have discussed throughout this chapter the primacy of relationships in professional services and the factors that either reinforce or undermine those relationships. In speaking to corporate counsel about their relationships with their advisers, there was one factor that was nearly universal in all these conversations. They want a relationship of trust with outside counsel.

They understand that law firms are businesses and need to turn a profit. They are struggling in this new world just as much as law firms are to get their heads around the dizzying arrays of fee arrangements and trying to sort out matter budgets from competing firms to understand whether they are getting value for money.

Your clients believe that if your firm prices a matter unrealistically, they may get substandard work, or that the fees will greatly exceed the estimate. In other words, it is possible to underbid and lose credibility. If the price is too low, they suspect that there is something the firm is not considering and that it is therefore less qualified to do the work.

An example of where trust can be reinforced or undermined is shadow billing, an increasingly common practice on fixed-fee work. This is where a firm has to submit both the fixed-fee bill and the hours spent on the matter. Many firms take exception to shadow billing on fixed-fee matters. They see it as a lack of trust from the client in the firm's integrity to work and bill appropriately. This is the wrong approach to take as, while partners are under pressure to sell work and maintain profitability, your clients equally are under tremendous pressure to hold down cost. There is an opportunity here to share information, promote transparency and build trust, or undermine it by being secretive and confrontational.

Trust is the key to relationships and, in turn, relationships are critical to selling professional services.

# LESSONS ON RELATIONSHIPS

From our contributions on the theme of Relationships, here are our top 10 lessons for marketing and business development leaders:

1. **Core clients:** developing long-term, mutually beneficial relationships with core clients is probably the best route to success and sustainability for most firms.
2. **Client involvement:** at the very least, clients should know and agree that they are on your relationship management programme; at best, they should participate in the programme with you. Involving the client in the planning and decision-making will enhance and deliver greater opportunity.
3. **Analysis and objectives:** such is the ubiquity these days of relationship management programmes that it is easy to skip over why you have one, who is involved and what you want to achieve. Ensure that before you start you analyse your client base, then set some objectives and make the right choices.
4. **Mutual benefit:** it will be obvious what your firm is looking to get out of its relationship management programme (increased revenue and profit, secure income streams, wider work portfolio, and so on), but don't forget to consider what the client is getting – a relationship should be mutually beneficial.
5. **Measurement:** this is going to be a big investment for the firm – maybe not in terms of direct cash outlay, but certainly when you consider partner or senior management time. So, make sure that you measure impact and take decisions accordingly. Ideally link incentives and reward to performance.
6. **Personality and trust:** when setting up and managing your programme, don't forget that relationships are all about trust and commitment between individuals. Don't lose the personal touch among your corporate objectives. Personality fit and one-to-one connections should certainly influence strongly who is involved.
7. **Marathon, not a sprint:** core client relationship management (CRM) should not be a fad or short-term activity. It should be a way of life and therefore requires the investment of time, commitment and mutual benefit over the long term – just like any good relationship.
8. **CRM systems:** you will probably want some sort of CRM system to complement your programme, but it shouldn't dominate proceedings – relationships come first, systems second.

9 **Internal and external relationships:** sponsoring a core CRM programme is one of the most valuable additions a marketing or business development team can make to their firm. Marketers have a critical role to play, but their success will depend on their ability to develop great relationships with internal stakeholders as well as external clients.

10 **Training and coaching:** CRM doesn't come naturally to all professionals. Training and coaching will be a big part of the set-up and running of any programme.

# THEME FIVE
## Managing

# Introduction to the Managing theme

> *Rank does not confer privilege or give power. It imposes responsibility.* (PETER DRUCKER)

In the days when the expectations of a professional services marketer were set at the level of discipline specialist, the step up to manager was not significant. The progress from unit to team to department head was usually gradual and the sphere of influence limited.

A marketing department was probably not significant in terms of the number of people and included like-minded individuals whose skill sets and aspirations broadly matched those of the person asked to take a lead. In addition, the position was probably not considered to be at the senior management level – unlike Finance and maybe HR. The marketing manager or head of department was probably asked to report to a marketing partner or equivalent director, someone who may not be a discipline specialist, but was considered to understand the views and opinions of clients and the partnership or director group.

As firms started to accept marketing as a valued discipline and began to wrap business planning, and even strategy, into the brief, a new generation of leaders stepped forward. Marketers were promoted or recruited into senior management roles on a par with other functional heads and, depending on the firm's culture, the operational partners and directors. Reporting lines shifted to managing partner or chief executive to reflect that change in status.

At this level, marketers need to influence not just the agenda and performance of their discipline colleagues, but also the wider partnership and senior leadership group. The measure now is not can you get the best out of a fellow marketer, but can you help your professional colleagues step up in their role as client relationship managers and business developers?

This is a role where advisory and influencing skills are more valuable than traditional line management ones. People will take advice and act on it because they like what they hear, are convinced by the argument and see both firm-wide and personal benefit. They don't act because someone has told them to. They also want a role model – someone who can walk the talk, not just preach from a pulpit.

In this model, a marketing leader has two distinct audiences to influence: a smaller group of direct reports and a wider group of functional colleagues and professionals, the latter extending from the top of the professional pyramid – partners and directors – right down to the bottom – newly qualified professionals and graduates.

Into this mix has now been thrown an additional audience, who probably don't report directly to the marketing leader, but do fall more closely into the discipline group than the wider professional set. In recent years, firms have started to professionalize the business development and sales processes of their firms and have recruited discipline specialists into those roles. These positions typically have not been taken into a central functional team, as with marketing, but placed out with the operational teams and businesses.

Whatever the overall marketing or business development leader's background, technical skill or discipline brief, the expectation is now that this individual will combine management, influencing and leadership skills to get the best out of all the relevant marketing, business development and sales resources in the firm, irrespective of the level of direct control. That implies a significant sphere of influence with a varied and flexible set of skills. In any one day, that leader can expect to cover any and all of the following:

- Set or measure performance on specific objectives for a junior report.
- Review strategic progress with the senior management team.
- Plan a development programme with a fellow director.
- Influence discipline and programme development in other functional areas, for example professional development programmes, recruitment and quality control.
- Teach or role-model client development best practice with a team of professionals.
- Challenge a partner or senior director on client behaviours.
- Interview or explain the firm's capabilities to a client.
- Contribute to a business development team's latest proposal or sales pitch.

Beyond being able achieve all of the above personally, the same individual needs to help all the audiences above work together successfully without the marketing leader being in the room!

If this doesn't seem too much to ask of one individual, two other capabilities have moved sharply into focus for a leader looking to manage a marketing organization. The first concerns marketing as a stimulus and cause for a change. The second is the need for marketing and business development metrics to match more recognized financial and performance measures.

Throughout this book we have covered the changing requirements of clients and the resulting need for a professional services firm and its marketers to adjust and evolve accordingly. If a marketing leader is going to be a client champion within their firm, the marketing agenda must act as a stimulus for change. It conveniently serves the ambitions of the marketing leader, but the modern marketing and business development agenda is likely neither to reinforce the status quo, nor restrict its impact to activities usually seen within the function's sphere of influence. We discuss elsewhere aspects of professional development, recruitment, project performance and quality control where marketers will need to get involved. As a marketing leader, change will be the only constant.

Finally, to bring marketing right to the fore and establish its influence on a par with all other aspects of professional firm management, marketing leaders must drive the agenda on measuring performance and judging return on investment. Across the marketing discipline, not just in professional services firms, leaders complain that they don't carry the influence or command the respect of other functional heads, most notably finance. There are a number of factors at play here, including history, precedent and professional qualifications, but without doubt the major one is measurement.

The inclusion of sales and business development into the portfolio of responsibilities has helped, but traditionally marketing has been seen as a discipline of the 'black arts': a necessary evil where whatever you try to measure, you are never sure if you are getting value for money. Rather than challenge that viewpoint and suggest realistic metrics, marketers have revelled in their elusive and illusory status and put forward cogent but frustrating arguments as to why they should just be trusted to deliver.

Marketers should lead the agenda and set metrics that become as critical to performance as operational utilization, charge-out rates and retention. Whether those measures are related to awareness and recognition at one end of the spectrum or opportunity conversion and client profitability at the other, the marketing leader will not be able to help manage the organization successfully if they cannot demonstrate how to measure it.

In this section we cover all the points introduced above in much greater depth through the eyes of five experienced marketing leaders. Matthew Fuller from White & Case and Jessica Scholz from Freshfields, two global law firms, separately share their experiences and keys to success of leading marketing and business development teams. Amy Kingdon and Eleanor Campion from the design, engineering and project management consultancy Atkins look specifically at the marketer's role in leading change in their organization. We finish with Giles Pugh from management consultant Sutherlands Pugh giving his advice on the all-important topic of marketing metrics.

# It's all about value
## managing marketing and business development

**MATTHEW FULLER,** Director of Marketing and Business Development EMEA, White & Case LLP

**Profile:** Matthew has nearly 25 years' experience working for international law firms. He has led the global business development teams at Allen & Overy and at Herbert Smith and spent time working in Germany. He is currently Director of Business Development and Marketing in EMEA at White & Case LLP. Matthew was also on the board of PSMG from 2006 to 2009.

In this chapter we look at the role of marketing and business development leaders in professional services firms and ask how they can deliver real value to their clients and the firm. We look at the issues and challenges faced by marketing and business development teams and explore the behavioural aspects of successful team management. We use a case study on improving the pitch process to illustrate how a marketing and business development leader needs to consider all aspects of the firm and partner and team engagement to succeed.

## The change in the professional services market

I recall, many years ago, the managing partner of the firm I was working for saying: 'There are just three basic levers of profitability in a professional services firm – cost-cutting, equity management and revenue generation.' As a perceptive and forward-thinking leader, he then went on to comment that 'firms like ours spend too much time on the first of the three and not enough on the last – revenue generation is the only one that can fundamentally turn around the business'.

As you might expect, I wholeheartedly agree with this view. All three levers must be continually and rigorously reviewed, and will, if properly planned, work together, but it is only by bringing in new work that you can make a successful and profitable business.

The basic economics of professional services firms has not changed in decades. What have changed are the buyers of services from those organizations. Clients no longer purchase just the expertise of the professional: they now buy value – the complete service and relationship. They are savvier and more sophisticated, keen to squeeze as much knowledge and experience as possible from the supplier in the most efficient way possible.

They are 'street wise' too. Many clients grew up in private practice and they understand well the dynamics of both the professional services firm and the market, and hence demand the best and most valuable service at the most competitive price. The clients no longer want a 'doctor–patient' arrangement where they call up their lawyer or accountant because they need a particular service, for example M&A advisory work or advice on a joint venture contract.

They want a relationship – and a relationship and partnership with a firm prepared to invest time in their business and markets, getting to know individuals and the sectors in which they operate. They also want ideas and proactive actions – being alerted to problems that might lie ahead, such as opportunities to invest in new companies or geographies. They want the professional firm to train their people, second their staff and share the risks on big projects. In short, they want a lot more… but for less.

This seismic shift in the client–professional service relationship has been developing for around 15 years. The 21st-century partnership may have the same economic dynamics as the late-20th-century firm, but the marketplace has been turned upside down and revenue generation demands a very different set of requirements and nature of support – all centred on value.

## So how are professional service firms adapting to this change?

This change in the marketplace, together with the globalization of the economy and the impact of the financial crisis, has created a more complex, fast-moving environment with larger, multi-office and multifaceted firms keen to retain the partnership principles but acknowledging (often reluctantly) the importance of adopting more 'corporate' structures and the professionalism of their business service support. Firms have begun to acknowledge that without more efficient internal structures and dedicated professional support, they cannot compete, sustain client relationships or ultimately generate more revenue.

This realization has driven firms to begin to organize themselves more around clients and move away from marketing solely along product or practice lines. Key client programmes, focused around the priority clients of the firm, are now the norm, with roles carved out for relationship partners and systems and processes established to support these relationship teams.

Accountancy and consultancy firms have been doing this for years with considerable sophistication and with relationship partners becoming role models, taken off fee-earning work and allowed to identify opportunities for fee-earners to follow up. In these firms, client relationship managers have also been hired with the expectation that they will spend time with clients, build relationships and generate revenue. Others within the professional services arena have been slower to follow, but are beginning to make significant changes as the clients in their markets become more demanding.

But what of the business development director/chief marketing officer role – the senior professional who heads the business development team in these professional services firms? Without doubt, the biggest change I have observed over the past 10–15 years, driven as a response to this very different market, is the new status that this role has been given. There is now widespread acceptance that professional expertise is of value and these directors have now been empowered to guide and contribute to the firm's strategic conversations and plans, as well as being given responsibility for executing these plans. This shift, which I have directly experienced, also comes with the expectation that senior members of the business development and marketing group, reporting into the director, will also be able to provide strategic advice and thinking, in addition to completing and delivering the basic business development tasks.

So, what exactly is this strategic thinking and advice? From my experience, the answer to this actually correlates directly with the client–supplier change outlined above. It is all about value. In other words, what insights, contacts or opportunities can the business development professional offer? These are the kinds of contribution that professional services organizations are looking for from their business development team and are a very large part of how marketing and business development professionals are now measured.

As an example, when I was leading business development at another firm, I quickly realized on joining that there was, first, a thirst for information from the partnership, and secondly, a need for someone to tailor and interpret this information. I also realized that not only for myself, but also for the whole team that I led, it would be hugely beneficial to have a proper research capability in-house, which could support us in providing intelligent and user-friendly reports on clients, markets, sectors, practices and geographies.

My very first hire at the firm, Ian Gilbert, was a young but dedicated researcher who had relevant experience at another leading international law firm. He immediately made an impact – producing informed reports, either in conjunction with business development colleagues working on projects or a particular pitch, or directly for a partner. There is no doubt that this work boosted the perception of the business development function at the firm and allowed for business development professionals to have conversations with partners, which they would not have managed before.

By the time I left the firm, and in the run-up to a major merger, the research team had expanded to four people and played a central role in supporting the due diligence process and advising the management executive on the clients and markets to pursue and prioritize after the merger.

# Issues and challenges

So, in this changing market, what are the issues or barriers facing the business development and marketing team and what are the challenges as it strives to add value?

The fundamental issue revolves around managing expectations. Most professional services firms acknowledge the changes that have happened in the market and the need to become more client and relationship focused. They also understand that bringing in professional support to help address this challenge can make a significant difference. However, firms often do not set realistic expectations of what one individual can achieve quickly, in particular if they are a new recruit, and then accept and allow them to operate within the partnership.

Partnerships are strange animals, with their own rules and ways of operating. While many are changing, and changing fast, to a more 'corporate' structure, they are not listed companies or highly structured corporations in which a small handful of individuals can make decisions speedily, setting the direction and quickly cascading orders down the organization.

The partners in a great many professional services firms are the shareholders and continue to want to have a say in the direction and, to an extent, the running of the firm. Managing partners, partners in charge of offices and practices, and client relationship partners all need 'buy-in' for decisions and the head of business development and marketing and their team have to learn and be taught how to operate in this culture.

The number of experienced and highly paid marketing professionals who have joined, failed and left professional services is very high. The most common report heard is that the firm believes that the business development director achieved little and offered no value, while the individual in question's view was that there was too little autonomy and delegated decision-making power and the management failed to drive change and make speedy decisions. This mismatch in expectations has also sadly tended to run through the 'ranks', with one former colleague commenting that 'the average business development executive at a law firm lasts as long as a sub-lieutenant in the First World War – about three months'.

The challenges facing the business development professional can be broadly split into two – those that are 'operational' and those that are more 'behavioural'. I will drill into these in a little more detail before addressing the common challenge for everyone in professional services – dealing with a lack of time.

## *Operational challenges*

First, for properly planned, joined-up and targeted business development to be successful, the objectives have to be part of the firm's and its practice groups' strategic plans and, in turn, included in individual fee-earner objectives. There must be total alignment and transparency.

Secondly, proper metrics have to be in place – clear, concise and realistic measurements. For fee-earners, a 'balanced scorecard' annual appraisal should be a part of the firm's overall performance programme, with individuals' personal business development origination and initiatives reviewed and a return on investment (ROI) analysed alongside their personal billing records. Plans and progress of business development objectives and targets should also be a prominent part of partner meetings and regularly featured in e-mail and presentation updates.

Thirdly, the firm needs to have the relevant marketing support tools in place to enable individuals and teams to generate ideas and plans, to execute on these and then to ensure that they are followed up and measured. Without user-friendly basics, such as an integrated contact management system, pitch templates and an up-to-date curriculum vitae (CV) database, all the best plans and intentions will be wasted. Even if they are in place, they will be wasted if there is no training on how they should be used – training that covers the technical essentials, but also drives the benefits to the user, so that they become embedded and part of the culture of how to do business in the firm.

For the business development team in particular, there are some important operational challenges that must be addressed to ensure maximum effectiveness and success. These are:

- The business development director or chief marketing officer must be given the status within the firm to be able to lead advice and make critical decisions. Ideally, the director should be on the board or the firm's executive and have the equivalent status to a partner. The leader's position will have a direct effect on the rest of the team and the way they are viewed within the firm.
- The business development team must be given access to information – key financial data as well as relevant strategic information, which could impact on the way the firm goes to market or the clients and targets with whom it communicates. Within reason, the team should also be allowed access to partner meetings and be on the relevant e-mail distribution lists.
- The business development team should be co-located with the practice groups they support – in other words, sitting on the relevant business floors, immersed with the business and visible and accessible to all. The only exception to this should be those people within the team who have more 'central' roles – the events, design and operations/systems professionals who are not dedicated to one particular practice.

## *Behavioural challenges*

In most cases, it should be possible to meet and resolve these operational challenges. Behavioural challenges, however, pose very different demands and often concern deep-seated cultural and organizational approaches, with long histories and traditions, frequently involving individuals unwilling to change. Successful business development in a professional services firm can only come about in an environment conducive to promoting transparent communication, open dialogue, a flexible attitude and forward-thinking leadership, which thinks in a commercial way.

The principal challenges that therefore have to be addressed are:

- How to make the organization client-focused, so that all the structures and approaches 'mirror the client' and are outward facing. Take a look at many of the professional firms' websites, their shop window to the outside world, and note the way the sites describe and organize the firm and, too often, offer an internally focused profile, rather than a client-oriented one.

- The ability to acknowledge the differences in an organization's offices, practices and regions. A firm should be flexible in how it approaches its different business development needs and understanding; it should celebrate uniqueness and thus appreciate that 'one size does not fit all'. Individual practices, however, must not use the defence of being 'different' as an excuse for inaction and non-conformity. A balance needs to be struck!

- Looking beyond your desk. This is a real challenge to many in the professional services world who have been brought up and trained to be specialists in a particular field, with its own distinct market, people and nuances. Of course, there is always a place and need for specialization. However, how individuals link up and communicate with other specialists is key. Many client needs are not neatly packaged around a particular specialism covered by an expert. They are broader and therefore require a joined-up approach from the professional services firm in response. This is as important when reacting to a client request, as it is in thinking of potential marketing opportunities from the clients' perspective. Specialists need to get up from their desks and talk openly about their clients and not just one practice area.

- How to get the firm to take a more 'commercial approach'. Professionals, lawyers, accountants, surveyors and so on have been trained to draft precise and professional technical reports and documents for their clients. However, this approach and style of writing is very often not needed when reaching out to prospective clients to profile the firm or gain attention on a particular issue. It is a huge shift for many to write or summarize an issue in an eye-catching form. Often this has to be done with extreme speed, so that your firm is the first out in the market with the alert on a topical issue. In my experience, all too often 'perfection is the enemy of the good' as professionals agonize over precise wording, resulting in the moment being lost as issues become history or are addressed by a competitor.

- Putting interested and passionate partners in charge of key marketing initiatives or client relationships. It is a fact that without enthusiastic leadership in these roles (which includes, of course, dedicating quality time), progress will not be made. If firms are serious about revenue generation, the best 'rainmakers' must be put in charge.

Finally, I have a word about confidence. I have noticed that many partners lack self-belief in their business development skills. Maybe it is a British malaise, but excessive modesty and self-effacement does not lead to distinct messaging and differentiation. In a world where everyone has less time and there is more competition, the ability to put your message out there in a punchy and succinct fashion is of paramount importance. It also has to be delivered with conviction and backed up with facts. Refining key selling messages, whether they be for a firm, a practice or an individual, is as important as how they are delivered.

There are also some fundamental behavioural challenges facing the business development team. These principally involve a shift away from a traditional comfort

**FIGURE 13.1** Balancing proactivity and reactivity in business development

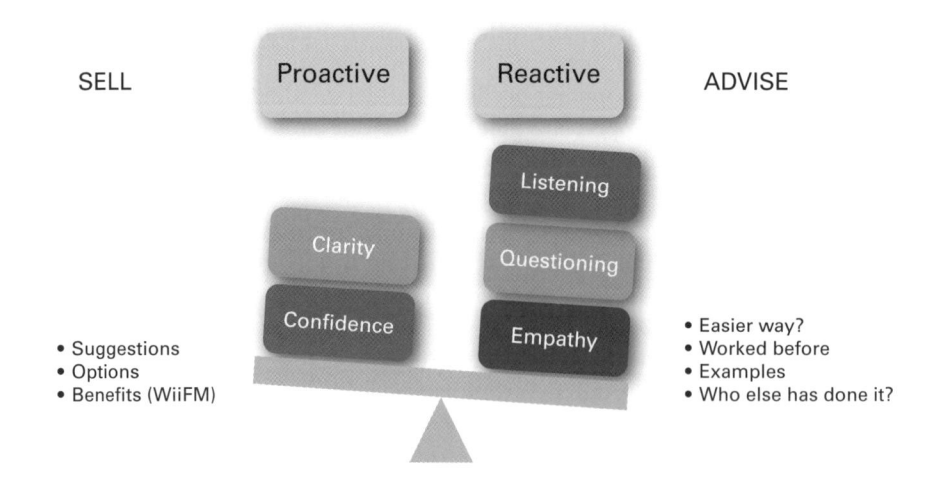

```
         Proactive              Reactive
SELL                                              ADVISE

                              Listening
              Clarity
                              Questioning
              Confidence
• Suggestions                 Empathy             • Easier way?
• Options                                         • Worked before
• Benefits (WiiFM)                                • Examples
                                                  • Who else has done it?
```

zone of sitting behind a desk reacting to queries and requests and communicating via e-mail. What I hear from partners constantly is a desire for their business development colleagues to be highly visible and totally engaged in the business and, above all else, coming up with ideas and suggestions to attract clients and win more work. As with all jobs, there will always be an element of administration that must be done, but currently, in most professional services firms, typical practice business development professionals spend too much of their time being reactive rather than proactive. John Timperley from The Results Consultancy has a useful diagram which summarizes this balancing act and what this means for the business development professional (Figure 13.1).

What this diagram illustrates is the essential split in the two basic behaviours for business development professionals. On the one side, we have proactivity requiring selling. For business development professionals to operate effectively, they need to have confidence in what they are selling and clarity in the way they deliver messages and propositions. Within any such discussion, the 'seller' (business development manager) needs to provide suggestions and options that ultimately explain very clearly what the benefits are to the 'buyer' (or partner). And for passing the benefit test – or the 'what's in it for me?' (WiiFM) test, the partner will want to know if it will help him or her to:

- win new clients?
- save me time?
- make me look good?
- raise my profile?
- make my life easier?
- hit my financial targets?
- achieve my plans?

- show I'm a team player?
- get an important action done?

On the reactive side of the chart, the key is to turn this into an advisory role – and away from a perception of just responding to a request. The key components around this involve listening, questioning and empathizing with the partner around their need. Business development professionals must plan better for these discussions and consider whether there are other options or opportunities to benefit from best practice.

Partners repeatedly demand ideas and creative thinking from their business development teams. When they have ideas themselves, they want to be challenged and expect well-thought-through advice. Presently, the balance is often not there in professional services firms, with the scales tilted towards a more reactive approach. This must change if the value of the service is to be sustained.

Underpinning both the operational and behavioural challenges facing business development professionals is the challenge over how best to use limited time. To allow the balance to move towards being more proactive, something has to give – with some traditional, mainstay business development work being moved away from the business development team's responsibility.

This is exactly the issue that was identified at my current firm, White & Case. The case study below outlines a project that was set up to tackle this issue, together with plans for taking this forward to the next level.

## CASE STUDY   The pitch improvement project

We identified that unnecessary tasks and actions were hampering progress in assigning business development support time onto key client relationship-building and development activities. To resolve this issue we set up an internal team, led by our Global Business Development and Marketing Operations Director, Jeremy Ford, and aided by a third-party consultant to help us scope out and deliver a solution.

Our starting position was to establish how the business development and marketing team typically spent their time on a per week/per day basis. We surveyed all the individuals in the team using in-depth, face-to-face interviews (no easy task in a global organization spanning 40 offices and around 200 business development or marketing personnel). The results were astonishing, with 42 different types of work identified, ranging from creation of brochures and publications to pitch production, events, research and database administration. These work types were then split into broad task baskets such as administration, or client targeting. In consultation with the senior manager group, 10 core areas were identified as the most important, with pitch production at the very top. We identified that pitching was not only the task taking up the most time, but also the one commonly perceived by the partners as the most valuable and relevant to the business.

With this initial work complete, a formal pitch steering committee was established, comprising mid- to senior-level business development managers, and an external project manager to support the initiative. The goal was to drill down in detail through the pitch process, with a view to considering options on how pitching could be done more efficiently and, ultimately, to free up the time of business development professionals to focus on client relationship-building.

The steering committee and project manager liaised with the business development function and partners to pull together a clear 'as is' for current practices as well as capturing the 'to be' where people felt we needed to go. The result of this diagnostic work was the identification of two broad phases for the project.

### Phase I

Phase I looked at how to get some of the basics in place. There were four key components:

1. Templates – the establishment of a small suite of easy-to-use, clear and accessible templates that could be controlled locally rather than having to go via a central design team.
2. Resources centre – the building of an intranet site which contains all the key databases required when assembling a pitch – CVs, credentials, pricing information, library of previous pitches, boilerplate templates of useful descriptions.
3. Best-practice guide – a complete guide on how to produce a pitch and the various steps and processes. Hard copies and soft copies were produced and a training schedule put in place for all business development members.
4. Pitch-feedback pilot – we thought it important that we gather our clients' views on our pitches, so we set up a pilot in a number of practice areas and offices.

In support of Phase I we had a sounding board of partners, drawn from different practices and offices around the globe, whom we asked to give feedback on thinking and production for these four key areas. Not only were these partners enthusiastic and provided extremely useful insight, they also helped to sell the project more readily into their practice areas.

Furthermore, we set up a global pitch help desk comprised of business development specialists who could be e-mailed to help people with simple questions, and we trained around 60 people in our global document services team on the new pitch templates. In this way we can support the partnership on a 24/7 basis around the world. Finally, we fine-tuned our communication, ensuring both transparency and awareness within the firm through sharing all global RFPs with the business development team and interested partners, as well as regular reporting of overall pitch results.

### Phase II

Phase II is under way and involves five key areas:

1. Review – looking back at what we have achieved so far and ensuring that we are producing world-class pitches with robust supporting systems and process. We continue to speak to clients through our post-pitch programme as well as interviewing users around the network to elicit responses and iron out any problems.

2. Hiring a central pitch team – a variable we identified in our due diligence in the early stages of this project was the need to bring in better general and project management expertise on our proposals, and, most notably, large panel and cross-practice pitches. We have hired someone to oversee the total pitch infrastructure plus dedicated and experienced pitch managers in the larger practices, who have reporting lines both to their practice manager and to the new global head of proposals. With this team in place, we feel that we are not only beginning to improve the quality of our pitches and are able to share best practice more readily, but also freeing up time in the practices for business development people to focus on client development work.

3. Associate involvement – another key objective for Phase II is to engage associates more in the pitch process. It is good experience not only for the associate, but also for the firm in giving the partners of tomorrow proper experience and understanding of how to sell the firm and win work. It is also good for the business development support, as they can share the responsibilities for pitch production. However, getting associate involvement is not an easy achievement, as there needs to be buy-in from the partnership, which, of course, wants to see the value, and will require an accompanying training programme and a discussion on the impact to the associate bonus scheme.

4. Reporting – with our improved systems, it is now possible to rely more on available data, as well as having the ability to analyse and break down our pitch statistics and share these with the partnership. These statistics, combined with the post-pitch feedback, enables us to generate a clearer picture on where we are having success in our pitches and where there are areas for improvement. Our reports typically break down by geography, sector and client and are beginning to provide insightful intelligence to the partnership.

5. Pricing – Phase II also involves how we can capture our pricing in pitches more readily. Working closely with our colleagues in the finance department, the aim is to give partners better and more informed advice on pricing decisions for our pitches. Included in this initiative is pricing software, which we now use to facilitate these discussions, as well as an alternative pricing booklet, which we have written and intend to distribute to the partnership. Finally, we are launching a series of workshops on pricing for partner groups, with the intention of improving awareness of issues and providing pointers and tips on pricing negotiation and best practice.

Finally, it must be stressed that implementation of a central pitch team, together with associate involvement in bids, does not mean that the business development support team absolves itself from any involvement in pitch writing and production. Pitches remain critical for the business, with some practice areas extremely reliant on successful bids. There is no better way of being at the heart of the business than to be involved in a competitive proposal.

The practices we are putting in place provide more shared responsibility, as well as expertise, but also allow business development time to focus on client development and pitching, tailoring and refining selling messages – another real value-add.

## Conclusion – key takeaways

Fundamentally, there needs to be an acknowledgement of, and buy-in to, the need for change within business development for professional services firms. Because of the structure and idiosyncrasies of most firms, this change requires both a bottom-up and top-down approach.

While there are certainly some basic and practical things that can be done to facilitate a more client-focused and sales-led culture among both the fee-earner and business development and marketing support teams, there are also certain best-practice approaches, which can make all the difference.

Key practices I would highlight to everyone in business development leadership positions in professional services firms, large or small, are:

- Be patient: everything takes time in professional services firms.
- If you have a 'burning platform', use it: there's no better way to galvanize people and make things happen.
- Acknowledge cultural differences, be flexible and practical, and always be aware that one size does not fit all.
- Celebrate successes and make sure that they are well publicized, as this invariably garners and gathers support.
- Lead by example and make sure that you are visible. Get involved and be prepared to get your hands dirty.
- Make sure you have the right people around you. There's not one change agent in a professional services firm – it needs a team who share responsibility and the passion to make things happen.

Finally, I would demand that you and those around you constantly and continually question whether the ideas and changes you are proposing will add value and will help with the ultimate objective of being more client focused and bringing in more revenue.

As Ben Hunt-Davis and Harriet Beveridge (Hunt-Davis and Beveridge, 2011) asked in their ground-breaking and inspirational book, will it make the boat go faster?

# Managing transformational change

## 14

**AMY KINGDON,** Marketing & Communications Director, UK & Europe, Atkins
and **ELEANOR CAMPION,** Communications Executive, UK & Europe, Atkins

**Profiles:** Amy is UK Marketing Director at design, engineering and project management consultancy Atkins. She has a strong track record in leading and managing strategic marketing in the professional services sector. Her previous roles include EMEA Marketing and Business Development Director for business advisory firm FTI Consulting, and UK North Region Marketing Manager for EY.

Eleanor is UK Communications Executive at Atkins. She has worked in the charity, public and private sectors in a range of marketing and communication roles. Her background includes Campaign Coordinator on the international GREAT initiative at UK Trade & Investment and Marketing Coordinator at the architecture education charity Open-City.

Managing significant change in any organization can be difficult, in particular if it requires a long-term cultural shift in a non-technical area such as marketing, while working within the structure and culture of a professional services organization.

In this chapter we explore the different types of challenges facing individuals and teams who are responsible for designing and delivering ways of improving marketing and business development strategy and operations in professional services firms. We will look at the implications of the specific characteristics of engineering firms (outlined below) for marketing professionals, and how these can be best approached, as well as looking at the industry more broadly.

We will focus on: influencing leadership, identifying the needs for change, leading marketing communities through change, changing culture and behaviours, and key project management skills for marketers. We will explore drivers for change, lessons learnt in approaching specific projects and some general success criteria.

# The nature of professional services firms

The professional services industry has many common factors running through it. Many of these relate to culture, structure, behaviours and the basic focus of delivering services – through a technical and highly qualified workforce – to other businesses. However, there are nuances and specifics to different sectors within the industry.

To provide further context to the examples in this chapter of our experience within Atkins, some of the particular characteristics of a firm with a core focus in engineering, design and project management need defining. This group is focused on solving problems and will usually look to identify the core problem in a situation. There is a natural tendency to probe and challenge information that stems from this. They are focused on logic and tend to interpret information and situations literally.

This type of workforce, of course, is a highly intelligent and qualified group of individuals. They may be less comfortable with ambiguity than those in other professions. The nature of their work means that individuals tend towards a strong process-orientation and, in our experience, this differs from other professional services disciplines. Engineering leaders will apply rigorous process and structure to internal functions and ways of working, just as they would to managing a client project. Structuring internally focused work into individual projects, with a professional project management approach, is definitely a particular characteristic of operating in such firms.

# 'Playing the long-game' – gaining leadership recognition and buy-in to significant change

One of the key elements needed to achieve long-term change in any organization, and particularly in professional services firms, is senior leadership support. Marketing professionals must find effective ways to inspire and therefore influence senior leadership so that they not only understand the case for change, but actually feel the need for it themselves and start to act as champions.

A pitfall for marketers in the professional services organization is becoming isolated within our own function. While we can clearly see the things we want to do differently, and are immersed in our plans for change, we can't achieve it on our own. Often our stakeholders are not as close to the situations we observe and have other priorities that consume their time and focus. Although it can be very difficult, one of the lessons in achieving widespread buy-in to change is to let go and trust others to help build and achieve your vision.

For business development and marketing change that we've been responsible for within Atkins and in the professional services firms that we've worked in previously, senior buy-in has been critical. Achieving this has meant tackling the specific challenges of our industry in the types of leader that tend to inhabit it. Partners and their equivalents in professional services organizations tend to be highly accomplished individuals who have developed very strong careers and experience in a technical field, be that accountancy, engineering, law, management consultancy or others.

What usually results is a strong core of analytical, logical and at times risk-averse leaders. Individuals with these characteristics naturally need significant evidence for, and the facts behind, a need for change. Critically, this is usually quite different from the way in which marketing professionals think and work. A typical professional in a marketing role tends to be creative, less analytical and more able to work with ambiguity and instinct, basing decisions on 'gut feeling' and emotional as well as logical reasoning. It can be a challenge to influence leaders who have a much more analytical bearing to accept the change that we are aiming to drive through, when the core characteristics and backgrounds are very different.

The first lesson, therefore, is to adapt your case for change to suit the interests and drivers of leadership. An example of this would be a brand-repositioning project for Atkins. Creating the belief among the leadership team that this was something that deserved investment required more than just conveying a sense that it's 'the right thing to do'. We've learnt that it can sometimes be challenging to achieve buy-in to a piece of investment or change of this scale. Talking solely about an opportunity is less tangible and therefore has less impact than talking to them about the risk of not acting. Our leaders were much better able to understand the need for change when we demonstrated what our competitors were doing in the area and the risk to our competitive position in remaining static. This helped open the door to embarking on this work in the first instance. Secondly, we ensured that we conducted robust research internally and – most importantly – with our clients to establish the specific needs for our brand development. Having our clients tell us that we needed to do this enabled our leaders to relate this work very directly to a risk around major clients and therefore revenue.

Another insight into how to influence leaders of professional services firms relates to appealing to their own profile, impact and success in the market (and therefore within the firm). Relating these ideas and needs to the individual partner/leader and the challenges they are personally experiencing is much more likely to result in them lending their support to the piece of work. In short, this is a case of demonstrating 'what's in it for me' to an individual who will then be personally motivated and rewarded.

## *What not to do?*

In some cases there can be a risk of potentially alienating senior people within an organization if you to try to win their support for lots of separate, individual projects or change pieces. For instance, trying to get the attention of a senior partner/managing director one month about a project to identify weaknesses in the bidding process, the following month about key account management and the next about a change in internal communications strategy risks sending them a message that these are discrete and possibly low-impact projects. They may then be seen as low-importance items, which in that individual's mind and in a busy world could be assigned forever to the 'marketing box'.

Instead, marketers need to be effective in making a connection between these sorts of component pieces and what the organization – and therefore the leader themselves – is trying to achieve strategically. To do this, we need to craft compelling stories around our projects. An overall vision for the change that you are trying to achieve, and a visual way of representing this, becomes critical in conveying a clear picture of the end goal and 'what good looks like' to the firm's leadership. This approach will more easily gain their support.

An example of this in practice is the 'business development transformation story' we have developed in Atkins, which crystallizes an end goal for a complex programme of change projects; establishes the what, how and – critically – 'why' of the programme; and works back from the end goal to include more detail on individual projects and interventions. This has laid the foundation for us to gain much more traction for individual pieces of work that we can clearly link back to our overall transformation. It has also provided us with the discipline to identify projects that may not be core to our overall vision and can therefore be postponed or even challenged completely.

## Establishing what needs to be done

Generally, types of organizational change can be narrowed into three categories:

- Strategic (change to the overall direction, purpose and focus of the organization).
- Structural (change to the way the organization is structured and run. This will include systems and processes).
- People (employee performance, skills, behaviours and attitudes, rewards etc).

The change we are concerned with in this chapter, relating to marketing and business development specifically, spans all three of these areas but with a particular focus in strategic and people-oriented change.

In order to determine the needs for a change programme within any firm, marketing professionals need to bring a combination of their previous experience, a solid understanding of the business itself and some form of thorough insight and research into its challenges, current situation and culture/appetite for change.

## Leading and inspiring marketing and business development communities through periods of change

Often, marketing and business development functions in professional services firms are formed of separate groups of individuals sitting in the different elements of matrix structures that include geographic areas, practice areas/disciplines, sectors and 'corporate'. In addition, individuals will be focused on different aspects of marketing and business development, from internal communications to sales. It can therefore be very challenging to influence, inspire and 'steer' fragmented communities when you're trying to achieve change. It is highly likely that individual teams have a much stronger affinity and allegiance to their divisional leadership than to the central marketing function initiating the change.

In the sorts of structure described above, corporate/central marketing functions are unlikely to be able to influence through authority alone. The individuals you are trying to reach may have no degree of reporting line to your area at all. By influencing the leaders that the marketing teams report to, as described previously in this chapter, you are more likely to create the space and mandate for the individuals that report to them to behave in a certain way, work on certain initiatives and add their support and resource to initiatives that you may need to run.

Creating a sense of community is critical across a fragmented function. Where a formal team structure doesn't exist, making individuals feel as if they have something in common and that working together will boost their own career prospects and profile within the organization can create the sort of collaboration and shared goals that underpin successful change programmes. Initially, face-to-face interaction becomes important in achieving this. With 'virtual' communities that are dispersed across different structural elements, primary communication methods will be electronic and remote. Periodically investing in bringing people together in person is hugely powerful in creating a sense of 'we're in this together'; it's also a good forum for surfacing new ideas and best practice, breakthroughs that wouldn't happen in more closed environments.

Leadership style is also incredibly important. 'Pulling rank' exerts little influence, for the reasons outlined above, and therefore a collaborative and inclusive style can be very effective. Gathering input from individuals, understanding their perspectives and welcoming their ideas helps people realize a sense of opportunity in the change you represent; this makes them feel less threatened by it, but more inspired, energized and therefore productive. However, before you embark on this 'softer' leadership approach, it is critical to demonstrate that you have the experience and the know-how to drive change forward. While you want to convey that you need their knowledge, skills and ideas in order to be successful, you also need them to be confident in your ability and leadership.

## *Challenges*

The practical challenges of gaining face time with a geographically dispersed community can constrain efforts to build stronger communities and to gain the benefits of 'in-person' forums. Unfortunately, it is a fact of modern working practices that remote communications will tend to prevail.

Time is another potential barrier. When individuals have priorities to address in their 'day jobs', it can be difficult to get them to see the benefit of taking time out to understand and align with longer-term change initiatives. Without influencing their senior management, it may not be possible to gain their understanding and cooperation. They may simply not be responsible for making decisions on how they spend their time.

Some challenges obviously stem from people being resistant to change because they're worried it will make them vulnerable in their position. It is important to demonstrate that transformation programmes overall are about marketing effectiveness across an organization, and are not related to individuals' roles.

## Solutions

In summary, we have found the following to be the key measures in achieving traction and active support from a dispersed marketing community:

- Influencing the leadership across the businesses, so that they can enable and inspire their marketing teams to be involved.
- Highlighting the personal development opportunities for the individuals involved. For example, if a change programme is oriented around giving marketing more strategic focus within the firm, that in turn offers everybody involved in that function the opportunity to be perceived as more strategic, adding more value in the organization and therefore gaining access to more senior people. That leads to the opportunity to work on more interesting projects and to reflect more credibility. The development of an integrated marketing community also opens up career development opportunities for people outside of their immediate team.
- Where there is resistance, it is important to put this into perspective and try to understand what people's personal motivation might be. You may need to spend time with individuals to understand their concerns rather than taking their comments too literally or, worse, excluding them because they create barriers. Sometimes the most sceptical people are the ones you have to spend more time with to bring them on board.

## When restructuring is part of the solution

There are various different options for structuring the marketing function across a professional services firm and we've seen almost all variations of this. The decision really comes down to the degree to which resources are focused at a practice/sector area level (ie 'in the business') or centrally (at a 'corporate' level) or a hybrid of the two. Within Atkins we have a hybrid approach, but there are always questions about whether it would be more effective to restructure in some other way.

Ultimately, formal structure may not actually be the best way to achieve a change, particularly if you can achieve strong alignment, collaboration and mobility across more of a virtual community, as outlined earlier in this section. This has certainly been our focus at Atkins: enabling individuals within business-focused teams to feel part of a common journey/vision and one common community, even if their reporting line is within their own area. Having said that, it can be more efficient to centralize tactical delivery areas; for instance, event management, graphic design and document production can be more cost-effective for the business if delivered centrally rather than in practice/sector areas.

Perhaps even more importantly, it becomes much more likely that alignment from a brand, messaging, positioning and quality perspective will be achievable. The centralization of these elements then allows focus in the business areas for professional marketers who are responsible for fully understanding that business and its drivers; they can develop market plans based on its objectives and therefore the strategy and planning aspects of marketing management. The execution, which is largely centralized, is less business-specific.

# Culture and behaviours – how to instil change beyond systems and processes

Already in this chapter we have touched on aspects of culture and behaviour as critical factors in designing and successfully implementing change programmes. Here, we focus more specifically on this area and address some of the challenges and solutions involved.

In order to achieve sustainable change in any organization, culture and behaviours are pivotal. It can be extremely tempting to focus on systems and process change alone. These elements are relatively straightforward to assess and address and can be controlled and changed in the short to medium term. It is much harder to determine how to challenge an organization's behaviour, values and beliefs. It also takes much longer to achieve real transition at this level, which means that patience and determination are essential.

Owing to the long-term nature of cultural change, it is important to remember that this change will be achieved last in the sequence of transformations you are seeking to make. It is almost inevitable that it will take a long period of time for change to be embraced across the entire organization. The project team needs to be prepared for stakeholders to be 'lost' along the way, for people to challenge and for the subsequent consequences.

What does this mean in practice for the marketing professional involved in a project that requires such change? First, at the beginning of any change project, in any kind of business, it is critical to identify the potential cultural barriers. This essentially means understanding the characteristics of the organization as a whole and its people's attitudes and behaviours, as they may represent obstacles in the journey you are about to undertake. Having identified any such barriers, the next step is to determine very clearly the profile of the new behaviours and beliefs that will support the change you are working on. What does the future need to feel like? Armed with this clear view, you are then ready to develop a plan to bring that change about.

Business development and marketing touches many elements of the professional services organization. This inevitably means that the areas of culture that need to be understood and addressed are widespread and involve most parts of the firm. Given that any client-facing individual within a professional services firm has some degree of marketing and business development opportunity, and therefore responsibility, it can be difficult to segment a more defined 'audience' to target with cultural change. Equally, even if the change project in question directly affects a narrower audience (for example, a formalized 'sales' force), it is likely that cultural change is required across the rest of the organization in order for those individuals to be supported and successful.

A specific example within Atkins would be our general overarching objectives of creating strong client – and ultimately sales – focus among our workforce. Training programmes that we have implemented to enhance sales and marketing skills across the organization target most directly those individuals responsible for sales. However, in order for the programme to be successful, HR professionals need to understand

and believe in the importance of the skills involved and to give these equal footing with more technical skills in the learning and development portfolio. Leaders in each division of the firm need to promote the programme, enable the right individuals to be given the time and space to attend and to activate the training afterwards. Line managers need to ensure that the impact of the training and the development of the associated skill sets are credibly assessed in the annual performance review process and so on.

## *Learnings and solutions*

As well as the importance of influencing leadership, which we have covered previously, the nature of the team responsible for driving change is also critical. Emotional commitment becomes as important as other strengths and capabilities when dealing with culture and behaviours. The marketing/business development project team must show that they truly believe in the 'cause', demonstrate emotional intelligence in connecting with stakeholders across the organization on the subject, and be resilient enough to deal with the sometimes reduced pace of progress that will be involved.

We would recommend avoiding the use of the 'language of change' when trying to instil fundamental shifts in behaviour. In fact, instead of referring to 'projects', which risks a perception that these are short-term interventions with start and end dates, try to find ways to make the desired culture and behaviours feel like business as usual. Introduce the concepts and the associated language into regular communications and make the terms familiar.

Identifying potential 'blockers' to change should be part of your stakeholder mapping early in the planning process; ensuring that the team is clear on where these barriers may exist will help them work with or around them. In addition, identifying and promoting 'quick wins' along the way can also be very effective. This involves understanding and celebrating, through various forms of internal communications, what has happened as a result of the changes you are implementing in the short term. Because the overall project aims will be long term, near-term successes that align with the overall direction can help win over hearts and minds along the way and maintain energy and motivation within the team. This can be particularly useful in silencing the cynics in the organization.

If you are able to influence incentives and rewards, reflecting desired behaviours here can obviously be powerful. Calling out desired values and ways of working in performance review language, in line manager meetings and in training and development initiatives reinforces the importance of culture to the business. Equally, working with HR colleagues to factor behavioural elements into the recruitment process ensures that future generations of the organization are aligned at a cultural level.

Ultimately, patience and determination are critical in any endeavour to change or evolve culture and behaviours. Be prepared to have to repeat sentiments and rationale frequently and to achieve traction one step at a time.

# Project management essentials for marketers

Marketers can benefit from a good grounding in project management skills to aid all fields of their work, not just change projects.

The Project Management Institute defines a project as a 'temporary group activity designed to produce a unique product, service or result' with a 'defined beginning and end in time, and therefore defined scope and resources'. It goes on to define project management as 'the application of knowledge, skills and techniques to execute projects effectively and efficiently. It's a strategic competency for organizations, enabling them to tie project results to business goals – and thus, better compete in their markets.'

With this in mind, many marketing communications activities could be defined as having project characteristics. An event or a direct communications campaign, for example, involves planning, organization, motivating (teams, senior professionals who need to input to, or attend, the campaign) and controlling (budget, assets). They are short-term or 'temporary' endeavours and are designed to produce a specific result. They always have a defined time frame and often limited budget. They are undertaken to meet marketing and sales goals and objectives to create value and possibly some degree of change (to reputation, market profile, quality of relationships and so on).

So, what are the key skills within project management that marketers really need to understand and develop? Our experience within Atkins as a design, engineering and project management firm is useful. Our professionals are rightfully immersed in the discipline of project management for the delivery of technical excellence, which means that this degree of structure and rigour is applied to the organization's approach to internally focused projects too. In turn, our marketing and business development team has been best served by adopting formal project management processes and methodology when designing and running our change projects. We are not suggesting that this type of emphasis needs to be given to the practice of managing marketing projects or individual, tactical marketing activities in every professional services firm. However, there are some basic skills and principles that should be appreciated:

- developing the overall plan: ensuring that the piece of work is properly scoped and has realistic and clear objectives;
- breaking down and prioritizing the specific tasks within a plan and creating a work plan for each if necessary;
- stakeholder identification: detailing and understanding the key stakeholders in the piece of work and establishing how you will engage/manage/communicate with them;
- resources: organizing the team, defining roles and responsibilities, clarifying deliverables, deadlines and milestones;
- clear communication of the plan, roles and responsibilities and relevant specific details to all involved throughout the piece of work;
- perhaps most importantly: evaluation of the project or campaign, not just in terms of measurement against objectives but also in terms of how the piece of

work itself was run. Conducting a 'lessons learnt' exercise with key team members and stakeholders can be invaluable in informing the approach to future pieces of work.

## Conclusion

As we have suggested throughout this chapter, perhaps the most important ingredients for successful change 'campaigns' in professional services organizations relate to the nature of the approach and to behaviour. By types of approach we mean the style adopted in driving through the change and in engaging both marketing communities and the organization's leadership as a whole; by behaviour we mean both that of the team responsible for shaping and delivering the change and also that of the organization in general – that is, the behavioural change required to sustain the change.

Ultimately, these requirements will ensure that marketers focus on developing some specific skills and qualities in addition to their technical capabilities. Building strong relationships at all levels, demonstrating leadership, influencing, inspiring and listening are all key. Adapting your style of communication, and the case you are presenting, to the nature of your stakeholders is a valuable capability to build, as are collaboration, patience and resilience. In addition, in order to remain focused and productive when faced with a broad potential remit, an organized approach to work, incorporating key project management principles, stands the marketer in good stead.

As marketers, we have a unique responsibility for creating a clear vision of what a better future could look like within our organization, and for designing interventions to help the firm achieve this vision. We have the opportunity both to contribute to strategy at the highest level and to see that strategy through to tactical execution.

We are perhaps one of very few functions within the professional services organization that can see and work beyond systems and processes in order to create long-term change and to foster in our more technical colleagues a sense of the imperative of addressing culture and behaviours in order to succeed.

# Understanding and exceeding partner expectations

## 15

**JESSICA SCHOLZ,** Business Development Manager, Freshfields Bruckhaus Deringer, Germany

**Profile:** Jessica is a senior business development manager with 14 years of experience. She leads the client relationship programme at Freshfields in Germany and Austria, having previously worked with various international law firms. Jessica is qualified in business and law and completed her MBA with a thesis on managing law firm marketing.

This chapter will look in particular at the evolution and current position of marketing and business development (MBD) in the German legal sector. It shares the insights and learning of a research study conducted by the author into the MBD practices of leading German law firms. It then sets out a series of recommendations for MBD leaders in the sector.

## An overview of marketing and business development in the German legal market

Marketing and business development is an established service function in German business law firms today, although its history spans less than 20 years. More than 80 per cent of the top 75 law firms in Germany now employ MBD professionals or operate integrated MBD teams. If we include teams or individuals who work in these functions in firms of all sizes, this community totals an estimated 150 professionals plus a small army of freelances.

Before 1987, legal marketing was prohibited by professional regulation in Germany. Lawyers were not allowed to display or communicate areas of expertise. The largest law firm at the time only had 25 lawyers and one office. Cross-regional firms were forbidden. In 1987, the restrictive professional regulation was abolished by a ground-breaking decision of the German Federal Constitutional Court.

Marketing activities by lawyers were also allowed under a few lawyer-specific rules and the regulation imposed by German unfair competition laws. Yet only in the mid-1990s, close to 10 years later, did a major law firm in Germany hire the first non-legal marketing professionals and the first wave of marketing recruitment start in the German legal market. This coincided with newly merged US and UK firms entering the German legal industry at the end of the 1990s and in the early 2000s.

The first decade of German legal marketing was spent developing brochures, websites, placing law firm advertisements in legal directories, writing lengthy newsletters and discussing how clients and non-clients could be invited to events and whether or not to serve food and drinks afterwards. Press work rarely featured as part of the communications mix and marketing tasks were assigned to a diverse range of people: from senior partners to junior lawyers, secretaries, HR people, translators, office managers and so on.

During the early 2000s, there was a trend to professionalize functions, and relevant departments grew and developed specialized teams for marketing, communications and business development. The early movers were the merged international firms, which brought in expertise from their UK and, to a lesser extent, US MBD functions. Today in Germany, it is commonly recognized in the law firm community that 'marketing and communications' stands for the specialization covering press and media relations, brochures, merchandising, branded materials and so on, whereas business development (BD) covers proposal management and writing, client and market research, client relationship management and so forth.

Today, the international firms in Germany have the largest MBD teams, with up to 20 or more employees. German independent firms have invested in the function as well and employ teams of up to 10 marketers and business developers.

Over the years, law firm MBD work has become more strategic. However, even in firms that are more managed than others, there is considerable variation in the application of a strategic approach to marketing and the extent to which marketing and business development is planned, executed and controlled in line with the firm's strategic framework. Anecdotal evidence from the German MBD community suggests that the function in German law firms is still not operated in a sustainable and strategic manner.

Most partners in law firms in Germany that employ MBD professionals do want to see a new breed of marketers in their firms, but they are not finding it easy to identify them – and if they have them, they often don't know how to utilize them to their full capacity and talents. For partners, it is hard to distinguish between 'designing the product' in a technical sense, where the marketer will have less knowledge than the legal/tax/engineer expert, and 'marketing the product', which is the genuine marketing task. Since many partners are not used to working with an MBD function, they often bring colleagues into the process too late.

In Germany, we might be one step behind more mature markets such as the UK, but I think we are at a critical point where partners are challenging what we have and how we do things. Many feel that it is time to take marketing and business development to another level.

Based on my case study, I will outline recommendations on measures that MBD leaders can take to improve the value their function adds to their professional services firm.

## CASE STUDY  Building partner support for MBD activities

### Background

Until recently, the field of professional services marketing, and law firm marketing in particular, was not widely researched (Hodges and Young, 2009). In those academic works where professional services marketing featured, the focus was mainly on the application of standard marketing tools. The managerial aspects of marketing functions were not covered, and especially not in the German and other continental European legal markets. The following quote neatly summed up the consensus among legal marketing practitioners, consultants and authors familiar with the legal industry: 'Marketing and BD specialists can become frustrated by the inability of partners to let them contribute as fully as they might' (Young, 2010).

Research and anecdotal evidence showed that law firms did not use MBD staff in an effective manner, which resulted in: internal clients (partners and fee-earners) being unhappy with the services delivered by their firms' MBD function; and MBD employees proving dissatisfied because they could not apply their skills to their full extent, resulting in high rates of attrition. Considering that law firms usually invest 1.5 to 5 per cent of their annual revenue in their MBD function and corresponding activities, it is clearly a problem if both partners and MBD staff are unhappy with the outcome of that investment.

### Assessing partner expectations and perceptions of marketing and business development

I designed a quantitative study of partners in law firms in Germany to ask about their expectations and perceptions of what they get from their MBD function. The questionnaire tested for preference and perceived delivery by the MBD function on 10 service attributes:

- understanding my needs;
- understanding my business;
- reliability;
- responsiveness;
- attitude and assurance;
- individual attention to me as a partner;
- acting in the best interests of the firm;
- visual quality of work;
- content quality of work;
- helping me to win work.

In addition, I conducted a series of interviews with a number of partners from German and international firms to gain more detailed insight into their individual views. In both cases, a range of firms that employ their own MBD professionals was covered.

The most insightful question on the quantitative side proved to be about how important specific MBD services were to the responding partners, and the gap between the importance and their perceived delivery of those services.

Of the 10 service attributes, the four that ranked as the most important for the responding partners were:

1 understanding my needs;

2 understanding my business;

3 content quality of work;

4 overall effectiveness in helping me to win business.

However, those that scored highest in terms of what the partners perceived on delivery were:

1 responsiveness;

2 reliability;

3 individual attention;

4 acting in the best interest of the firm.

These findings indicated that MBD staff are responsive (quick), behave professionally and pay attention to partners, but they don't understand their partners' business, don't know what they need and thus can't help them win business. In short, MBD people are nice to work with, but not helpful to partners in the critical activity of developing new business.

The interviews I conducted with a number of partners from various firms reinforced the findings from the quantitative study, but also highlighted other points and issues.

On quality and service levels they said:

- MBD services and service quality are not well defined or standardized. This is not surprising given the variability in the sector and the differing relationships and expectations between the MBD function and partners in the firm.

- There was little or no agreement on service levels with marketing and business development and a variability in service quality. This was consistent with the survey gap between expectation and service attributes for 'content quality of work'.

- All interviewees from UK or US firms perceived a quality gap on the adaptation of marketing materials or BD concepts when rolled out in the German market. They perceived a failure to adapt to local market conditions and customs as a corresponding quality gap.

- Almost every interviewee pointed to a limit in MBD capacity and how difficult they often found it to get MBD support on an individual service task. Partners did not know whether there was a process for prioritization, nor escalation if they were unhappy.

On services available they said:

- Although understanding was lacking in larger firms with established MBD teams, the situation was worse in smaller firms. In these firms, partners did not seem to understand at all what to expect from their MBD function.
- Partners identified a lack of clarity and transparency in the MBD service portfolio.
- Only partners in larger firms and with larger MBD teams could formulate specific gaps in the services offering, for example the need for a more sophisticated approach to providing forward-looking market intelligence or more differentiated brand messages.
- Partners expected their MBD team to understand the business and know the best course of action on marketing and business development. They should advise the partners and, as with the firm's external clients, provide advice and ideas ahead of the partners' requests.

On the relationship between partners and the MBD team:

- Many partners are interested in building and maintaining relationships with their MBD staff that go beyond the service transaction. More or less all interviewees indicated that the quality of these relationships depends to a great extent on individuals' characters (on both sides) and on the 'chemistry' between the individual parties. However, interviewees also admitted that in their respective partnerships not everyone is open to building sustainable relationships with MBD staff. Cases where partners expect marketing and business development to act as 'silent servants' were reported.
- Partners located in different offices from the MBD team find relationship-building more difficult and would like more face-to-face time with MBD staff members. They want their MBD team to be visible. The results leave room for the assumption that visibility is directly linked to transparency of the MBD service offering and partners' understanding of which MBD services are available.
- The experience of partners is that there are cases where MBD professionals do not show sufficient interest or effort in wanting to build rapport with partners and rely on a more transactional relationship. Reasons for this can be over-utilization as well as the wrong personality for the job.

However, overall, partners did not necessarily blame MBD staff members for their lack of understanding and recognized that they were responsible for failing to educate and engage. The partners also recognized that they need to be ready for change and to accept advice from strategic and creative MBD people, but the MBD team needed to build a track record and reputation of being able to offer such advice. One of the most encouraging findings of the study in this regard was that the vast majority of partners responded with agreement to the statement that 'partners do not do enough to make MBD understand us'.

# Recommendations for MBD leaders

In summary, my research uncovered that partners receive significantly less of the MBD service attributes they desire most and more of what they say they find least important. Thus, something in the service design of MBD departments in Germany's law firms must be wrong. In addition, there also appears to be a number of gaps with respect to the recruitment, training and utilization of MBD staff. This seems to be particularly relevant within German law firms, but might also be the case in professional services marketing departments in other countries. Last but not least, there is a gap in communication between partners and marketing and business development, which is closely linked to a fundamental gap in understanding on both sides.

Based on these findings, I have identified a number of recommendations to help close these gaps and not only satisfy partners but also help them win more business. I have grouped my recommendations around the following three topics.

## *Understand your internal clients*

Just like partners, who are service providers to their external clients, MBD specialists should understand the business and needs of their internal clients.

David Maister has suggested that partners of professional services firms need to become 'trusted advisers' to their clients (Maister, Green and Galford, 2000) in order to establish successful and sustainable client relationships. We marketers need to think the same way. We need to aim to become 'trusted advisers' to our internal clients: the partners and fee-earners of our firms. Otherwise we can't lead any marketing function in our firms. To achieve success, we first need to establish mutual understanding between 'us' and 'them' – and try to overcome the 'us' and 'them' mentality at the same time.

The existence of an understanding gap between partners as internal clients of marketing and business development and MBD professionals implies that often partners and marketing and business development have a different understanding of *what marketing and business development is* – as a *service* from the partners' perspective and as a *job* from marketing and business development's perspective. If possible, law firms should codify a definition of MBD services and responsibilities so that misunderstandings can be avoided. My recommendations are:

- If marketing and business development is not defined in your firm, find agreement with your firm's management on what it covers and excludes. Encode this and live it. If no one else initiates the discussion, bring it up in a top-level discussion.

- Talk to each other, and give partners more chance to understand what marketing and business development is.
- Bring marketing and business development into senior associate training, so that the next partner generation has the chance to understand it better than previous generations. Remember: these things are mostly not taught in law school.
- Establish more face-time between marketing and business development and partners. Give your MBD people a platform where they can showcase their professional skills beyond correcting a proposal or sorting name tags alphabetically.
- Establish MBD skills trainings where MBD people train younger lawyers. They will be grateful for it and your MBD staff can build an expert profile with the fee-earners.

With regard to Germany: in the past, German law firms appear to have spent more effort on defining marketing and business development tools to be applied by MBD teams but less time on strategically structuring the service function itself. The question 'what to do in MBD' has been discussed, but the question of 'how to do it' seems to have been neglected. This is particularly true in German national firms, which do not benefit from the best practice applied in their UK or US operations, where the MBD function will have been established for a longer period of time. I recommend that the German firms ask their UK or US colleagues for examples of best practice and don't reinvent the wheel.

## *Rethink recruitment and training for marketing and business development staff*

The case study shows that there is a need for MBD people to understand better the legal market, legal products and the partners' business. Bearing in mind that the skills needed to gain this understanding are diverse and usually not covered by a single syllabus of study, the introduction of new forms of professional training for law firm marketers should be considered. To better match the required skills, recruitment of MBD people could be focused more on existing skills rather than formal qualifications. This might be particularly true for Germany, where the business culture is still highly focused on formally documented skills and a match between academic background and professional occupation. Professional development for MBD job holders in law firms should be considered to help MBD staff gain the skills required to fulfil partners' expectations, which are, as we see in the case study, understanding the legal business and partners' business development needs.

A central theme of the research was that partners want their relationship with MBD colleagues to match their own relationships with their external clients. However, MBD staff need not only to understand their internal clients better, but also to understand the firm's clients better. Although there is little interaction between MBD staff and a firm's clients (in Germany and elsewhere) today, MBD staff need to recognize that strategic understanding and management of client relationships is increasingly important. MBD leaders therefore will have to focus more on supporting client relationships when defining their team's structure, instead of just assigning business developers to all of the firm's practice and sector groups. And firms would be well advised to include external client orientation into MBD job profiles to a much larger extent than is common today. My recommendations are:

- When recruiting, clearly define what skills are needed and look beyond formal qualifications; also look for skills required in a professional services environment.
- Consider both aptitude and attitude when recruiting. There are ways to build the specific technical skills needed by someone in an MBD function, but it's much harder to train someone on the attitude required.
- Empower your MBD people: enable them to build credibility and to influence people in powerful positions. There is excellent training and workshops available to develop these skills. That money will be extremely well invested.
- Do not be afraid to question whether the things that have been done for ages in MBD in your firm are right for today. This includes questioning whether the firm should continue to hire the same type of MBD candidates as they have done before.
- As law firms rethink the classical pyramid structure of their firms, MBD leaders should consider moving away from the linear structure of many MBD departments and introduce a more (flat) pyramid-like shape to their teams. A group of strategically sound and partner-communication-friendly MBD professionals, with some support resources, will be more homogeneous than a large group of MBD staff with a higher diversity of skill levels. This model would also leave younger colleagues more time to grow and develop their individual skills.

## *Develop leadership and make sure you have management's support*

Last but not least, the MBD function requires strong leadership and the support of the firm's management. MBD leaders need to have a voice at the highest management level. If the MBD leader does not have a seat at the board table, the team needs a strong advocate for the function that represents them there.

MBD leaders who do not have the power to influence what services should be offered and in what manner will struggle to gain recognition for their team members as respected professionals and as 'advisers to the advisers'. Law firms need to consider empowering the MBD function and individual people to take relevant decisions. This might require a different type of person, so that MBD professionals are more capable of working and communicating with partners as peers. Given that, traditionally, the legal profession has maintained a high degree of social closure, this part might be challenging. But times are changing and lawyers today work together with other professionals much more cooperatively. Of course, not every single marketer will aspire to this level, but that then calls for more of a mix of people and capabilities within the MBD teams and more diversity in training backgrounds, communication skills, professional attitude and specialist knowledge.

The findings from the research prove that neither marketing nor legal skills alone are enough to advise and support partners in developing their business. This case study therefore might prove that it is time to support the development of a 'new breed of law firm marketers'.

The 'new marketers' will not only master the metrics of measuring marketing's success to underpin marketing's 'right to exist' in a professional services firm. They will also embrace technology to a much larger extent than previous generations of marketers and employ technology with more sophistication. They will even be able to move marketing's efficiency and internal processes to an entirely new level. This might sound anachronistic in times when digital has moved to the core of strategic thinking, but in law firms, where partners still mark up documents on hard copies and send these back via scan, the importance of digital and the strategic use of technology can't be emphasized often enough.

In short, my recommendations for developing leadership are:

- If you are the divisional head of marketing and business development, seek a place at the management table. If you don't get there, find a strong ally who speaks for you and your team. You will find these advocates, because there are already a number of partners out there who are waiting impatiently for the 'old world' to turn and for the arrival of the 'new marketer' who is listened to at the board level.
- Focus on relationships with the partners and fee-earners, ideally those who go beyond the service transaction. Building trust and rapport with partners largely depends on the breadth of relationships, so go out and seek to build them. Most of the partners at your firm will be grateful to know you and your team members better than just by your e-mail address.
- If you are coming from a non-professional services background, learn to understand how law firms work and how lawyers tick. A marketing leader who was hired from a consumer business might think that politics exist in every company – and of course this is true. But law firm politics, opinion-building and the coexistence of formal and non-formal leadership within a partnership can be much more complex than expected.
- Be an exceptionally good internal marketer. We are, of course, experts in marketing the services of our firms to our target markets and audiences out there, but when it comes to positioning ourselves within our firms, there seems to be a lot of room for improvement of our own marketing.

## Summary

One of the partners I interviewed for my research said:

> In the ideal world, you tell us what we need and what we need to do, not vice versa! You are the marketing experts! Tell me, please! Do tell me, for example, 'Why don't you try this approach instead of doing that?' If we can trust you to understand our work well enough, including the legal aspects, that you can make suggestions to us, that's brilliant.

I think this quote captures the essence of managing the marketing function in a professional services firm. We need to be really good at marketing the firm's services externally and our own plus the firm's services internally. And we need stable and trusting relationships with our internal clients – so that we have the chance to understand our external clients, too.

In firms that have a mature and well-developed marketing function, this will be much easier to achieve than in firms where marketers are still treated like silent servants. But we are on a positive path in many firms, which will motivate others too. Of course, we still need to work on the further professionalization of marketing and BD in our industry. To reach this, both partners and MBD professionals need to contribute to that development. In the end, it might help to understand that this professionalization is not only a desire of the marketing professionals, but that our clients expect it too.

Competition in our markets will not decrease and clients will not cease to ask for more. We will only be able to contribute sustainably to our firms' response when we manage our firms' marketing, internally and externally, on a par with partners'.

# The role of marketing KPIs in professional services firms

16

**GILES PUGH,** Principal, SutherlandsPugh

**Profile:** Giles is the co-head of a consulting firm focused on the professional services firm sector, advising on strategy, marketing and performance. Giles has been Chief Strategy and Chief Marketing Officer in various global professional services firms following an earlier career in strategy consulting and investment banking.

This chapter looks at how marketers can use key performance indicators (KPIs) to measure, track and provide evidence of the impact of their activities on the firm. It looks at all aspects of a KPI dashboard, from who should use KPIs to what to measure. It outlines the pitfalls to look out for and takes a particular look at the KPIs for digital marketing.

## Background

Marketers know from the earliest days of their career and training that KPIs are a cornerstone of an evidence-based approach to marketing. Yet in many professional services firms, KPIs are marked more by their degree of absence than by their ubiquity. This is in contrast to marketing in many other sectors, so it is first worth examining why. The reasons are partly evolutionary and partly cultural.

When professional partnerships were limited to 20 partners and marketing consisted of a few people organizing events, performance was immediately apparent and KPIs were largely unnecessary. Since then, the growth in the knowledge economy has transformed both the scale and the scope of professional services firms, to levels that were previously unimagined. Now, professional services represent (depending on the definition used) at least 15 per cent of developed economies. Firms have grown in some cases to thousands of partners and there are a number with revenue figures in the billions. This evolution has necessitated a growing professionalization of both marketing and management. Hence the growing interest in using KPIs to provide the evidence and information on how to achieve value from the growth in budgets, marketing staff and marketing activity.

Culturally, however, there remains a constraint. Professional services firms, unlike corporate structures, are designed to provide autonomy to talented individuals operating with shared values under a common brand. KPIs can be perceived as marching in a different direction. The notorious financial ratios of Hal Geneen (of ITT) or Arnold Weinstock (of GEC) were all about accountability, which sits less comfortably in a collegiate partnership culture.

This suspicion of KPIs is reinforced by those marketers who feel that their subject is fundamentally about intangibles and is not something that can be readily quantified. For fee-earners guarding their marketing budgets, on the other hand, there is the natural desire that the available funds should be spent exclusively on actual marketing, not on metrics.

These perceptions are, however, incorrect. First, marketing at its core is about winning client preference for the firm and for its practitioners. It is clients that produce the firm's cash and you can't get much more tangible than that. The intangibility is fundamentally no more than a lack of technique: even opinions and perceptions can be measured.

Second, if used effectively, KPIs are not about quantification and control. They are about building consensus on future direction, which is invaluable in professional services. In contrast to 'blue-sky thinking', which is often suggested by senior fee-earners when they want to consider the future, a discussion about KPIs enables a firm to coalesce and align its thinking in a way that is both tangible and specific.

Lord Kelvin put it rather well at the turn of the 19th century: 'When you can measure what you are speaking about, and express it in numbers you know something about it; when you cannot express it in numbers your knowledge is of a meagre and unsatisfactory kind.'

From which follows the third point: beyond a certain size of operation, investing in metrics is a small but necessary overhead to achieve effectiveness. The axioms 'if you can't measure it, you can't manage it' and 'what gets measured gets done' have an undeniable logic. KPIs are therefore a necessary feature of professional services firms that have grown to such a scale and scope that they need to be run and managed professionally. A firm's marketing is at the core of client and income generation, so determining how those client relationships will be, and are being, developed is essential to a firm's success. This means that the top tier of marketing KPIs should be the concern of every managing partner and every firm's executive committee.

Heads of marketing functions often find their role challenged or doubted by firms' partners who think they also know a thing or two about marketing. KPIs are the way of demonstrating undeniable evidence of direction, effectiveness and success: the one thing all professionals appreciate is evidence.

## What firms do and should measure

Most management information in professional services firms originates from accounting departments. Professional services firms are no exception to the strong influence of accounting in the business culture of Anglo-Saxon-inspired commercial organizations. This has advantages, for example in the integrity of the data. Accounting is, however, primarily about record keeping. Accounting information is often the picture through the rear-view mirror: it measures revenues and profits, which are the outputs and outcomes of the firm.

To influence the destiny of the firm, something different is required: the quantification and measurement of the whole value chain, not just its financial outputs. KPIs are most effective when they are holistic; they should encompass the measurement of the:

- ingredients used to operate the firm;
- effectiveness of the processes in transforming them;
- success in terms of the revenue and profit achieved.

This balanced scorecard approach, developed in the 1990s (Kaplan and Norton, 1992), was underpinned by thinking of the organization as a complete entity and measuring inputs and processes as well as outputs.

## The purpose of KPIs

A good way to think of this holistic role of KPIs is by analogy. Let's assume you are having a flying lesson. The days when people climbed into a Tiger Moth, flew across the Channel and sent a cable home to report on the outcome – that you had arrived at Le Touquet for lunch – have passed. While this outcome-based approach may have had a certain charm, flying is now safer, quicker and more reliable despite crowded skies, because it is also more advanced. So what happens now?

The first step is that you spend some time devising your flight plan. You will work out how much fuel you need to reach your destination, familiarize yourself with the conditions en route and develop a set of waypoints as you work out your route to get there.

When you get into the cockpit you will be surrounded by instruments that help you with direction (such as GPS, altitude, course and bearing), the condition of your aircraft (for example: engine thrust, fuel state, artificial horizon, hydraulic pressure) and that supply the information from ground control to allow you to operate the aircraft with other flights happening around you. You are measuring and acting on the inputs and the process of flying the aircraft.

Running a professional services marketing function is very similar. You will normally develop your marketing strategy and plan based on the prevailing conditions in the marketplace. This is your 'flight plan', which articulates what you are going to do and how you are going to do it. KPIs are then an essential feature of any plan to flag the route to your team and to your partners. These act as your waypoints on the journey that you and your team are undertaking. These KPIs allow you to monitor the health of your firm's brand and your marketing operation as you travel to your objective. Your instructions from air traffic control are in the form of the firm's strategy and instructions from your managing partner. This will ensure that your approach is aligned with the direction and other component parts of the firm.

The telemetry from your aircraft can be used to adjust the set-up and running of its engines; similarly, KPIs will provide the evidence for you to communicate to colleagues and for you to change actions and behaviour across your firm.

## The audience for marketing KPIs

We have said that marketing is about winning client preference. As clients are the *sine qua non* of any firm, so marketing KPIs are relevant to everyone in the firm, but in different ways and at different levels of aggregation. Ideally, each person should have six to eight key dials tracking the elements of the firm that are important to them. If a dial moves into the red, that is the time to access more detailed diagnostic data to understand what is moving the parameter away from its objective and what to do about it. So while the firm's executive or management committee needs to track the parameters at the top of the pyramid, other members of the firm need to track dials that monitor other levels.

## How to develop KPIs

What are the parameters that should be developed into KPIs? Tim Ambler (Ambler, 2003) has a well-structured approach that converts well to the often-different professional services firm environment. There are some metrics that are fundamental to all firms. However, if a firm is to be more than a 'me-too', if it is to have a clearly identified place in the market, it needs performance measures that relate to its own specific market positioning.

So how does one get to a consistent set of dials that are relevant to your particular firm? There are four stages, which are illustrated in Figure 16.1.

### 1. Define markets and segments

The first stage is to define the markets and market segments you are interested in. This seems at first blush no more than a truism. Sadly, the world of metrics is littered with KPIs where the numerator and the denominator of the measure are incompatible,

**FIGURE 16.1**  Stages in the development of KPIs

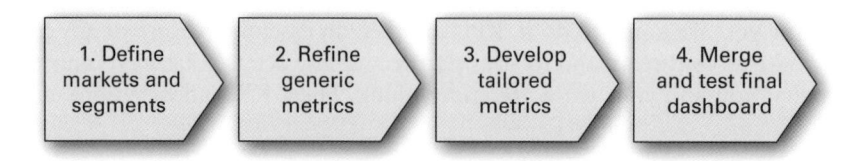

1. Define markets and segments → 2. Refine generic metrics → 3. Develop tailored metrics → 4. Merge and test final dashboard

so it is an important piece of initial due diligence. This ensures that you have correctly defined the contestable market in which you are operating, and have addressed the issue of availability of data at the outset.

## 2. Refine generic metrics

The good news is that there are some KPIs that everyone should have in their portfolio, because they are fundamental for any business. They are:

- the top line – the change in revenue by segment;
- marketing investment – the market budget per period of time;
- the bottom line – the profitability of the firm, ideally analysed by client and by work-type.

The profitability of each assignment, project or matter is the starting point for some powerful analysis. It gives insight into the success of different parts of the firm (clients, sectors, practices, work types). It also allows you to gauge the relative attractiveness and your competitiveness in different parts of the market. However, beware of using (as is still quite common) just the realized fee rate as an analogue for profitability. It is insufficient: arithmetically, partner gearing, fee-earner utilization and margin, as well as fee realization, drive professional services firm profitability.

Every firm needs to be able to answer the following marketing questions:

- Are potential clients aware of your firm?
- How are the number of clients and the value of work that you do for them changing?
- How do they rate your quality?
- How satisfied are they with their experience of your firm?
- Do they have the habit of using you – are they loyal?

Associated with these questions are a core set of marketing metrics which every firm should measure:

- awareness – unprompted/prompted awareness compared to other firms;
- penetration – change in the number of clients per period and the change in the average value per client over the same period;
- how clients think, feel and behave about your firm:
  - quality: your firm's preference ranking compared to competitors;
  - relative satisfaction: rated on a scale of 1 to 5;
  - loyalty: percentage of clients who have used the firm for more than three years, or the percentage of clients who have produced no repeat business.

The measures of penetration and loyalty can be produced from internal data. Measures of awareness, perceived quality and relative satisfaction require you to speak to your clients. This is an unavoidable imperative. However, it is sometimes difficult to formalize the regular surveying of clients unless the value is clearly communicated and understood by the senior management team and the partnership as a whole.

## 3. Develop tailored metrics

Generic metrics, however, take you only part of the way. Pursuing the same KPIs as everyone else serves only to take you to the same place. Commercial success for any firm relies on differentiation, whether it is on non-price factors or on cost. This is where tailored KPIs are required that reflect a deeper understanding of how your particular firm works and how it can be improved.

There are a number of starting points for developing KPIs that are relevant to your firm. The first is if you have the luxury of an already well-defined and articulated strategy. From here the key metrics drop out fairly straightforwardly and indeed may already have been defined as part of the strategy process. The second is almost as good, which is when you are fortunate enough to work in a firm with a clearly defined and differentiated business model.

However, as we know both from experience and the work of Professor Mintzberg (Mintzberg and Waters, 1985), most firms have what are politely called 'emergent strategies', so one has to find the answer by other means. This requires a third starting point, determining what your senior management see as important and translating it into its marketing implications.

There are various techniques for doing this. One is to poll everyone on what they see as the most important key success factors for the firm, and then triangulate between them, sometimes going through a number of iterations. Another is 'success mapping', where you define what realistic success would look like three years out, quantify it and then work back, defining the actions and metrics that are appropriate for each intervening year.

If all else fails, and this smacks slightly of desperation, go through lists of KPIs and select those that fit best with the particular circumstances of your firm. The best way to do this is by asking: if you had a bit more performance on this parameter, would it notably drive forward your firm's specific objectives? We'll talk more about the dangers of lists shortly.

One checklist that is useful to have in front of you is the list of different categories of KPI to make sure you have achieved sufficient coverage with your KPIs. Table 16.1 will help you determine whether there are any glaring gaps.

## 4. Merge and test final dashboard

The process of identifying tailored metrics for your firm will throw up a longer list than is either feasible or required. Remember, the ideal is for each person to have a manageable dashboard of key dials to monitor. What you are seeking is to develop a one-page 'traffic light report' that gives you information that immediately leads to action.

The best way to do this is to distil down the long list through some common-sense filters. First, put each KPI on your long list through the following four tests and eliminate any that test positive:

- Does the chosen parameter change only infrequently?
- Conversely, is the parameter too erratic to be reliable?
- Does it change only in synchronicity with others?

**TABLE 16.1** Categories of marketing metrics for professional services firms

| Category | Explanation |
| --- | --- |
| 1. Brand metrics | Measures of the impact and perception of your brand |
| 2. Market metrics | Market share, penetration and other quantification of the market |
| 3. Client metrics | Distribution, size, profitability and other measures of the make-up of clients and client performance |
| 4. Business development metrics | Measures related to client pitches and converting prospects into clients |
| 5. Work-type metrics | Analysis of changes and developments in the portfolio of services offered to clients |
| 6. Pricing metrics | Measures such as average billing rates and the proportion of fees charged at an hourly rate or under other arrangements |
| 7. PR metrics | PR performance ratios and measures |
| 8. Advertising metrics | Advertising recall, reach, overall impact and cost |
| 9. Web metrics | The number, sequence, duration and actions from visits to the website – measures the impact of your digital marketing channel |
| 10. Marketing function metrics | The level of marketing investment and the number of different marketing actions to which it has been applied (seminars, receptions, newsletters, conferences attended, etc) |

- Does it simply explain change further up the pyramid, meaning it's more of a diagnostic measure than a KPI?

The second area to look at is whether the data are available. One needs to look carefully at the trade-off between the time and cost of generating the data and the value they will produce.

The third step is to do a bit of analysis. If you look retrospectively at the impact of the potential KPI measures on previous performance, can you identify any significant correlation? This is a good way to understand whether the metrics measured will genuinely produce the result you want.

Finally, it is always valuable to have your senior management team on board. It also helps move them towards a consensus on what is important to measure and monitor. From this point onwards you are ready for action. Or are you?

# The pitfalls

Notwithstanding the power of KPIs to coalesce, align and bring about change in an organization, there are also some notorious bear traps. Each report on some failing in the UK's National Health Service (NHS) highlights the often tragic consequences of a naive pursuit of targets. It is not confined to state-run bodies. I have seen managing partners of professional services firms issue edicts about partner utilization targets, resulting in clear unintended consequences. As a result, partner billable hours have gone up, but at the cost of hoarding of work, reduced partner gearing and, perversely, a decline in profitability. The best way to arm yourself against these types of problem is, first, to understand what they are, and second, to know how to avoid them.

The first pitfall is the one of data rather than information. In large firms it is not uncommon to find partners and managers surrounded by a sea of data but struggling to find a relevant drop of actual information to drink. The volume of data is such that they lack the relevant knowledge to make decisions, which then go by default. This can be the well-intentioned mistake of accounting departments who feel that they are providing a service with a proliferation of reports and performance data. In fact they are achieving the contrary.

The solution is to ensure that people have genuine *key* performance indicators put in front of them. This means enforcing a degree of constraint on the number of KPIs so that they form a single page of traffic lights. When a traffic light shows up red, analysis can quickly reveal what has gone adrift and the corrective action that is required. Good KPIs are like the tip of the iceberg: underneath there needs to be a large and well-organized data warehouse that provides access to diagnostic data.

The second pitfall is using KPIs that are not adapted to the particular business. You can, if you are so inclined, purchase a book called the *KPI Mega Library: 17,000 Key Performance Indicators*, described as 'the world's most comprehensive KPI list' (Baroudi, 2010). As Professor Tim Ambler puts it: 'simply rocking up to a metrics warehouse to buy the fashionable data is counter-productive' (Ambler, 2003). If you use metrics that are not adapted to your firm's differentiated strategy, you may well be driving your firm's marketing in the wrong direction; you are certainly not serving the interests of either you or your firm well.

The third pitfall is sub-optimization, which is a more serious issue than it may sound. It lies at the core of many of the NHS's target problems. The pursuit of reduced A&E queuing times and shorter waiting lists is in itself laudable, but if these are pursued at the cost of core patient healthcare, their impact is to create a serious imbalance in the operational process. However, there are ways to overcome this problem. First, KPIs need to be devised within a larger framework, so that the impact of a change in one parameter on others can be seen. Each KPI should sit ideally within a Dupont diagram. A Dupont diagram is similar to the pyramid of ratios in accountancy. It is a representation of the firm's activities in a series of ratios and arithmetic expressions that together make up a picture that describes the firm and its operations. These expressions should be mutually exclusive but collectively exhaustive. This way, the interrelationships of each metric can be understood. Second, a more intuitive approach should also be taken. For each KPI, the designer of the chosen set of metrics should ask themselves what are the likely behavioural consequences from change on this metric.

A fourth pitfall is data integrity. There are two aspects to this. First, data integrity can be poor owing to the paucity of controls on data entry. A common feature of many systems is that the basic data capture process is put in place but there is limited allowance for the human element. A feature of all data entry is the many different ways in which the same data can be entered. This means that your systems should incorporate data validation routines to ensure that what goes in is consistent and makes sense. Furthermore, data will corrupt or become irrelevant over time. Therefore periodic data audits and data cleansing are a necessity to ensure that the KPIs produced are accurate and relevant.

The other aspect of data integrity is that, by their nature, there is considerable institutional pressure behind targets and KPIs. Where bonuses or promotion rests on the attainment of a target, there is an incentive to game the system. This is another reason for ensuring both random and independent audits of your data.

A fifth pitfall is KPIs that are devised without being subject to management action, or don't have a large impact on performance. When selecting the right KPIs for your organization, make sure that they are measures that can be influenced by action within the firm. Simply put, KPIs need to be key with a capital K and critical for your business. If they have a minor impact on the performance of your firm and your function, they almost certainly don't qualify. Less substantive metrics are useful, but they belong in your data warehouse for when it is time to understand why your KPIs are showing a variance.

## KPIs and digital marketing

Lord Leverhulme, the founder of Lever Brothers, which is now part of Unilever, is reported to have said: 'I know half my advertising isn't working, the problem is I don't know which half.' With digital marketing, that has changed. The ability to measure each stage in the online component of the marketing and sales process has transformed marketing KPIs.

Perhaps the single most valuable aspect of online KPIs is the ability to measure the areas of your proposition that have the most salience. The use of web analytics allows you to track how frequently your website is visited and which parts gain the most traction. It is the acid test of the success of your inbound or content marketing, which is the staple of the digital marketing channel. Table 16.2 shows some of the metrics that are relevant to judging the effectiveness of your website and its content.

**TABLE 16.2** Web metrics and their effectiveness

| Metric | Description/technique | Notes |
|---|---|---|
| Page views | Number of times a web page is served. | Significantly more accurate than a website 'hit', which is affected by the number of 'files' (such as images, graphics etc) per web page. |
| Visits | Number of unique viewings of a website. When used relative to 'Page views' reveals the average number of multiple pages being viewed. | Measures audience traffic on a website. |
| Visitors | The number of unique visitors to a site over a period. | Measures whether the website is attracting a few loyal adherents or many occasional visitors. |
| First visit/ repeat visit | Number of first-time visits to the site and number of repeat visits. | Gauges the split between new visits and how often a user is drawn back to the site. Visitor recency measures the time between repeat visits. |
| Bounce rate | The percentage of visits that are single-page visits. | A useful measure of engagement with your site. |
| Visit duration | Refers to the time the visitor spends on the website. | Page duration can also be measured. |
| Exit rate | The percentage of visits to a page where that page is the final page viewed on the website. | Can indicate where visitor loses interest. |

No website is paying its way unless it works in terms of Google's 'Zero Moment of Truth' or ZMOT, the moment at which a potential buyer picks up their laptop, smartphone or tablet and starts searching for products and services.

Historically, the First Moment of Truth in professional services was when the client had the professional in front of them and asked: 'Is this someone I both like and would trust to resolve my issue?' With the wealth of comparative information on the web, this has changed. The ZMOT is when someone with an issue to resolve grabs their laptop and your firm both comes up high on the search list and has relevant content that corresponds with the client's problem. For this reason, tracking search engine optimization (SEO) KPIs is critical to an effective digital presence. Commissioning an analysis of your on-page and off-page SEO metrics is therefore often a worthwhile investment, particularly for getting a picture of your and your competitors' performance.

Closely associated with the success of both your content marketing and SEO is your success in social media marketing, but look beyond just 'follows' and 're-tweets' to more tangible measures of your influence. Measure the proportion of your activity on Twitter that is integrated with other platforms, such as your blog, website or YouTube account. In particular, quantify the uplift in newsletter subscriptions and white-paper downloads. Use influence-monitoring tools to calculate your online influence score based on activity around your profile.

In the world of digital marketing there is considerable discussion about lead conversion, but this needs to be looked at differently for professional services. What you are seeking to achieve is a client's action that leads on to that First Moment of Truth. So 'conversion' is success in achieving, through your online presence, a prospect either clicking through to e-mail an enquiry (as a precursor to a meeting) or registering their details to receive content from you on a regular basis. The 'lead-nurturing metrics' most commonly used are click-through rates to forms and client contacts from the web. Analysing the path forwards and backwards from conversion points and calls to action on your site gives an insight into how effective the site is in driving visitors through to these conversion points.

Finally, e-mail remains an integral part of any digital marketing strategy, and there are relevant metrics in this area as well. These include: the opening rate, the rate of click-through to the content, the unsubscribe rate and the bounce rate. Each tells a story about either the quality, form and appropriateness of your content, or the quality of your database. There are analytical services that help you understand whether your e-mails are resonating with clients.

Web-based metrics are opening up a new dimension in marketing KPIs. However, while they are more available and more accessible, the key principles for using KPIs remain the same.

# Key principles

Bringing all this together, there are seven core principles in using KPIs. KPIs should be:

1　**Tailored to your strategy and business model**: generic KPIs will take your organization only part of the way. You should be aiming to produce KPIs that act as waypoints for the delivery of your specific market proposition. You need KPIs that promote your competitive positioning and your route to achieving it.

2　**Like Goldilocks, you should have not too many and not too few**: the Goldilocks principle is fundamental here. The most common problem is too many KPIs, resulting in a proliferation of data with the user unable to extract the information and knowledge necessary to make a decision. Conversely, a narrow focus on too limited a number of KPIs can promote sub-optimization and a lack of balance, neglecting equally important areas of a firm's success.

3. **Organized within a balanced framework**: the best way to avoid sub-optimization, the pursuit of one or more goals at the expense of others, is to use KPIs within a framework. A quantified set of metrics that shows the interaction of each KPI, as is possible within a Dupont diagram, is an ideal way of doing this. The KPIs must be organized to produce a balanced impact on the organization, not to skew performance in a way that results in an adverse effect.

4. **Understood in the context of their behavioural effects**: a necessary intellectual exercise is to assess what behaviours will be engendered by the pursuit of each KPI. The 'cobra effect', named after the experience in Delhi in the 1900s, is a common phenomenon. This was when a bounty was given for dead king cobras to rid the city of this dangerous snake, but resulted in an increase because people bred cobras in captivity to earn the reward. As we have seen, if you incentivize greater billable hours, the law of unintended consequences can result in hoarding of work, less partner gearing and lower profitability.

5. **Subject to management action and have a material impact**: ensure that the KPI you are monitoring will respond to management action. Tracking parameters that you cannot influence is largely pointless and detracts from the credibility of using KPIs to steer and guide your organization. The KPIs you track should, when achieved, be parameters that will have a significant impact on the fortunes of your firm. It is worth going through the exercise of mapping out your metrics as in Figure 16.2.

6. **Readily and often measured**: there is a trade-off between gaining valuable KPIs on the one hand, and cost and availability on the other. If you have a set of KPIs that are incredibly powerful but where the information is both expensive and difficult to obtain, the chances are you won't track those KPIs very often. It is far better to have less ambitious and less expensive KPIs that are regularly tracked, measured, and engender action.

7. **Accurate and checked**: finally, with the advance of digital technology, information has become significantly less expensive. But, if it is not accurate, it is neither credible nor useful. There must therefore be an effective process of data capture, with data validation routines and audits in place to ensure that the metrics are what they purport to be.

Evidence-based management is, in the final analysis, the only way to operate. KPIs remove the ecclesiastical debate from management discussions. They enable you to communicate effectively to your team and to your colleagues. They allow you to signal what needs to be achieved, and the waypoints on the route to get there. Finally, when achieved, they provide incontrovertible evidence of your success.

# The Role of Marketing KPIs in Professional Services Firms

**FIGURE 16.2**  The impact of KPIs and influencing change

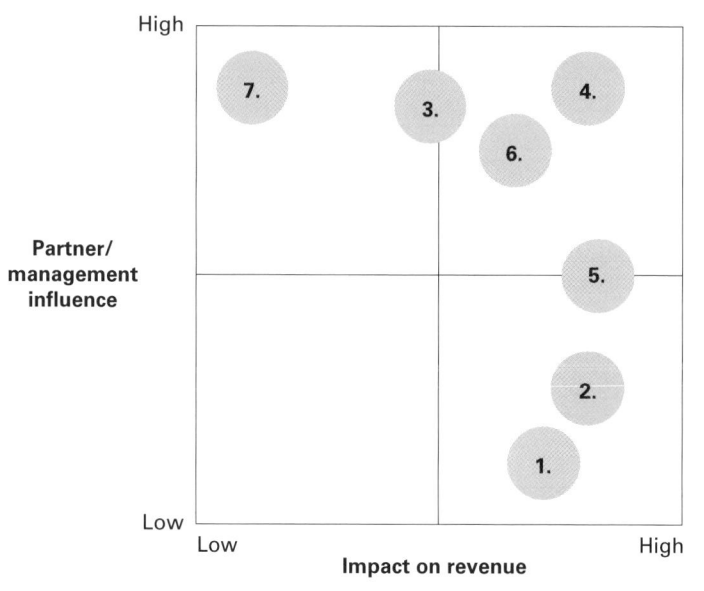

1. Market growth
2. Competitor BD visits
3. Newsletter frequency
4. Number of client meetings
5. Price realization %
6. Business development training frequency
7. Number of brochures

# LESSONS ON MANAGING

From our contributions on the theme of Managing the marketing organization, here are our top 10 lessons for marketing and business development leaders:

1. **Client champion:** your central role should be to understand, communicate and organize the interests of your clients within the firm through the facilitation and management of client-focused activities – both behaviours and formal programmes.

2. **Role model:** as a leader, you will need to 'walk the talk'. Live and demonstrate the client champion behaviours you want everyone in your firm to adopt.

3. **Develop a great team:** you cannot do it all yourself – build a great team around you and think about what further skills and capabilities you all need to develop. Like others in the firm, you will need to build much more than a team of individual discipline specialists.

4. **Understanding and empathy:** build understanding of your external and internal audiences. If partners or senior management are your direct clients, make sure you know what they are trying to achieve and the challenges you face. If you show empathy and help them achieve, they will reciprocate.

5. **Clarity of purpose:** develop a clear vision of what you are trying to achieve and how that will benefit the objectives of the firm. Set and communicate the benefits of your programmes and projects within that vision. Be disciplined, stick to the script and don't launch random or sporadic initiatives.

6. **Flexible and adaptable:** you need clarity of purpose, but you will also have to be flexible and adaptable in how you achieve your aims. It's more important to win the war than to triumph in every battle.

7. **Persuasion:** you can do some things yourself and command others occasionally, but ultimately your success will be determined by your ability to persuade. For this you will need buckets of emotional intelligence, alongside the usual professional traits of rational thinking and logical arguments.

8. **Patience:** material change in a professional services firm takes time. Be determined and push hard, but be patient too – Rome wasn't built in a day!

9. **Opportunities for change:** you will probably lead an agenda for change and need to shift your firm from the status quo, so work with enthusiasts, identify agents of change, leverage a 'burning platform', celebrate success, don't waste

too much time on perennial naysayers, and so forth. Benefit from every opportunity to drive change.

10 **Smart measurement:** understand how you can measure the success of your marketing and business development objectives and do so religiously. Think carefully about what measures matter and make a real difference to individual, team and firm-wide behaviours and performance.

# Conclusion

# 17

# The future for professional services marketing: becoming a client champion

Each of the themes and chapters in this book has outlined the priorities we believe should sit high on the agenda of a professional services marketing and business development leader. Each highlights the issues and solutions our contributors consider critical to ensure that they have a positive and enduring impact on their firms.

In this concluding chapter we pull together the lessons from each of those themes and propose how the future will look for people and teams who want to lead their firms in marketing and business development. We put forward the case for a marketing and business development professional to be a true client champion within their firm and identify what that will mean in terms of role, responsibilities, activities and outcomes.

## Lessons learnt

The five themes we have talked about through this book are (Figure 17.1):

- Growth – identifying and choosing markets and clients;
- Understanding – listening and responding to client needs;
- Connecting – building a conversation with clients and stakeholders;
- Relationships – developing and managing client relationships;
- Managing – influencing the marketing organization.

Our contributors have raised a range of scenarios, issues and solutions, in part driven by the circumstances of their firms' particular market or situation. No two firms are the same, and so situations and appropriate solutions will vary, but we see a number

**FIGURE 17.1** The five themes for the marketing and business development leader

- Growth – identifying and choosing markets and clients
- Understanding – listening and responding to client needs
- Connecting – building conversations with clients and stakeholders
- Relationships – developing and managing client relationships
- Managing – influencing the marketing organization

(Centre: Marketing & BD leader)

of important lessons cut through each, which should hold true whether you are a global accountancy practice, regional law firm, provincial property consultancy, multidisciplinary engineering practice or any variation thereof.

We have summarized what we consider to be the principal lessons at the end of each theme, but in short they are:

## Growth

- You need to be clear on your **reasons for growth**.
- Equally you will need to consider carefully **market selection**.
- **Following your clients** is a sensible starting point for your growth strategy.
- **Brand clarity** will help attract the clients and people you need.
- Strong client **relationship** management (CRM) is always likely to feature.
- You need to build **trust** with your clients and between your teams to **cross-sell services**.
- Growth can be achieved using a variety of **business models**.

- Growth is dependent on your people having strong business and client development **skills**.
- Introduce **innovation** and new, **disruptive** services and business models.
- Identify when continuity is important and where you want to drive **change**.

## *Understanding*

- Most firms claim to be client-focused, but they are still not very good at **listening**.
- **Everyone needs to listen** to and understand their clients.
- It is best practice to run a structured, **formal client listening** or feedback programme.
- Understand your **objectives**, then that will help influence programme design.
- Client listening needs to be **open, positive, engaging** and forward-looking.
- You will get the best response when your interviewers are **independent**.
- You need to listen, understand and **improve continuously**.
- Clients are now more demanding and looking for **commercial partners**, not just technical advisers.
- Capabilities in listening to and understanding your clients' business needs can be **taught and learnt**.
- Listening to and understanding your clients' priorities is worthless unless you then take appropriate **action**.

## *Connecting*

- Professional services firms have a privileged **opportunity** to build brand, increase authority and establish leadership.
- Develop a **new mindset** and ditch many of the traditional marketing models for 'pushing' out communications.
- Marketers need to accept that they are no longer in **control**.
- Recognize that **trust**, timing and context are as important as the message.
- The route to your target audience will increasingly be through **engaging with your employees**.
- **Multi-channel** conversations and content consumption is the new norm.
- **Thought leadership** content offers an excellent opportunity to engage a client and stimulate a conversation, but it needs a **purpose** and should instigate action.
- **Thought leadership and sales** are on the same continuum; they are not separate activities.
- Consider **bespoke content** for a particular audience on a major pursuit or sales opportunity.
- Your content needs to be **engaging**, visually strong, digestible and easy to share.

## Relationships

- Developing long-term, mutually beneficial relationships with **core clients** is probably the best route to success.
- **Involving the client** in planning and decision-making will enhance and deliver greater opportunity.
- **Analyse** your client base, then set some **objectives** and make the right choices.
- Don't forget to consider what the client is getting – a relationship should be **mutually beneficial**.
- Make sure that you **measure** the programme's impact and take decisions accordingly.
- Don't forget that relationships are all about **trust** and commitment between individuals.
- Core client relationship management is a **marathon**, not a **sprint**.
- A **CRM** system should complement, not dominate, your programme.
- Your success will depend on your ability to develop great relationships with **internal and external** clients.
- **Training and coaching** will be a big part of the set-up and running of any programme.

## Managing

- Your central role should be to understand, communicate and organize the interests of your clients – a **client champion**.
- You will need to 'walk the talk' and role-model client champion behaviours.
- You will want to **develop a great team** around you.
- You must build **understanding of, and empathy with,** your external and internal audiences.
- You must have **clarity of purpose** and communicate the benefits of your programmes and projects within that vision.
- You will need to be **flexible and adaptable** in how you achieve your aims.
- Ultimately your success will be determined by how good you are at **persuasion**.
- Be determined and push hard, but be **patient** too – Rome wasn't built in a day.
- Benefit from every opportunity to **drive change**.
- Understand how you can **measure** the success of your marketing and business development objectives and do so religiously.

Not every lesson will be of equivalent relevance or value to every firm or marketing and business development professional. Equally, it will be hard for any individual to understand and interpret the consequences of all these lessons for their firm, but taken together, they should touch every aspect of your role and outlook.

# The client champion role

Throughout this book we have been talking about how to achieve the best, mutually beneficial future for the firm and its clients. In addition, we have considered how a marketing and business development professional or team can increase their impact and influence. Both objectives are consistent with a firm taking a more client-focused view of the issues and opportunities that will shape its future.

In order to create that future, we believe that the leaders of a firm should understand and interpret the needs of the client first and then shape a response that permeates the whole firm's beliefs and actions. An individual, or more likely a group of people, will need to be the catalyst for that process of change. That team must step forward and think and behave as if they were the client within their firm. In short, they need to be a client champion.

To be a client champion, you will want to understand the key themes that this book has covered and interpret the appropriate response for your clients. That means you will be their eyes and ears within your firm. You will be their conscience, interpreter and voice – the person or team who will speak out and say with authority and conviction in any situation: 'I think the best solution and outcome for the client here is…'

Some may contend that this is going too far, and that always seeking to interpret the world through the clients' eyes could prejudice the best interests of the firm and conflict with the foundations of the client-to-adviser relationship. There will be a concern that the independent objective stance held by a professional adviser will be compromised.

We don't believe that the advisory role is compromised here or that acting in the best interests of the client conflicts with those of the firm. In a world where clients are increasingly looking for partnership and a shared commitment to achieving common goals, what is best for one party will, over the long term, be the best outcome for both. Looking out for the firm first might benefit financial performance or your risk profile in the short term, but it won't foster mutually beneficial, long-term client partnerships, which should be the foundation for success of any professional services firm.

Even if the firm's role remains that of independent adviser and the client is not looking for a long-term partnership, shaping advice within the client's frame of reference still makes sense. We have heard throughout the book how professional advice and technical excellence need to be placed in a commercial context. Seeing the world through the eyes of the client and responding accordingly always makes sense.

If you strive to be the client's champion and both parties see the relationship as mutually beneficial, your client will reciprocate and similarly champion your cause. The characteristics of a professional services firm outlined earlier in the book highlight how interdependence can foster competitive advantage. If you are looking for competitive differentiators that are defensible and sustainable over the long term, adopting a client champion mentality is probably your only option.

If you consider the likely response of a client champion to the challenges of the key themes we have identified through this book, you can see how the outlook and response of the firm could change (Table 17.1).

**TABLE 17.1** The traditional response vs the client champion response

| Theme | Traditional response | Client champion response |
| --- | --- | --- |
| **Growth** | Which markets are growing fastest and with the least competition? How can we maximize revenue and profit from any particular opportunity? What growth model will allow us to exploit the opportunity fastest? | In which markets are our clients developing and what additional skills, resources and coverage do we need to help them succeed? How do we prioritize the pursuit of our best clients' objectives? What business model will maximize our opportunity to match those clients' needs? |
| **Understanding** | What do we know about our clients? Do we know the right people so that we can tell them what we do and sell more? What do they buy and who else do they use and why? | What is on our client's agenda – what are their business objectives and priorities? Where do we fit into their business model and are we performing? Where are they going and how can we help them get there? |
| **Connecting** | What's our ideal brand positioning? How do we get our message out into the marketplace? What's the cheapest, most efficient communications channel that reaches the majority of our clients and contacts? | How do we initiate a valuable conversation with our key audiences that progresses their agenda? What are the best channels and networks to develop those conversations? Can we share and develop ideas together? |
| **Relationships** | Who do we want a relationship with – how much money are we making out of them now and is it worth investing in getting more? How do we get our partners/directors to take on this role and still stay billable? | Which of our clients are looking for long-term relationships? How can we engage in and manage that process to the benefit of both parties? How do we measure mutual benefit? |
| **Managing** | Who is responsible for what and who is in charge? Do marketing and business development professionals add value in this firm? What do you need to do to get promoted in this firm? | How do we work together to deliver value for our core clients? What complementary skills do we possess and how do we develop together? How do we measure and demonstrate collective and individual progress? |

# The client champion today

The painful truth for most marketing and business development teams in professional services firms today is, as we have intimated through this book, that they are a long way from being the client champion.

If you were to approach a managing partner or chief executive of a professional services firm today and ask who best understands their clients and represents their interests, the most likely response would be 'the partners/directors of the firm'. They are the individuals who today get closest to that position. The partners or directors typically guard tightly their key client relationships and that knowledge which comes with personal interaction. Those relationships are, after all, often the principal source of power, influence and income within a firm.

However, we would contend that professional culture and historical precedents do not encourage most partners or directors to behave as true client champions. Evidence, examples and feedback throughout this book bear that out.

There are too many competing forces to allow the client's perspective to shine through. There are precedents and contrasting pressures from professional training, technical proficiency, team management and performance metrics to confuse the picture. If you were to ask most clients about the key individuals in their professional advisory firms, they would often be very complimentary, but they are unlikely to describe a relationship consistent with that of a client champion.

There will hopefully be examples of people demonstrating client champion behaviours and competences in most firms. These are the people who demonstrate a real understanding of their clients and shape their decisions based on what they know the client is looking for. However, we believe that they are the exception rather than the rule. These individuals tend to be one-offs – identified as exceptions from the norm and people who are typically described as 'really good with clients'.

In truth, every business needs its client champions. Whether by accident or design, there will be people, values or processes that bring the essence of the client into the heart of the organization. It often originates with the initial owner or founding partners of a business and their inspiration for starting things in the first place. For some great businesses, the original 'reason to be' was a desire to solve a particular customer issue or conundrum, and that desire to create solutions and solve problems permeates through the value and culture of the business today.

## *'Outside in' vs 'inside out'*

There is a perspective that some businesses are inherently better at understanding and responding to customer needs. This picture is often painted of innovation-driven, consumer-facing businesses – think about Apple with the smartphone, easyJet with low-cost airfares or Unilever with environmentally friendly personal care products, as three examples.

A contrary view is that such firms are not being client-focused because their focus is innovation and inventing new products that customers haven't even considered they want, let alone revealed the need for in a survey or market research. The argument goes that if such businesses are just responding to what customers ask for, they're already at least one step behind the competition.

We would contest, though, that these perspectives are consistent. If you are really listening to your customers and interpreting their behaviour, you will uncover insights and opportunities that they are not even aware of. It's not just about straight interpretation of what they say.

You are looking for a potent combination that brings together perceptive insights of the market and your clients' needs with a deep understanding of what is technically possible. In other words, you are drawing together the 'outside in' market and client perspective with the 'inside out' skills and capabilities of your business.

The business of technology innovation and consumer-led product development often feels a world away from the professional services sector, but we believe that the same concepts apply here.

As Figure 17.2 highlights, what a professional services firm has to offer – the 'inside out' view of the world – is captured by a blend of knowledge and capabilities ranging from the tangible to the more intangible. This view combines everything at the 'softer' end of the spectrum, such as values, culture and people skills, together with everything that is more tangible, such as metrics, experience, processes and systems. At the other end of the spectrum, there is the client's view of the world – the 'outside in' – which combines the 'hard' expectations around business objectives and project outcomes with more intangible requirements of empathy and relationship development.

**FIGURE 17.2** 'Inside out' vs 'outside in' views of the world

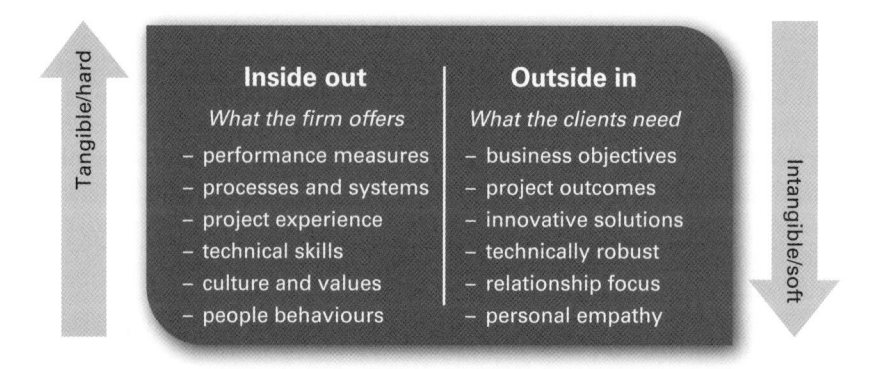

| Inside out | Outside in |
|---|---|
| *What the firm offers* | *What the clients need* |
| – performance measures | – business objectives |
| – processes and systems | – project outcomes |
| – project experience | – innovative solutions |
| – technical skills | – technically robust |
| – culture and values | – relationship focus |
| – people behaviours | – personal empathy |

Tangible/hard → Intangible/soft

## *The opportunity for marketing and business development professionals*

The challenge for any business is to balance the 'outside in' and 'inside out' views of the world. The 'sweet spot' is where the two meet and match. In an ideal world, one view will feed off the other, but in a fast-moving environment where external shocks and customer demands are ever-changing, a business should never settle into a position where the 'inside out' view dominates.

Of course, a client champion is always thinking 'outside in' – that is their steady state – always enquiring what the client wants next and anticipating new opportunities and challenges. If you are a marketing or business development professional in an organization where you own the customer relationship and/or you capture and control most of the information on your customers' requirements and behaviours, the role of client champion should come naturally. Your business leadership will expect it and you will have the tools and information necessary to deliver.

As we highlighted above, the closest person a professional services firm today has to a client champion is probably the partnership or directors – the people who 'own' the client relationships. However, they are also the group most likely to concern themselves with the 'inside out' view of the world. They will obsess about performance measures, be the best source of project experience and skills in the firm and be responsible for the development of technical resources and people.

In all likelihood, while the best will be able to balance 'inside out' and 'outside in' views of the world, they probably need help in ensuring that the firm remains honest to its clients and that their view is the dominant one. This is where the opportunity arises for marketing and business development professionals. While they need to understand the firm's 'inside out' view, they should have the independence, mindset and skills to champion the clients' 'outside in' perspective. The client champion role is there for the taking!

## *The marketing and business development professional as client champion*

If the marketing and business development professional is going to step forward and take on the mantle of client champion, they need not only the right mindset and licence to operate, but also the skills and knowledge to know where to lead, advise and act throughout the life cycle of interaction with the client (Figure 17.3). Each point in this life cycle is critical to a successful and sustaining client relationship, and yet firms handle many haphazardly; marketing and business development professionals tend to focus on only a few steps. In addition, firms typically take an 'inside out' perspective where the established position of the firm is prioritized over an 'outside in' client view.

Table 17.2 shows the actions that 'inside out' vs 'outside in' firms would take at each step in the process. We then identify whether the marketing and business development professional as client champion should play a lead or partnership role for each step. Critically, the true client champion is not only involved at each stage; they have a perspective on the whole life cycle and how each stage benefits the others.

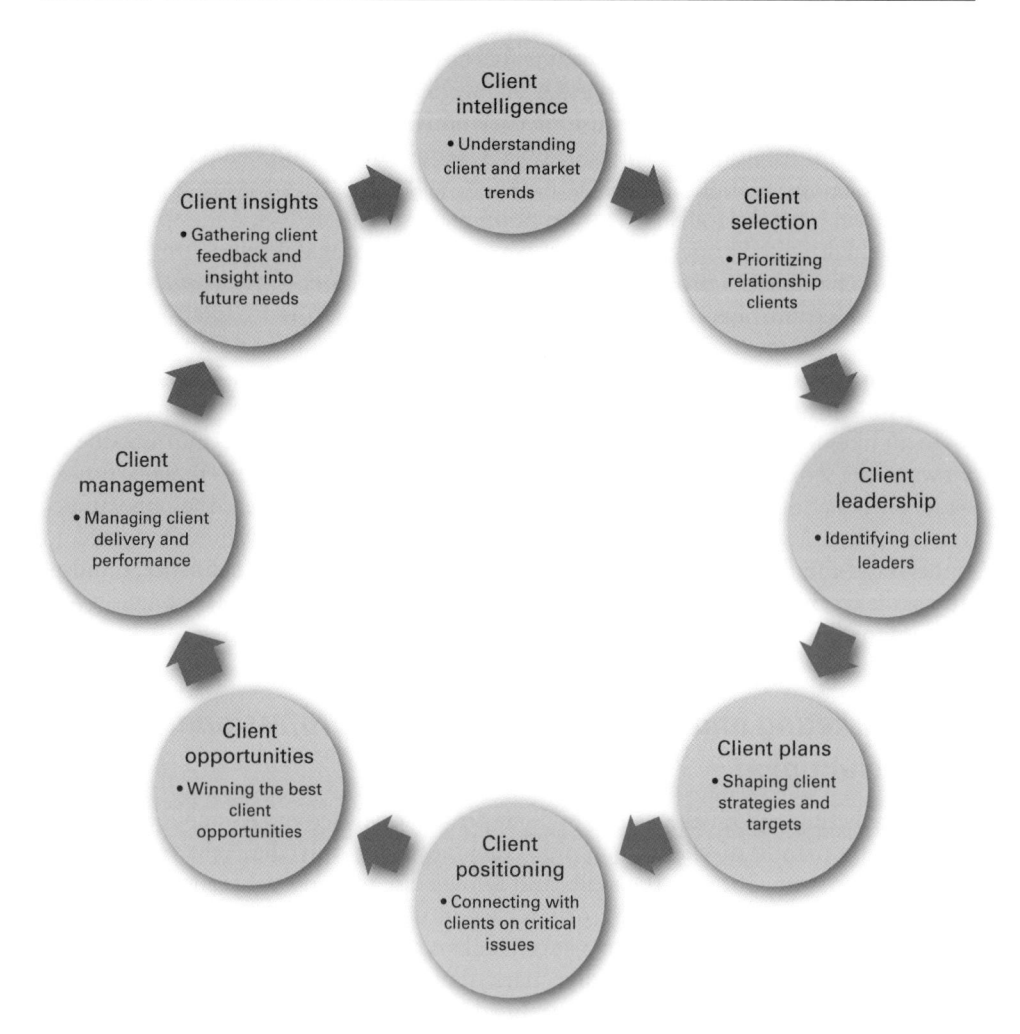

**FIGURE 17.3** The client life cycle

- **Client intelligence**
  - Understanding client and market trends
- **Client selection**
  - Prioritizing relationship clients
- **Client leadership**
  - Identifying client leaders
- **Client plans**
  - Shaping client strategies and targets
- **Client positioning**
  - Connecting with clients on critical issues
- **Client opportunities**
  - Winning the best client opportunities
- **Client management**
  - Managing client delivery and performance
- **Client insights**
  - Gathering client feedback and insight into future needs

**TABLE 17.2** The client life cycle response

| Client life cycle step | 'Inside out' view | 'Outside in' view | Marketing/BD as client champion |
|---|---|---|---|
| Intelligence | Study market research and client performance data. | Research and compare market trends, talk to clients, interpret behaviour and needs. Share and discuss insights with clients and the firm. | Lead – this should be home territory for client champions. |
| Selection | Pick the top 10/20/50 largest and most profitable clients from the past year. | Assess whether clients will benefit from investment in a client relationship. Agree their expectations from the investment and set shared objectives. | Partner – advise partners/directors and clients on who should be on the client relationship programme. Agree how to manage those who suit a different relationship. |
| Leadership | Appoint those people who are 'good with clients' or currently own the relationship. Avoid 'gurus' with high billability, so that short-term performance doesn't suffer. | Assess the skills, competences and compatibility of your people. Match people to client objectives. Agree with the client who will be in their client team. | Lead/partner – advise partners/directors on who best should be involved in client leadership from across the firm, including marketing/BD teams. Depending on the client and skills, marketing/BD may lead. |
| Planning | Reluctantly write a plan or update last year's using a standard template. File away once completed. Only refer to when predetermined milestones are reached. | Shape and share the plan with the client. Involve the whole client team and make it a living document. Set milestones and review dates with the client. | Partner – work with the appointed client team and the client on the development and delivery of the plan. |

**TABLE 17.2** *continued*

| Client life cycle step | 'Inside out' view | 'Outside in' view | Marketing/BD as client champion |
|---|---|---|---|
| Positioning | Identify the messages you want to communicate to clients and the market and choose the most efficient channel to get your message across. | Understand the topics and conversations that would benefit the client and your relationship. Shape the engagement to further the relationship. | Lead – leverage marketing and communications skills, but be wary of slipping into traditional 'push' marketing mode. |
| Opportunities | Focus on the biggest opportunities in the short-term pipeline. Prioritize deals you would like to win and bids you feel you should go for. | Ideally, shape an opportunity with the client. Identify early on with the client the differentiators you bring to the solution. Reject anything where you can't show the client how you will make a difference. | Lead/partner – depending on the stage of the opportunity and the make-up of the client team, take the lead or partner. |
| Management | Focus on technical excellence, agreed scope and deliverables, and internal performance measures. Internal reviews, checks and problem fixes. | Work to shared deliverables, milestones and metrics with the client. Check progress together, identify issues early and collaborate on resolution. | Depending on project size and scale, marketing/BD may not have a role, but as client champion you will want to stay abreast of progress and highlight any situation where the firm might be slipping back into 'inside out' mode. |
| Insights | Possibly ignore, especially if it's an awkward client, and at best focus on metrics and measures that check up on the firm's historical performance. | Gather objective and independent views on performance and the relationship. Consult the client and the client team. Share everything with the client and shape next steps. Use to identify future trends. | Lead – these insights should combine with those gathered in Intelligence (above) to underpin the importance and primacy of the client champion role. |

# The future for professional services marketing and business development

This model of how a firm partners with its clients and the critical role of the client champion is a world away from how most professional services firms operate today. It's also a massive shift for marketing and business development professionals and teams.

Some firms will be reluctant or unwilling to make the necessary change. Equally, many marketing and business development professionals will struggle to step up. They will lack the skills, temperament and ambition to move into such a pivotal role within their firm.

Ideally, everyone in a firm will have a client champion mindset – thinking 'outside in' first, then 'inside out' – but it is not essential that they shift roles completely. To be a leader you will need to be fully immersed, but the firm still needs its teams to deliver on technical excellence, whether that is in its professional advice or how it goes about its marketing and business development activities.

People can hone their client champion skills as they progress through their careers and move into different roles. This is as true for technical practitioners as it is for marketing and business development specialists. For both groups, the more direct exposure they get to clients and their challenges, the easier it will be to move up towards their client champion 'black belt'.

We strongly believe that those firms that adopt a client champion ethos and have leaders in key roles that can demonstrate and teach the behaviours of a true client champion will be the firms that succeed in the future. They will have the best client relationships and the most sustainable path to future growth and prosperity. Their clients will flourish too!

We urge you to take the lessons and experiences of our experts and the other ideas in this book back into your firm. Become a client champion for the benefit of everyone and put the client at the heart of your organization.

Your firm will prosper and so will you.

# REFERENCES

Acritas (2013) *Sharplegal 2013 Global Elite Brand Index* [Online] http://www.acritas.com/globalelitebrandindex2013

Allen & Overy (2014) *Unbundling a market: the appetite for new legal services* [Online] http://www.allenovery.com/SiteCollectionDocuments/Unbundling_a_market.PDF

Ambler, T (2003) *Marketing and the Bottom Line*, 2nd edn, FT Prentice Hall, London

Baroudi, R (2010) *KPI Mega Library: 17,000 Key Performance Indicators*, CreateSpace Independent Publishing Platform, United States

Chartered Institute of Marketing (2014) *Glossary* [Online] http://www.cim.co.uk/Resources/JargonBuster.aspx

Covey, S R (1989) *The Seven Habits of Highly Effective People: Powerful lessons in personal change*, Simon & Schuster, London

Dixon, M and Adamson, B (2013) *The Challenger Sale: Taking control of the customer conversation*, Portfolio Penguin, New York

Dixon, M, Freeman, K and Toman, N (2010) Stop trying to delight your customers, *Harvard Business Review* [Online] http://hbr.org/2010/07/stop-trying-to-delight-your-customers

Economist (2013) Wasting time: India's demographic challenge [Online] http://www.economist.com/news/briefing/21577373-india-will-soon-have-fifth-worlds-working-age-population-it-urgently-needs-provide

Epley, N (2014) *Mindwise: How we understand what others think, believe, feel, and want*, Allen Lane, London

Financial Times, Meridian West, MPF (2012) *Effective Client-Adviser Relationships* [Online] http://ftcorporate.ft.com/professional-services/

Fleming, N and Cooper, S (2013) *Insight Trading*, Sinclair Knight Merz Pty Limited, Melbourne

Forbes (2014) *The World's Biggest Public Companies* [Online] http://www.forbes.com/global2000/list/

Fortune (2014) *Fortune Global 500 2014* [Online] http://fortune.com/global500/

Gates, B (1999) *Business @ The Speed of Thought*, Warner Books, New York

Hodges, S and Young, L (2009) Unconsciously competent: Academia's neglect of marketing success in the professions, *Journal of Relationship Marketing*, 8 (1), pp 36–49

Hunt-Davis, B and Beveridge, H (2011) *Will It Make the Boat Go Faster? Olympic-winning strategies for everyday success*, Troubador, Leicester

Information Technology Services Marketing Association (2014) *Increasing Relevance with Buyer Personas and B2I Marketing* [Online] http://www.itsma.com/research/pdf_free/ITSMAPersonasandB2I_AbbSum.pdf

International Monetary Fund (2010) *Regional Economic Outlook: Asia and Pacific* [Online] http://www.imf.org/external/pubs/ft/reo/2010/apd/eng/areo0410.htm

Kaplan, R S and Norton, D P (1992) The balanced scorecard: measures that drive performance, *Harvard Business Review*, **69** (1), pp 71–79

Kirby, N (2013) *Think you're a thought leader? Think again* [Online] http://www.businesslife.co/Features.aspx?id=think-youre-a-thought-leader-think-again

Maister, D (1997) *How to Give Advice* [Online] http://davidmaister.com/articles/how-to-give-advice/

Maister, D, Green, C and Galford, R (2000) *The Trusted Advisor*, The Free Press, New York

# References

Market Research Society (2014) *Code of Conduct* [Online] https://www.mrs.org.uk/standards/code_of_conduct

Mintzberg, H and Waters, J A (1985) Of strategies, deliberate and emergent, *Strategic Management Journal*, **6** (3), pp 257–72

National Business Research Institute (2011) *The Importance of Employee Engagement – Infographic* [Online] http://www.nbrii.com/blog/infographic/

Neighmond, P (2007) *Toddlers Outsmart Chimps in Some Tasks, Not All* [Online] http://www.npr.org/templates/story/story.php?storyId=14224459

Nisus (2004) *Seeing the world through clients' eyes* [Online] http://www.nisus.net

Ofcom (2014) *Adults' Media Use and Attitudes Report 2014* [Online] http://stakeholders.ofcom.org.uk/market-data-research/other/research-publications/adults/adults-media-lit-14/

PwC (2013) *Breakthrough innovation and growth* [Online] http://www.pwc.com/gx/en/innovationsurvey/

Shirky, C (2008) *It's Not Information Overload. It's Filter Failure* [Online] https://www.youtube.com/watch?v=LabqeJEOQyI

Social Chorus (2014) *The Definitive Guide to Employee Advocate Marketing: A seven step guide to ensure success* [Online] http://info.socialchorus.com/rs/socialchorus/images/The-Definitive-Guide-to-Employee-Advocate-Marketing-SocialChorus.pdf

Sperry, R (2003) *The Split Brain Experiments* [Online] http://www.nobelprize.org/educational/medicine/split-brain/background.html

Stein, S J and Book, H E (2000) *The EQ Edge: Emotional Intelligence and Your Success*, Jossey-Bass, San Francisco

Technorati (2013) *Engaged Employees Build Engaged Customers: How does Addvocate help you engage?* [Online] http://technorati.com/engaged-employees-build-engaged-customers-how-does-addvocate-help-you-engage/

Tönnies, F (2003) *Community and Society*, Dover Publications, Mineola, NY

United Nations Global Compact (2010) *A New Era of Sustainability* [Online] https://www.unglobalcompact.org/resources/230

Whitmore, J (2002) *Coaching for Performance: The principles and practice of coaching and leadership*, Nicholas Brealey, London

World Tourism Organization (2013) *China – the new number one tourism source market in the world* [Online] http://media.unwto.org/press-release/2013-04-04/china-new-number-one-tourism-source-market-world

Young, L (2010) *Business Development for Lawyers: Principles and practice*, Ark Group, London

Young, L (2013) *Thought Leadership: Prompting businesses to think and learn*, Kogan Page, London

# FURTHER READING

Broderick, M (2011) *Managing Professional Services: Insights from leaders of the world's top firms*, Prentice Hall, Upper Saddle River, NJ

Hodges Silverstein, S (2013) I didn't go to law school to become a salesperson – the development of marketing in law firms, *Georgetown Journal of Legal Ethics*, **26** (2)

Koku, P S (2007) Turf wars or a misunderstanding of roles: an examination of the relationship between marketers and lawyers within the corporation, *Journal of Services Marketing*, **21** (1), pp 15–23

Kotler, P, Hayes, T and Bloom, P N (2002) *Marketing Professional Services*, 2nd edn, Prentice Hall Press, Paramus, NJ

Maister, D (2000) *True Professionalism*, Simon & Schuster, London

Maister, D (2001) *Practice What You Preach*, The Free Press, New York

Malhotra, N and Morris, T (2009) Heterogeneity in professional service firms, *Journal of Management Studies*, **46** (6), pp 895–922

Morgan, N A (1990) Communications and the reality of marketing in professional service firms, *International Journal of Advertising*, **9** (4), pp 283–93

Rasiel, E (1999) *The McKinsey Way*, McGraw-Hill, New York

Schultz, M, Doerr, J and Frederiksen, W (2009) *Professional Services Marketing*, John Wiley & Sons, Hoboken, NJ

Stevens, R F, Loudon, D L and Williamson, S (1998) Getting it done: achieving law firm objectives through the development of effective marketing strategies, *Journal of Professional Services Marketing*, **17** (1), pp 105–18

Tschida, M H (2010) The Impact of Market Orientation on the Performance of Professional Service Firms, PhD thesis, University of East Anglia, Norwich

Vickerstaff, A (2000) Legal sector marketing: a contested case, *Management Decision*, **38** (5), pp 354–61

Williams, T (2010) *Positioning for Professionals*, John Wiley & Sons, Hoboken, NJ

Young, L (2005) *Marketing the Professional Services Firm*, John Wiley & Sons, Chichester

# INDEX

Page numbers in *italic* refer to pages and tables.

ACC Value Challenge   178
access to information   107, 108, 114, 192
account management   131
account management programmes   31, 85
account managers   151, 160
account performance measurement   155
account plans   155
account selection   153–5
account teams   151, 155
accounting   221
accuracy, of data   230
Acritas   89–102
Adamson, Brent   134
adaptability   15, 232
'advanced' positioning   30
advertising metrics   225
advice, and relationship failure   97
AECOM   148–61
aggregation of content   113, 115, 116
Allen & Overy   22–36, 128–9
Amazon   131, 132
ambiguity of purpose, avoiding   124–5
Ambler, Tim   222, 226
Apple   132
archives, content material   139–40
ASEAN   39, 44
Asia Pacific, growth strategy implementation   37–47
Asia Pacific Services Marketing Association (APSMA)   133–41
associate involvement, in pitch process   197
Association of Corporate Counsel (ACC)   178
Atkins   199–208
Australia   27, 29, 44, 46, 47, 73, 175
authority   169
auto-enrolment, thought leadership (case study)   126–7
autonomy   44, 45, 50, 191, 220
awareness, measures of   223

B2C organizations   131, 132
Baker & McKenzie   37–47
'balanced scorecard' approach   191, 221
behaviour(s)
    and change programmes   205–6
    of highly effective people   165–6
    KPIs and   230

behavioural challenges, business development   192–5
behavioural change, sensitivity to   94
bespoke content   131, 142
best-friend alliances   29
Bird & Bird   64–77
blue-sky thinking   220
brand(ing)   *13*
    clarity   57
    and client understanding   100–1, *102*
    compulsory global   50
    content marketing and   135
    global vs local dichotomy   44
    growth and globalization   30
    metrics   225
    as part of organizational culture   31
    positioning   25
    power of   54–5
Breakthrough innovation and growth   122–3, 130
BRICS   39
brochures   40, 42, 44
budgeting, client feedback programmes   99–100
business
    contexts, advice and understanding of   81
    conversations *see* conversation(s)
    internationalization of   48–9
    winning new   179–80
business case, for thought leadership   123–4
business challenge, thought leadership   119–20
business development
    metrics   225
    *see also* marketing and business development
business development teams   192
'business development transformation story'   202
business model   57
buy-in
    business development   198
    client feedback programmes   98–9
    client relationship management   155, 159–60, 164
    communication and   83
    transformational change   200–2

campaign topics, choosing the best   125–6
capital markets   23
challenge   10
Challenger Sale   133, 134, 136, 137

# Index

*The Challenger Sale* 134
change
    client listening and 74–6, 104
    commerciality and need for 84
    continuity and 57
    corporate counsel and 175–6
    danger of overlooking pace and scale of 56
    driving 34, 42–3, 136, 206
    impact of KPIs *231*
    instigating 41–2
    opportunities for 232–3
    organizational characteristics and attitudes to 166
    in professional services market 188–9
        firms' adaption to 189–90
    technological *see* digital media
    *see also* behavioural change; organizational change; transformational change
cherry picking, client feedback programmes 99
chief marketing officers 192
'chimp vs child' experiment 61, 62
China 38–9
choice 107–8, 142
clarity 57, 98, 122, 232
client champions
    current 243–8
    response to challenge *242*
    role 232, 241
client concentration *12*
client control 142
client engagement 133, 138–9
client expectations 31, 97–8, 160
client feedback
    acting on 100, 104
    client management programmes 155–6
    engagement with (case study) 76–7
    learning from 32
    programmes 98–100
    relationship development 167, 168, 170
client innovation panels 126
client life cycle *246*, 247–8
client loyalty 66, 90, 94, 98, 135, 223
client metrics *225*
client relationship management (CRM)
    and growth 32, 33, 57
    need for strategic understanding 215
    professional roles and titles 3
    programmes 149, 177–8
        future trends 160–1
        issues and challenges 158–60
        major argument for 151
        measurement criteria 156
        setting up 151–6
        success factors 161
        systems to support 156–8, 181
    support of best friend alliances 29

client selection 247
client signals, reading 94, 100
client understanding 89–102
    brand and reputation 100–1, *102*
    building 91–2
    client-firm relationship cycle 92–102
    importance of client feedback programmes 98–100
    recommendations for MBD leaders 214–15
    Sharplegal research 90
    value of 90
client-care partners 165, 168–9
client-firm relationship cycle 92–102
client-focused capability 3
client-focused organizations 192–3
clients
    CRM programmes
        analysis of current 152
        identification 153, *154*
        inclusion/involvement in planning 158, 181
    diversity, and globalization 22–3
    future challenges for 79
    listening to *see* listening to clients
    matching/following 5, 57
    new demands and changing role of professional services 1–2
    nurturing 44–5
    relationships with *see* relationships
    thinking, understanding 95–6
coaching 159, 182
*Coaching for Performance* 167
cobra effect 230
cohort marketing 114–15
    employee engagement 116–17
    honing content (case study) 117
    network behaviours 116
cohorts 114
collective branding 50, 51, 54, 55
commerciality 78–88, 103
    appetite for change 84
    client dissatisfaction with 79–80
    getting the balance right 88
    professionals and the struggle for 83, *84*
    'seven habits of a commercial adviser' framework 80–3
    skills, building 85–7
    transformational change (case study) 86–7
commitment 43, 206
communication 107, 108
    and client understanding 94
    commerciality and 82–3
    growth and globalization strategy 25
    importance in relationship development 167
    online *see* digital media
    *see also* conversation(s); strategic communication

# Index

Community and society 113–14
competition 77, 97, 179, 218
competitive advantage 3, 56, 101, 153, *154*, 241
conferences, and trust-building 52
confidence 83, *84*, 193
conflict resolution 170–1
connecting 7
  from communities to cohorts 110–18
  introduction 107–9
  lessons for 142, 239
  thought leadership
    business challenge 119–32
    and sales 133–41
  traditional vs client champion response 242
consistency *10*, 54, 169
content
  aggregating 113, 115, 116
  cohort marketing and 115–16
  thought leadership
    archiving 139–40
    curating 132
    drafting 137–8
    need for engaging 142
    and work-winning 135
content marketing 135, 136
continuous improvement 77, 100, 103
conversation(s) 7, 32, 71, 81, 83, *84*, 108, 120, 128, 133–41, 142, 192
core clients 181
corporate counsel 175–6
Covey, Stephen 165
credibility 3, 50, 56, 122, 150
CRM *see* client relationship management
cross-selling 33–4, 57
culture(s)
  hierarchical 41
  and listening programmes 74
  *see also* organizational culture; timesheet culture
curating content 132

damaged relationships, repairing 169–71
data analysis 69, 71–2
data collection 69
data integrity, KPIs and 227
data synthesis 127–8
data volume, KPIs and 226
decision-making 26, 72, 81, 108, 114, 165, 191
dedicated account leads 160
deliverables, mismatch between outcomes and 81
desired outcomes, understanding clients' 81
desk research 128
desktop publishing technology (DTP) 114–15

differentiation 174, 224
digital media
  access to information 108
  and marketing 56, 110
    challenge of mobile devices 112
    client engagement 138
    from communities to cohorts 113–14
    *see also* cohort marketing
    implications 111
    key performance indicators 227–9
    pros and cons of change 112–13
    thought leadership 120, 130–1
  in MBD 217
  *see also* social media
directness 41
directors (business development) 192
disruption 57
disruptive technologies 113–14
Dixon, Matthew 134, 135
'do the ordinary extraordinarily well' 45
drafting content 137–8
Dupont diagram 227

e-mail 229
economics, understanding 81
*Effective Client–Adviser Relationships* 78
efficiency 125, 131, 174, 176
egocentrism 62
emerging markets 23, 38–9
emotional commitment, to change 206
emotional intelligence 100, 165, 171
emotional quotient (EQ) 165, 171
empathy 61, 62, 136, 232, 244
employee engagement 116–17, 142
entertainment 179
enthusiasm 193
entrepreneurialism 26
Europe 21, 38, 39, 40, 43, 73, 74
evidence-based marketing 219, 230
executive sponsorship 159
expensive services, and relationship failure 96–7
experience pitch 176
external oversight, international network development 55–6

face-to-face research 128
Facebook 52, 115, 145
failure, fear of 166
fee-earners 4, 32, 33, 135
financial fluency 81
financial regulation 23
First Moment of Truth 228, 229
first-mover advantage 27
flexibility 15, 44, 193, 232

flexible fees   93
focus   40–1
Forbes Global 2000   22
formal listening   103
Freeman, Karen   135

Gates, Bill   169
Geneen, Hal   220
generic brochures   40, 42, 44
generic metrics   223
geographic insight   122
German legal sector, MBD in   209–18
Gilbert, Ian   190
global networks   27, *28*, 49, 54
   *see also* international network development
global vs local brand dichotomy   44
global vs local client management   159
globalization, growth and   22–36
   best friend alliances   29
   brand   30
   building strong relationships   31–3
   capturing opportunities   22–3
   cross-selling and sectoral approach   33–4
   cultural alignment   31
   global reach, local depth   26–7
   key lessons   35–6
   market entry   27–9
   new services, products and models   34–5
   partnership model   26
   and quantitative approach   70
   strategy   23–6
goal clarity, client feedback programmes   98
Goldilocks principle   229
Google   114, 120, 228
ground rules   94
GROW model   167
growth   6
   Asia Pacific   38
   and globalization   22–36
   implementing a growth strategy   37–47
   international network development   48–56
   introduction   19–21
   lessons for   57, 238–9
   pressure for   19
   thought leadership   125, 131
   traditional vs client champion response   242
growth strategy   20
   for globalization
      setting   24–6
      single vs multi-country matter profitability   23, *24*
   implementation   37–47
      challenges   40–3
      recommendations   43–7
   lessons for   57

hierarchical cultures   41
honesty   93, 159

ideas generation   125–6
in-house teams, building client understanding   91–2
independence
   of client interviewers   103
   of local firms   50
India   39
influence-monitoring tools   229
influencing   168–9, 185, 204
information
   access to   107, 108, 114, 192
   sharing   158
   *see also* digital media; online information
information channels, choice   108, 142
information sources   108, 112, 115
innovation   57
'inside out' vs 'outside in' perspective   243–5, 247–8
insight(s)   85, 122, *248*
*Insight Trading* (case study)   140–1
insights libraries   132
intangibility   *11*
intellect   *10*
intelligence
   client life cycle response   247
   *see also* emotional intelligence; social intelligence
interdependence   165–6, 241
internal clients, understanding   214–15
internal communication   25
internal relationships, building   166–8, 182
international network development   48–56
   the future of   56
   power of branding   54–5
   regulation and external oversight   55–6
   three basic models   49–51
   trust
      building   51–3
      reinforcing   53–4
international outlook, need for   46
internationalization, of business   48–9
interviews, and client listening   71
intimacy   150
ITSMA   130

Kelvin, Lord   220
key client programmes   31, 45, 77, 165, 189
key performance indicators (KPIs)   219–31
   audience for   222
   background   219–20
   client programme management   153–5, 156, 159

key performance indicators (KPIs)   *cont'd*
  client services   72
  development   222–6
  digital marketing   227–9
  holistic   221
  impact of   *231*
  key principles   229–30
  pitfalls   226–7
  purpose   221–2
knowledge, and client understanding   91
knowledge sharing   29, 86, 94, 158, 164
*KPI Mega Library: 17,000 Key Performance Indicators*   226
KPIs *see* key performance indicators
Kreston Reeves   48–56
Kurtzman, Joel   134

language   74, 81, 98, 206
lateral thinking   95
lead conversion   229
lead-nurturing metrics   229
leadership
  barriers to   4
  brand health   *102*
  client life cycle response   *247*
  commerciality and   85
  and MBD
    recommendations for   214–17
    through periods of change   202–3
  need for international outlook   46
  support
    client feedback programmes   98–9
    transformational change   200–2
  themes *see* connecting; growth; managing; relationships; understanding
  *see also* thought leadership
left brain vs right brain   134–5
legal markets   23
Leverhulme, Lord   227
liability fears   83, *84*
liking   168–9
LinkedIn   52, 92, 115, 116, 125, 130, 145, 178
listening programmes
  adapting the approach, internationally   73–4
  analysis and reporting requirements   71–2
  assigning responsibility   70–1, 72
  making change happen   74–6, 104
  qualitative vs qualitative approach   68–70
  selecting target respondents   73
  as a tool for growth   32
listening to clients   64–77
  barriers to   65–6
  as bedrock of marketing   66–7
  strength of relationships   94
  top lessons in   103
local autonomy   45, 50

local strategies, within a global context   43–4
long-term commitment   43
long-term planning   26
long-term relationships   94–6
long-term view   95
loose associations   49, 50, 56
'losing face'   45

magic circle firms   13, *175*
Maister, David   1, 150, 214
management, client life cycle response   *248*
management action, KPIs subject to   230
management support, MBD function   216–17
managing   7–8
  introduction   185–7
  lessons for   232–3, 240
  marketing and business development   188–98
  role of KPIs   219–31
  traditional vs client champion response   *242*
  transformational change   199–208
market entry   27–9
market forces, relationship failure   96
market metrics   *225*
market research   101
market segmentation   23, 174–5, 222–3
market selection   23, 57
marketers
  as choreographers   135–41
  as external communications experts   3
  new breed of   4–5
marketing
  defined   2
  failure in   110–11
  *see also* professional services marketing
marketing and business development (MBD)
  barriers to leadership   4
  failure to embrace   65
  future for   249
  German legal sector   209–18
    building partner support (case study)   211–14
    overview   209–10
    recommendations for leaders   214–17
  leadership themes *see* connecting; growth; managing; relations; understanding
  need for international outlook   46
  processes, concurrent growth   46–7
professionals
  balancing 'outside in' and 'inside out' views   244–5
  as client champions   245, *246*, *247–8*
  moving up the value chain   45–6
  skills   3, 57, 137, 185
  and value   188–98
    balancing reactivity and proactivity   *194*
    change in professional services market   188–9

firms' adaptation to change   189–90
    issues and challenges   191–5
    key practices   198
    pitch improvement (case study)   195–8
marketing function metrics   225
material impact, of KPS   230
MBD *see* marketing and business development
meetings, client management   155
Megatrends Map   125, *126*
mentoring   86
Meridian West   78–88, 119–32
metrics   125, 223, 224, *225*, 228, 229
mobile devices   112
momentum, CRM programmes   155, 158
multi-channel delivery   121, 142
multi-service teams   165
mutual benefit   158, 181
'myopia professionalosia'   65–6

negative client feedback   170
negotiation   170–1
network behaviours   116
new business, winning   179–80
new clients, building understanding with   92–3
Nisus Consulting study   66, 67
no-go decisions   41
non-fee-earners   4

objectives
    CRM programmes   152–3, 181
    listening to clients   103
online diagnostics   130, 131
online feedback   155–6
online information   112, 114, 132
    *see also* digital media
online research   128
openness, in listening to clients   103
operational challenges   191–2
opportunities   142
    for change   232–3
    client life cycle response   248
    global growth, capturing   22–3
organic growth   26–7
organizational change   202
organizational culture
    client feedback as part of   100
    globalization, brand and   31
    ownership structure and   14
    and transformational change   205–6
outcomes, understanding clients' desired   81
'outside in' vs 'inside out' perspective   243–5, 247–8
outsourcing   56
over-charging   96–7
over-promising   93, 95
overspecialization   83, *84*
ownership structure, of firms   14

Pareto principle   152
partner support, building (case study)   211–14
partnership(s)   14, 26, 47, 103, 158, 191
patience   232
PDF   115, 120
peer groups, and trust-building   52
penetration, marketing metrics   223
people
    commerciality and understanding   82
    and organizational change   202
perception vs reality   170
performance management   160, 165, 170
perishability   9
personal contacts, building   52
personal development opportunities, highlighting in change programmes   204
personality   151, 181
personalization   130, 131
persuasion   232
piloting   43, 136
pitch   174, 176
pitch improvement (case study)   195–8
planning
    in business development   191–2
    client feedback programmes   99
    client life cycle response   247
    thought leadership   124–5
    *see also* account plans; strategic planning
point of view, clarity in   122
positioning   25, 30, *248*
PR metrics   225
pricing   93, 96–7, 197
pricing metrics   225
priority client programmes   45
proactivity, balancing reactivity and   194
problem-solving, practical   82
procurement   93–4, 108
professional pyramid   9, 216
professional services firms
    adaptation to change   189–90
    characteristics   8, 9–13
    differences between   13–14
    and KPIs *see* key performance indicators
    nature of   200
    role for both qualitative and quantitative approach   70
professional services marketing
    and business development *see* marketing and business development
    digital *see* digital media, and marketing
    lack of differentiation in   174
    need for   2–3
    new client demands and changing role of   1–2
    *see also* cohort marketing; content marketing; marketers

professional training
   change programmes 205–6
   client feedback 99
   client listening 71, 104
   and commerciality 83, *84*, 85
   CRM programmes 159, 182
   MBD staff 215–16
   to insure international outlook 46
profitability 188–9
programme design, client relations 153–6, *157*
project, defined 207
project management 207–8
project risk *11*
purchase complexity *12*
purpose, clarity of 232
push-pull dynamic 130, 131
PwC 110–18, 122–3, 130

qualitative vs quantitative approach 68–70
quality
   brand and 30
   and relationship termination 97
   thought leaderships and 120
quality assurance 50, 54
quality of service 97, 98
questioning, and client understanding 92

rapport 70, 90, 101, 217
reactivity, balancing proactivity and *194*
reality, perception vs 170
reciprocity 169
recognition, reward and 45, 160
recruitment 83, 215–16
regulation 23, 55–6, 74
relationships 7
   building strong 31–3
   client listening 71
   in client situations *150*
   developing internal and external 162–72
   failure 96–8
   gap between individual and firm-wide capability 2
   importance of good 164–5
   important aspects of 149–51
   introduction 145–7
   lack of understanding as damaging to 78
   lessons for 181–2, 240
   management *see* client relationship management
   nurturing clients 44–5
   primacy of 148–51, 173–80
   repairing damaged 169–71
   seismic shift in 189
   skills, need for 2
   stages of development *149*

   traditional vs client champion response *242*
   value of 176–7
   *see also* client-firm relationship cycle
relationships marketing 162–3
reliability 150
reporting
   client listening 71–2
   pitch process 197
reputation 45, 101, 135, 136
requests for proposal (RFP) 176
research
   leadership campaigns 127–8
   qualitative vs quantitative approach 68, 69
   *see also* market research
resistance, to change programmes 204
responsibility, assigning
   client feedback programmes 99
   client listening programmes 70–1, 72
restructuring 204
return on investment (ROI) tracking 132, 191
review, pitch improvement 197
reward(s) 45, 86, 160, 163
Riddell, Warren 29
right-brain-left-brain theory 134–5
risk *11*, 125, 131, 166
role models 232
RSS 112

sales *see* thought marketing, and sales
*Science* 61
scope/scoping 82
search engine optimization 228–9
sectoral insight 122
sectoral knowledge 91
Seeing the World Through Clients' Eyes (Nisus) 66, 67
self-awareness 62
self-importance 62
self-orientation 150
sense of community 203
service quality 97, 98
*The Seven Habits of Highly Effective People* 165–6
shared understanding 168
Sharplegal study 90–102
Shirky, Clay 112
Sinclair Knight Merz 140–1
single international firms 50
skills, MBF professionals 3, 57, 137, 185
small niche firms 50
smart measurement 233
SMART targets 155
smartphones 112
social intelligence 61, 62

# Index

social media  111, 112, 113
   client engagement  138
   information sharing  158
   measuring activity  229
   relationships  145–6, 163, 177
   thought leadership  130
   see also Facebook; LinkedIn; Twitter; YouTube
social relationships  179
South Korea  39
specialists  193
speed  95
Sperry, Roger W  134
staff secondment, and trust-building  52
Stop trying to delight your customers  135
strategic change  202
strategic communication  25
strategic conversations  32, 190
strategic planning  26, 71, 72, 77, 101
strategic plans  191
strategic thinking  190, 217
strategic value  101
strengths and weaknesses  75, 77, 93
structural change  202
sub-optimization, KPIs and  226–7, 230
subservience  45–6
success mapping  224
support function/status, MBD leaders  4, 5
support tools, business development  192
switching costs  12

tablet computers  112
tailored metrics  224
targets
   business development  192
   client programme management  153–5
team development  232
team tactics  93
telephone research  128
'them and us' attitudes  14, 45–6, 214
thinking
   right-brain-left-brain theory  134–5
   understanding clients'  95–6
   see also lateral thinking
third party interviewers, client listening  71
Thomson Reuters Elite  173–80
thought leadership  119–32
   'advanced' positioning  30
   business case for  123–4
   business challenge  119–20
   campaigns
      choosing the best topic  125–6
      planning  124–5
      research and data synthesis  127–8
      roll-out  129–30
      secrets of successful  132

   case studies  122–3, 126–7, 128–9
   definition  120
   five criteria for excellence in  121–2
   future for  131–2
   purpose  142
   and sales  133–41, 142
      Challenger Sale  133, 134
      content marketing  135
      *Insight Trading* (case study)  140–1
      marketer as choreographer  135–41
      right-brain-left-brain theory  134–5
      top lessons  141
*Thought Leadership*  124
time factor
   client feedback programmes  99
   transformational change  203
timesheet culture  83, *84*
Timperley, John  194
Toman, Nicholas  135
Tönnies, Ferdinand  113–14
training *see* professional training
transactional marketing  162–3
transformational change  199–208
   achieving support  204
   commerciality and (case study)  86–7
   culture and behaviour in  205–6
   establishing a change programme  202
   leadership recognition and buy-in  200–2
   leading and inspiring fragmented communities  202–4
   practical challenges  203
   project management  207–8
transparency  167, 168, 180, 191, 192
trust  33, 142, 163, 168
   building  43, 51–3, 57, 94, 98, 217
   client listening  70
   importance of  180
   reinforcing  53–4
trust equation  150
trusted advisers  1, 32, 80, 133, 141, 214
Twitter  92, 112, 115, 145, 229

understanding  7, 232
   closing the commerciality gap  78–88
   internal clients, MBD and  214–15
   introduction  61–3
   lessons for  103–4, 239
   listening and responding to clients  64–77
   testing  167
   traditional vs client champion response  *242*
   what the client wants  89–102
unique selling points (USPs)  164
United Kingdom  26, 39, 44, 46, 48, 56, 67
United States  21, 26, 38, 39, 43, 46, 56, 73, 175, 176

value
    of client understanding   90
    importance of delivering   178–9
    and relationship termination   97
    of relationships   176–7
virtual communities   203
visual presentation   121

web metrics   225, 227, 228, 229
webinars   180
Weinstock, Arnold   220
what's in it for me? (WiiFM)   194, 201
White & Case   188–98

white shoe firms   175
Whitmore, John   167
win-win   149, 165, 168
win/loss analysis   178
work, asking for   139
work-type metrics   225
work-winning   44, 135, 136
written material   121, 193

Young, Laurie   124
YouTube   115, 229

Zero Moment of Truth (ZMOT)   228